The Home Front in Britain

MW00716455

To David and Gregg,

Thanks for all your support over
the years,

Lovely to have you home for Christmas,

Love to you both,

Janis
xx

The Home Front in Britain

Images, Myths and Forgotten Experiences since 1914

Edited by

Maggie Andrews
University of Worcester, UK

and

Janis Lomas
Independent Scholar, UK

palgrave
macmillan

First published 2014 by
PALGRAVE MACMILLAN

Palgrave Macmillan in the UK is an imprint of Macmillan Publishers Limited,
registered in England, company number 785998, of Houndmills, Basingstoke,
Hampshire RG21 6XS.

Palgrave Macmillan in the US is a division of St Martin's Press LLC,
175 Fifth Avenue, New York, NY 10010.

Palgrave Macmillan is the global academic imprint of the above companies
and has companies and representatives throughout the world.

Palgrave® and Macmillan® are registered trademarks in the United States,
the United Kingdom, Europe and other countries.

ISBN: 978–1–137–34898–2 hardback
ISBN: 978–1–137–34897–5 paperback

This book is printed on paper suitable for recycling and made from fully
managed and sustained forest sources. Logging, pulping and manufacturing
processes are expected to conform to the environmental regulations of the
country of origin.

A catalogue record for this book is available from the British Library.

Library of Congress Cataloging-in-Publication Data

The home front in Britain : images, myths and forgotten experiences
1914–2014 / edited by Maggie Andrews, University of Worcester, UK,
Janis Lomas, independent scholar.
pages cm
Includes bibliographical references.
ISBN 978–1–137–34897–5 (paperback : alk. paper)
1. Great Britain – History – 20th century. 2. World War, 1914–1918 – Great
Britain. 3. World War, 1939–1945 – Great Britain. 4. Great Britain – Social
conditions – 20th century. 5. Women in war – Great Britain – History – 20th
century. 6. Women – Great Britain – Social conditions – 20th century. I.
Andrews, Maggie. II. Lomas, Janis.

DA566.H66 2014

940.3′41—dc23   2014025708

Contents

List of Illustrations

Figures

Tables

Foreword

While it is axiomatic to state that 'no family was unaffected' in the United Kingdom by the two World Wars, it is more extraordinary to think that in nearly every family today, whose forebears lived through 1914 to 1918 and 1939 to 1945, stories will still abound of the Home Front and the many roles played by family members. Such stories will often stand out as the most significant features of people's – particularly women's – lives, for which they are recognised, remembered, and indeed honoured. The nature of human intergenerational interaction dictates that such accounts can be expected to be extinguished from family folklore within three or four generations, if not kept alive through the medium of photography, the written word, or the arts in drawings or music. In my own family, stories such as my grandmother's anecdotes from her late teens of undertaking agricultural labour, 'man's work', and of battling with rural and industrial prejudice against working women in the Welsh Marches and Norfolk during the First World War must be replicated in millions of other homes, as Chapters 6 and 12 of this book so eloquently explore. Similarly, my mother's experiences as a child, of sleeping under canvas for two winters of the Second World War as 'we had nowhere else to live' and it was 'warmer sleeping out when it snowed' must resonate with many who were dislocated, including the 'forgotten' Guernsey families described in Chapter 8.

What marks *Home Front: Images, Myths and Forgotten Experiences* as an important addition to the body of knowledge surrounding the Home Front is the multi-dimensional approach taken by the editors and chapter authors: from the mix of heart-rending personal reminiscence in Chapter 2 to the detailed analysis of the social and domestic effect of war in eight of the other chapters. Of particular interest to many will be the description of the extraordinary career of Ellen Wilkinson MP in Chapter 7 and the examination of the effect of the Home Front in framing governmental action on both pensions, and health and safety in Chapters 3 and 4. Also of interest will be the focus on the contemporary effect of media-driven social 'stereotyping' in Chapters 10 and 16 and the little-researched aspect of the impact of wartime on National Savings discussed in Chapter 13. My own family experiences, and the understanding of Remembrance that I obtained through my tenure as Chief

Executive of the National Memorial Arboretum and in working with the Royal British Legion as the national 'Custodian of Remembrance', lead me to welcome this work and to commend it to you.

Charles Bagot-Jewitt
Former Chief Executive
National Memorial Arboretum

Images from the photo album of Mary Kate Vick (nee Neville) who was in the Women's Land Army from 1916–1918.

Source: Images reproduced by kind permission of Mary Parsons.

Acknowledgements

The editors would like to acknowledge the role of both the Women's History Network and the National Memorial Arboretum in the development of this book. The Women's History Network has, since it was formed in 1991, aimed to promote the study of Womens History in Britain, it aimed to encourage anyone with a passion for women's history both within academia and beyond. The National Memorial Arboretum's 150 acre site in Staffordshire houses a range of civilian and military memorials, including a memorial to the Home Front. In 2010 with the support of the then Chief Executive, Charlie Bagot-Jewitt, the NMA began to host annual conferences organised by the Midlands Region of the Women's History Network. Many of the chapters in this book were initially presented at one of the five conferences that have taken place since then.

We would also like to acknowledge the help of a number of archives and helpful archivists who have assisted many of those who have written chapters in this volume. In the present stringent economic times when archives face cuts to their resources, a special thank you is due to those who continue to support so many historians undertaking research. The Imperial War Museum, the Mary Evans Picture Library and the People's History Museum were particularly helpful in identifying and providing images, as were a number of individuals; Ina Taylor, who provided the cover image, deserves a special thank you.

The completion of this book has been eased by the cooperation and support of colleagues and students, friends and families and we would like to thank them all. Both our husbands, Neil and John, have at times been somewhat inconvenienced by the writing of this book but they have with equanimity and good humour supported us through the project – we appreciate it, thank you. This book is dedicated to them and those who share an interest and enthusiasm for studying the Home Front.

Notes on Contributors

Maggie Andrews is Professor of Cultural History at the University of Worcester, and has worked in higher, further and adult education for over 25 years. She is the author of a range of publications including a feminist history of the Women's Institute movement entitled *The Acceptable Face of Feminism* (1997), *Domesticating the Airwaves: Broadcasting, Domesticity and Femininity* (2012), and was the joint editor of *Lest We Forget: Remembrance and Commemoration* (2011) and *Women and the Media: Feminism and Femininity in Britain, 1900 to the Present* (2014). Maggie is an AHRC-funded adviser to the BBC in the West Midlands on its *World War One at Home* project and is the historical consultant for the new BBC Radio 4 drama *Home Front*. She is a co-Investigator on the AHRC funded Voices of War and Peace First World War Hub, leading the Gender and the Home Front theme.

Paula Bartley has been promoting women's history in schools, colleges and universities for most of her adult life. She was Senior Lecturer in History at the University of Wolverhampton before going to live in Hungary for seven years. In 1983 she co-founded the *Women in History* series for Cambridge University Press aimed at school students. She co-edited ten books in the series and co-authored three of them with topics ranging from *Women in Medieval Europe* through to *Women in India and Pakistan*. Her sole-authored books include *The Changing Role of Women, 1815–1914, Prostitution: Reform and Prevention, 1860–1914* and *Emmeline Pankhurst*. In 2012 she won the Elizabeth Longford award, administered by the Society of Authors, to support her research on Ellen Wilkinson. Her biography, *Ellen Wilkinson: From Red Suffragist to Government Minister*, was published in 2014.

Paul Elliott holds a PhD from the University of Essex and lectures at the University of Worcester. He is the author of *Hitchcock and the Cinema of Sensations* (2012), *Guattari Reframed* (2012), an introductory guide to the work of the French psychoanalyst Felix Guattari and a monograph entitled *Studying the British Crime Film* (2014). He has also published articles on film theory, philosophy and British cinema. He teaches courses on counter-cinema, documentary and British cinema and is interested in the intersections between realism and the avant-garde.

Thomas George is a final year postgraduate student working towards a PhD in Welsh History at Cardiff University. He is also an undergraduate seminar tutor and a project coordinator for a local community engagement project. Under the supervision of Dr Stephanie Ward and Dr Tracey Loughran, his thesis examines female wartime employment in Wales during the First World War with a particular focus on those engaged in munitions and agricultural production. Prior to beginning his doctorate, he completed a BA in Modern History and International Relations and a Master's in Modern History at Swansea University. The subject of his MA dissertation examined British attitudes towards the American Expeditionary Force (AEF) during the First World War. This is his first publication.

Barbara Hately-Broad is Honorary Research Fellow in the History Department at the University of Sheffield. She has published a number of articles on prisoners of war and was co-editor of *Prisoners of War, Prisoners of Peace* (with Bob Moore, 2005). Her monograph, *War and Welfare: British Prisoner of War Families, 1939–1945* was published in 2009.

Karen Hunt is Professor of Modern British History at Keele University and is currently Head of Humanities Research at Keele, as well as Chair of the Social History Society (2014–2017). She is a former editor of *Labour History Review* and serves on various advisory boards including for *Twentieth Century British History*. Her publications cover many aspects of the gendering of politics (locally, nationally and transnationally) particularly from the 1880s to 1939, including *Equivocal Feminists* (1996) and *Socialist Women* (2002, with June Hannam). Her current research juggles a number of intersecting interests: the life and politics of Dora Montefiore; inter-war women's politics, focussing on the local and the everyday; and women and the politics of food in the First World War. She is an adviser to the AHRC/BBC World War One at Home project in the West Midlands.

Hilda Kean is visiting professor at the University of Greenwich and adjunct professor at the Australian Centre for Public History, University of Technology Sydney who has published widely on cultural/public history and on non-human animals. Her many books include *Deeds not Words: The Lives of Suffragette Teachers* (1990), *Animal Rights: Political and Social Change in Britain since 1800* (2000) and *London Stories: Personal Lives, Public Histories* (2004). Her numerous articles include those on animals and their representation published in *Anthrozoos, Australian*

Cultural History Journal, History Workshop Journal, International Journal of Heritage Studies, London Journal and *Society and Animals,* where she is an associate editor. Her most recent book is *The Public History Reader* (2013) edited with Paul Martin. She is currently writing a book on the animal-human relationship on the Home Front during the 1939–1945 war. She can be contacted via her website http://hildakean.com/

Elspeth King is currently a PhD student and part-time lecturer at the University of Worcester, following a twenty-year career in local government and educational administration. Her research investigates the tactics employed by gender and class groups to circumnavigate government rationing on the Home Front in the Second World War especially in relation to the idea of a 'People's War'. Apart from World War Two other areas of interest include the inter-war years and the Cold War.

Janis Lomas has worked as a social and women's historian at various universities for over 20 years and has been associated with the Women's History Network since 1992. She founded the WHN-Midlands Region and served on the National Steering Committee of the Women's History Network for several years. She was responsible for obtaining and cataloguing the War Widows' Archive at Staffordshire University and since 2009 has jointly coordinated, with Professor Maggie Andrews, the Annual Women's History Network–Midlands Region Conference on themes related to Women and War at the National Memorial Arboretum. Published work includes '"So I Married Again": Letters from British Widows of the First and Second World Wars', in *History Workshop Journal,* Issue 38; '"Delicate Duties"; Issues of Class and Respectability in Government Policy Towards the Wives and Widows of British Soldiers in the Era of the Great War', *Women's History Review,* Vol. 9, No. 1, 2000; 'They took my husband, they took the money and just left me': War Widows & Remembrance after the Second World War', in *Lest We Forget: Remembrance and Commemoration,* edited by Maggie Andrews, Charles Bagot-Jewitt and Nigel Hunt, (2011).

Gillian Mawson a postgraduate of the University of Manchester, is a freelance historian and author with a strong interest in oral history and community engagement. In recent years her focus has been on interviewing Second World War evacuees and gathering their living memories. In 2010, Gillian created a community group to empower evacuees living in northern England to share their memories with each other and with the public. She has worked with the BBC on Second World War documentaries, BBC Coast and local history programmes.

She works in partnership with museums to create historical exhibitions and develops educational materials, including documentary films. She creates workshops for schools which often involve local people who were eye witnesses to historical events. Her first book *Guernsey Evacuees: The Forgotten Evacuees of the Second World War* (2012) describes the evacuation of 17,000 civilians from Guernsey to England just before the German occupation of the Channel Islands. Her latest book, *Evacuees: Children's Lives on the WW2 Home Front* (Pen and Sword, September 2014) contains interviews with one hundred evacuees who spent the war years in Britain. It includes memories and photographs from children, mothers and teachers.

Bob Moore is Professor of Twentieth Century European History at the University of Sheffield. He has published extensively on the history of Western Europe in the mid-twentieth century, including *The British Empire and its Italian Prisoners of War, 1940–1947* (with Kent Fedorowich, 2003), *Crises of Empire: Decolonisation and Europe's Imperial States* (with Martin Thomas and Larry Butler, 2007), and *Refugees from Nazi Germany and the Liberal European States* (with Frank Caestecker, 2009). He has also edited a number of collections, including *Resistance in Western Europe* (2000) and *Prisoners of War, Prisoners of Peace* (with Barbara Hately-Broad, 2005). His latest monograph, *Survivors: Jewish Self-Help and Rescue in Nazi-Occupied Western Europe*, was published in 2010.

Rosalind Watkiss Singleton completed a PhD, using oral testimony to examine change and continuity in post-war working-class communities between 1945 and c.1970, in 2011. Recent research interests include post-war teenage consumption patterns, working-class employment experiences, working-class housing and theft from the workplace. Her current research project is exploring the influence of 1960s pop music, the cinema and magazines upon the romantic expectations of teenage girls and their attitudes towards love, sex and marriage. She is involved in several local community projects training volunteers, of all ages, in oral history techniques, including *Women of Wolverhampton* (2013) and *The Block Capital Project* (2013–2014), which is examining slum clearance and the transition to high-rise flats. Rosalind works as an independent researcher and is also employed as a sessional lecturer in the History and Politics Departments at the University of Wolverhampton and at Ruskin College, Oxford, where she teaches radicalism, feminism and socialism.

Angela Clare Smith has worked in the heritage and museums sector for ten years, as a historical researcher, interpreter and project manager.

After initially studying archaeology, she worked for the Royal Armouries for eight years on a range of exhibitions and events across the museum's sites of Fort Nelson in Portsmouth, the Tower of London and the Royal Armouries Museum in Leeds, exploring a variety of archives and collections. During this time she completed her Masters by Research at the University of Leeds. Most recently Angela has developed a new exhibition and series of events for Bankfield Museum in Halifax, drawing on regional stories and experiences to commemorate the centenary of the First World War. During her career she has found herself researching various periods and subjects, from Henry VIII's arms and armour to women's roles in the British military. Angela's interest lies in making historical research, collections and archives accessible and engaging for audiences, through exhibitions, events, live performance, television, radio and online.

Anne Spurgeon was formerly a Senior Lecturer in the Department of Occupational Medicine at the University of Birmingham. She originally trained as a psychologist and specialised in the health effects of occupational exposure to neurotoxic substances such as organic solvents, heavy metals and pesticides. For several years she chaired the Research Committee of the Industrial Injuries Advisory Council, which advises the Secretary of State for Work and Pensions on Industrial Injuries Benefit and its administration. Since retirement she has completed an MPhil in History at the University of Worcester, focussing on the work of the British Women's Factory Inspectorate, formed in 1893. She now carries out independent historical research in the field of occupational health and safety policy and practice. She has published and lectured on a range of occupational hazards including the problems of dust exposure in nineteenth-century needlemakers, solvent and lead exposure among painters in mid to late twentieth-century Britain, and the use of various different agents in sheep dipping over the past hundred years. She is currently writing a biography of Adelaide Anderson, Principal Woman Factory Inspector in Britain between 1897 and 1921, and a major player in the development of women's occupational health and safety during the First World War.

Introduction

Maggie Andrews and Janis Lomas

At the beginning of the twentieth century the term 'Home Front' was not part of popular vocabulary.[1] Yet as Britain begins to commemorate the centenary of the First World War the idea that modern warfare is experienced both by fighting forces and in the everyday domestic life of the towns, villages and homes of Britain is accepted. The Home Front is part of the public understanding of war and conflict which is gained not merely through visits to museums and the school curriculum but also in recent years through television and film. However, there is selectivity in these popular images of the Home Front, myths circulate and there is a tendency to perceive war as an agent of change, particularly in relation to women's position in society.

The origins of such a perspective lie in Arthur Marwick's social change thesis developed over fifty years ago in *The Deluge*[2] and then *War and Social Change in the Twentieth Century: A Comparative Study of Britain, France and Germany, Russia and the United States.*[3] Marwick argued that total war is so destructive and disruptive it inevitably causes change, particularly as the war effort requires the active participation of all social groups in society. Historians, including some in this volume, have challenged and rejected Marwick's thesis but it remains tenacious in popular television history, for example in Andrew Marr's *Making of Modern Britain* (2009) and *History of Modern Britain* (2009). In part this can be explained by an intrinsic desire to create narratives and myths which perhaps, if not actually empowering, are at least comforting. Both the First World War and the Second World War fractured families, displaced people, destroyed homes and ended lives, it is hardly surprising therefore that there is a desire in the popular imagination to search for something positive coming out of this.

1

Marwick's thesis has also had an influence on academic studies of the Home Front and much of the work exploring women and war has felt the need to at least engage or respond to his argument that there was an increase in women's participation in the workforce in the First World War and the Second World War which led to greater emancipation for women. This argument has now taken on the status of an oft-repeated myth. The evidence to support this seems weak and the interpretation has been challenged;[4] for example, prior to the First World War approximately one third of married women undertook paid work outside the home and in the 1920s this figure was almost identical.[5] One problem with overarching myths is that they generalise and simplify the complex nuances and variations in historical periods and processes. There was not just one experience of the Home Front but numerous infinitely varied experiences shaped by geographical location, class, gender, age, political and cultural attitudes and values. The studies in this volume, which explore women and work, are specific to region, industry, occupation, interest group or theme. Many chapters discuss experiences and lives which have not made it into history books, television dramas or into museums. All in some way serve to dislodge, stretch or rework myths of the Home Fronts of the First World War and the Second World War, they go behind the popular images and iconography of the eras and uncover forgotten experiences. By image we mean not only those popular images gained from television and film but also the images of the past that historians themselves help to create whether working within an academic sphere or in partnership with museums, community groups, heritage sites and public institutions.

Four of the chapters in this volume have a particular focus upon women's working lives and aim to widen the conceptualisation of how working practices and lives are influenced by war and conflict. Anne Spurgeon's 'Mortality or Morality? Keeping Workers Safe in First World War' explores the work of women factory inspectors and how the welfare system instigated in the First World War detracted from their work in health and safety. She draws attention to the many women who worked in industry and undertook dangerous jobs before the First World War and continued to do so. The experiences of these women have been overshadowed by the munitions workers who have an iconic status as First World War women workers. Thomas George's exploration of 'Female agricultural workers in Wales in the First World War' moves beyond the iconic image of the Land Girl, drawing attention to the range of women who undertook agricultural work in this era including those on family farms. Barbara Hately-Broad and Bob Moore's exploration of the women who worked on Britain's Inland Waterways during the Second World War indicates once again the complexity of women's wartime working experience. Women's work on the canals prior to the Second World War may have been hidden in family labour, and shifts in the industry itself in the post-war period influenced their future employment prospects. Finally Paula Bartley's chapter highlights the contribution of the Labour politician Ellen Wilkinson in the Second World War, a forgotten experience of war work.

A consequence of the academic pre-occupation with debates about how participation in the workforce in wartime might have changed women's lives is that there has been a tendency to overlook the larger number of women whose primary role as 'housewife'. This is particularly addressed in Karen Hunt's discussion of the housewife on the First World War Home Front as she seeks to bring the women in the food queues back into focus and thereby raise questions about what war meant for everyday life in Britain as the crisis developed and deepened between 1914 and 1918. A number of the chapters in this book serve as a reminder that the domestic space of the home and domesticity have often been marginalised in the study of the First World War Home Front and yet as Maggie Andrews' first chapter argues, domesticity was stretched and reworked during this period, leading to the cult of domesticity in the inter-war years.

Angela Smith's case study of the letters between Gert and Jack, provides a very personal account of everyday life for one lower middle-class couple coping with the separation of war. What these chapters also demonstrate is that many elements of the Home Front that are, in people's minds, identified with the Second World War – such as rationing – were developed in the First World War as the volunteerism, charity and ad hoc arrangements were steadily replaced by centralised government policy.[6] One area in which this was the case was the provision for war widows but as Janis Lomas's examination of the introduction and operation of the war widows' pension argues, there are strong continuities with Victorian attitudes, and class continued to govern social policy.

Arthur Marwick was not the only influential social historian of the 1960s to turn their attention to war; Angus Calder's *The People's War*[7] took apart the popular myth that the Home Front in the Second World War involved a unity of sacrifice and experience, or the idea of class unity in wartime. Instead he pointed out the working class worked longer and harder and suffered more than those who were wealthier. Yet the myth of the people's war, like the myth of social change, is tenacious. Elspeth

King and Maggie Andrews demonstrate that as citizens sought strategies to circumnavigate clothes and furniture rationing, class and wealth continued to be key deciding factors in shaping experience.

In the over-arching myth of 'all in it together' and the familiar iconography of food rationing, bombing and evacuation, there are a number of forgotten experiences which are brought to attention in this volume. Rosalind Watkiss's discussion of the National Savings Movement in the Second World War and Hilda Kean's exploration of animal and human relationships in Second World War diaries and letters are two such examples. Both these areas would have had a significant impact on the everyday experience of ordinary people on the Home Front. Some experiences are both particular and forgotten, as in Gillian Mawson's chapter which examines what happened when 17,000 Guernsey evacuees descended on towns in northern England such as Stockport, Bury, Halifax, Bradford and Oldham in June 1940, just before the threatened German invasion engulfed their island.

In one sense or another the majority of chapters in this volume have something to say about images of the Home Front, they all stretch and rework popular perceptions of these two key periods of time. However some chapters place image and media as their main focus. Paul Elliot takes as his starting point the perceptions of the Second World War Home Front which are contained in the popular sit-com *Dad's Army* (1968–1977) and interrogates discourses that surround non-conscripted masculinities in 1940s cinema in his chapter – 'The Weak and the Wicked' whilst Maggie Andrews' closing chapter explores contemporary images and ideas of the Home Front in popular television drama series.

This volume is not intended to be an overarching guide to the Home Front in Britain in the First World War and the Second World War, such a task would be impossible. We are well aware that there are inevitably many silences, a consequence of the paucity of sources and the serendipity of chance that leads to the production of a volume like this, the meetings and contacts, which brought these chapters together. It has also been shaped by the timing, which meant that particular research was ready for publication at this specific juncture in time. We acknowledge the problems in this, but hope that this collection will act as a stimulus to further academic work and provide a catalyst for a reappraisal of the place of the Home Front in British conceptualisations of war and conflict. We also hope that there will be, in the next four years of the First World War commemoration, more case studies of how war shapes the everyday experience of people within their domestic, working and leisure lives.

Notes

1. S. Grayzel (1999) 'Nostalgia, Gender, and the Countryside: Placing the "Land Girl" in First World War Britain', *Rural History*, 10, 2, pp 155–170.
2. A. Marwick (1965) *The Deluge: British Society in the First World War* (London: Macmillan).
3. A. Marwick (1974) *War and Social Change in the Twentieth Century: A Comparative Study of Britain, France and Germany, Russia and the United States* (Basingstoke: Macmillan).
4. See for example, G. Braybon and P. Summerfield (1987) *Out of the Cage: Women's Experiences in Two World Wars* (London: Pandora); P. Summerfield (1998) *Reconstructing Women's Wartime Lives* (Manchester: Manchester University Press).
5. G. Holloway (2005) *Women and Work in Britain Since 1840* (London: Taylor and Francis).
6. See A. Gregory (2008) *The Last Great War: British Society and the First World War* (Cambridge: Cambridge University Press).
7. A. Calder (1969) *The People's War* (London: Jonathan Cape).

1
Ideas and Ideals of Domesticity and Home in the First World War

Maggie Andrews (with thanks to Layla Byron)

Introduction

The munitions worker and the Women's Land Army are familiar images of the Home Front in First World War and the number of women in paid employment increased during the conflict; however the majority of women remained in the home[1] or retained domestic roles and responsibilities alongside paid work. Nevertheless domestic life can still be categorised by Gilbert and Gubar as part of the 'unofficial female history' of First World War [2] which has received limited academic attention. This chapter suggests that during the conflict, the home and women's associated domestic and emotional responsibilities for nurturing and supporting men were sustained, reworked, stretched and developed in Britain. A range of letters, diaries, memories, newspapers and posters, particularly from the West Midlands, will be utilised to draw attention to the significance of the domestic activities women undertook in wartime. Women cared for or supported men in their domestic lives and in voluntary activities beyond their homes; hence gender roles and status were not fundamentally challenged. Indeed the seeds were sewn for a new privileging of the domestic[3] within private life, the imagination and public discourses[4] in the post-war era.

The idea of home has been utilised in numerous ways; as a place of emotional belonging, a domestic space to inhabit, a physical building or a homeland which is idealised, dreamed about and fought for. Ostensibly, one of the reasons men enlisted was to protect their homes and families. A recruitment poster which addressed the 'Men of Essex' and encouraged them to 'Rally Round the Colours and Keep the Flag Flying' by joining others in the Essex regiment went on to ask them: 'Do you realise that these men are giving their lives to protect your homes from devastation, your wives and daughters from being dishonoured?'[5] The connection drawn between enlisting in the armed forces and protecting home was more credible after the shelling of Whitby, Scarborough and Hartlepool on 16 December 1914. These raids were referred to specifically in the recruitment posters which followed; one bore an image of a young girl holding her sibling in her arms in front of a damaged house. The accompanying strapline asked: 'Men of Britain! Will You Stand This?' and went on to explain underneath:

> No 2 Wykeham Street, Scarborough after the German bombardment on Dec 16th. It was the Home of a Working Man, four People were killed in this House including the Wife and Two Children the youngest aged 5. 78 Women & Children were killed and 228 Women & Children were wounded by the German Raiders. ENLIST NOW.[6]

The relationship between what became an idealised version of home to be protected and the lived experience of everyday domestic life could however be tenuous. Between 1914 and 1918, domestic roles and responsibilities expanded both within and beyond the home. Domesticity in wartime for women was varied, influenced by wealth, class, age and geographical location. Some women kept house not only for their families but also for billeted soldiers or Belgian refugees. Wives and children took on new roles and responsibilities in family farms, smallholdings and businesses when husbands or sons left for war. Some wealthier women were alarmed to discover the supply of domestic servants decreasing, whilst others with large houses converted part of their home into a convalescence hospital for wounded soldiers. As the conflict progressed it increasingly interfered with daily life in the home in ways unimaginable to previous generations, causing disruption and destruction. War fractured families, displaced people, destroyed homes and ended lives. Food shortages, queues and rationing, in the latter part of the war, added to the stress of housewives, as did the Zeppelin raids. Although arguably the civilian casualties in First World War were small, just under 1500 people, 'the Zeppelin's impact was more imaginative than factual'.[7] However for many, concerns about bombing were outweighed by more immediate practical and financial problems or anxiety over their relations at the front.

Not too far from home to be looked after

Men's decisions to enlist presented their wives and mothers with challenges in continuing domestic management, provisioning and caring.

Sylvia Pankhurst, who lived in the East End, noted that 'a poor neigh-bour of ours ... got into debt to buy new underclothing for her husband when he went to camp'.[8] Furthermore initial organisational problems meant that many women needed to provide their husbands and sons in the camps with food and other items whilst difficulties over the payment of separation allowances meant that working class women were them-selves short of funds. Mothers who had relied upon their son's contri-bution to the household struggled particularly in financial terms in the early days of the conflict. For some women, however, whose domestic arrangements were less than ideal, the war came as a welcome break:

> One woman with a very bad husband owned frankly that she would not be sorry if he were killed. 'But I suppose he'll be spared, and others as'd be missed'll be taken, for that's the way of things.' Said she, 'It's the only time as I and the children 'as peace, The war's been appy time for us.[9]

For others wartime separation was a very different story. Nancy Huston has suggested that 'women in the First World War were presented with a limited range of prescribed roles by propaganda, as mother, sweetheart, wife, sister or daughter'[10] and as such, whether in paid work or not, they took on the main task of writing and sending parcels to men in the armed forces. In so doing they provided the ammunition to keep the idea, and the ideal, of home alive for their men. Women's sometimes time-consuming emotional and practical labour was utilised to send letters and cigarettes, tobacco, chocolate or other comforts to the troops as they attempted to continue to nurture and care for the welfare of the men who were away from home.

As, Joanna Bourke has suggested: 'men's identities remained lodged within their civilian environment'.[11] Indeed the home and fighting fronts were intimately linked as recent scholarship has emphasised.[12] Adrian Gregory has pointed out one of the unfortunate consequences of the attention given by historians to the most famous First World War literature is an emphasis on the bond between soldiers whilst the strong bonds those in the armed forces maintained with their homes can be sidelined.[13] Soldiers' bonds and identification with their homes and communities were nurtured by a heavy traffic of letters; in 1916, for example, 5,000,000 letters were sent each week from the British Expeditionary Force in France and Belgium to Britain. One soldier claimed to have received '167 letters besides papers and parcels and [had] written 242 letters'[14] in the preceding twelve months. Michael Roper observes the post was something tangible which enabled the receiver to 'touch the very paper that the loved one had held.'[15] Letters came from relatives and friends; they provided news but also acted as a space for emotional exchange, ensuring that the lines of communication were maintained between those at home and the men living in grim or alien circumstances whether in training camps, hospitals or theatres of war. The letters of William John Brown, who was only eighteen when he joined up (see Figure 1.1), demonstrates this. He wrote regularly to his mother in Worcester, mainly about life at home, asking after the health of his father who was ill, and constantly anxious for news of his beloved pigeons – who for him represented home and freedom.

Dear Mother and Sister

I had a letter off Frank and he has written the address on for me if you write again. We are expecting to move this week to Tidworth so write before Saturday.

I am getting on quite well but it's a bit rough. We have plenty of food. The time I am writing this is Wednesday February 17th.

I am glad dad is getting better and I hope you are all in good health and happy. The other piece is for Ernie Noake as I want to know how the pigeons is getting on as there is no one down here only seagulls and a few german ships whats captured.

With best love to you all from Bill[16]

We have no record of William Brown's mother's response to this letter or her experience of war; many of the women's letters, diaries and memoirs that have survived are from women with more money, education and time than William Brown's working class Worcester mother. His letters indicate his delight when his sister Amy sent him a cake and cherries. Fowler has suggested that perhaps the 'sending of comforts to colleagues and friends at the front' should be seen as 'an extension of informal patterns of aid to neighbours in distress that had kept so many working class families going for generations'.[17] Similarly the correspondence that has survived between the middle class Vera Brittain and her fiancé Roland Leighton hints at the 'connectedness'[18] between the home and fighting fronts afforded by:

photographs, letters, parcels from home, newspapers and magazines; tangible objects were as much part of the dialogue as the words themselves. Thus, for example, Vera Brittain sent Roland Leighton the fountain pen with which he wrote to her, and he in turn sent her violets picked from the roof of his dug-out in Ploegsteert Wood.[19]

This led to what Carol Acton has termed 'interdependence' whereby the 'massive flow of communication between the two worlds', which took place through correspondence, challenges simplistic divisions between male and female wartime experience.[20] This flow of communication was supplemented by interactions with men in the armed forces, or women in support and nursing services whether in the field, in Britain on leave or to recover from injuries. The documentary of *The Battle of the Somme* in 1916 also provided an inkling of men's experiences of war for those on the Home Front, albeit a selective and partial one. It 'set box-office records in Great Britain'[21] as civilians seized the opportunity to catch a glimpse of their relatives or friends and strengthen their sense of connection with them. Women's sending of regular letters and parcels to their families was thus framed by an awareness of the danger that their loved ones might be in.

Some women wrote every day to their husbands or every week to several sons in different parts of the world, maintaining their domestic caring role even though their men were in armed forces. William Brown placed great emotional investment in the letters and parcels he received from home. On the 13 January 1916, he wrote 'I am expecting to go away, back to Salonika, so write back soon.'[22] Letters indicate how important any contact which reminded him of home was. He requested items which were not readily available such as Woodbines and in one letter a handkerchief saying: 'I want you to try and send me a handkerchief as we cant go out when we like, and I want a handkerchief bad', (see Figure 1.2).[23] Thus one of the responsibilities of women on the Home Front became to source and supply a range of items including socks and underwear. Better-off families also sent blankets, helmets, scarves, jerkins, equipment and overcoats[24] to men in the armed forces and when the poet and officer, Wilfred Owen got a parcel from home he apparently 'snuggled up in bed to open it' and said, 'It was like a look in at home, to burrow into that lovely big box and examine all the loving presents.'[25] Food and tobacco were very common ingredients in parcels although they did not always travel well, soldiers reported parcels arriving when strawberries had turned into a sludgy mess or rats had nibbled at loaves of bread. Some gifts were perhaps inappropriate but, as Rachel Duffett has suggested, 'the parcels were proof that the men at the Front were not forgotten and that their sacrifices were acknowledged and appreciated.'[26] The parcels and letters also helped to maintain the idea of the home in the men's imagination.

Providing domestic care at a distance, homely comforts and emotional support for men in the armed forces was a complex and expanding role for women in wartime, seen as their patriotic duty. Lois Turner, a young middle class girl from Stone in Staffordshire, corresponded with a number of young men, seeing it perhaps as war work. The letters she received indicate her efforts were valued, comments from recipients include: 'Thanks for the shirt, socks etc needless to say they are most welcome' and 'I must write and thank you for those dear little macaroons you sent in Billie's parcel especially for me' or even 'I am so jolly glad I came to see you. Dear Lois ... I can just picture you making that nice homemade bread' (see Figure 1.4).[27] In the carnage and death toll on the 'Western Front', which Hobsbawm has suggested 'became a machine for massacre',[28] holding onto images of home became an essential element of emotional survival.[29] To one of Lois's correspondents the image of her making bread, which he nurtured in his imagination, represented the ideal domestic world, for which he was fighting and to which he hoped to return. Women like Lois Turner extended their domestic caring and nurturing to men outside their immediate family and friends. In this she was not alone; the *Manchester Evening News* reported in December 1914 that 'many soldiers at the front had nobody to care for them, and nobody to write to them.' This resulted in 90,000 'godmothers' adopting lonely soldiers at the front[30] to whom they wrote letters and sent small comforts. Such charitable activities became an important extension of domestic women's war work.

Volunteering: extending domestic caring and nurturing to others

Women individually or through the 18,000 charities set up 'with the aim of relieving distress caused by the war or providing comforts to servicemen and their dependents'[31] extended their domestic, caring and nurturing duties beyond their own homes and families. Caroline Playne's 1931 remark about the outbreak of war that 'the great era of knitting set in'[32] is a little dismissive but women's domestic skills were certainly commandeered for the national war effort. As the *Worcester Herald* explained in an article addressed to women in the first week of the war, 'Now that the dreaded hour has arrived and our country has been asked to take its part in the terrible war which may devastate Europe, we women have to think how we can best aid our soldiers at the front and their families at home.'[33] Women's role was thus articulated in terms of supporting soldiers and their families and numerous local and national charities sprung up to help those on the Home Front with this undertaking.

Newspapers organised charities and campaigns; the *Daily Telegraph* mobilised its readers to send money to support Belgian refugees. Whilst *Sporting Life* ensured that footballs, boxing gloves and playing cards would be sent to soldiers, *The Weekly Despatch* focussed on providing tobacco.[34] Some 740 charities solicited help for prisoners of war in Germany, with women undertaking fund-raising activities. In Worcester, examples of such charitable activities include the Lady Mayoress's charity to help servicemen's wives and local residents, set up in 1914, and two years later organising a Christmas party for children orphaned by the war. Women's motivation to undertake charitable work was varied; for some it was about fulfilling their patriotic duty,[35] feeling useful, a connection to their loved ones, or a way to deal with grief and gain companionship. Wartime activities could provide communality, a female space for the exchange of gossip and chatter. The Women's Institute Movement set up under the auspices of the Agricultural Organisation Society to improve the food supply in 1915 epitomises this. Its slogan 'For Home and Country' linked the Home Front to the national war effort but for many of the women its appeal lay in the companionship, friendship and relief from domestic drudgery that it offered.[36]

Under the umbrella of charitable activities, domestic caring was stretched into public spaces through the provision of canteens, staffed by volunteers, set up to minister to those on their way to and from the front, hospitals or training camps. Miss Margaret Boulton and Miss Marietta Feurheerd opened the Victoria Station Buffet on 4 February 1915, serving tea, coffee, cocoa, Bovril, sandwiches and cake to soldiers and sailors.[37] A writing table was provided for the men's use and cigarettes, socks and mittens distributed. In Stafford, a plaque commemorates that the Empire Club in 1917 and 1918 in St Chad's School Room 'was privileged to provide rest and refreshment for more than forty thousand men of his majesty's forces.'[38]

Some undertook domestic activities much further afield, Sarah McNaughton set up a soup kitchen to assist refugees and troops fleeing the German army as it advanced through Belgium in 1914. She recorded that

> I am up to my eyes in soup! I have started a soup kitchen at the station and it gives me a lot to do ... The first convoy gets to the station about 9:30 a.m., all the men frozen, the black ones nearly dead with cold As soon as the train arrives I carry out one of my boiling marmites

to the middle of the stone entrance and ladle out the soup while a Belgium Sister takes round coffee and bread.[39]

Although it can be argued that both Sarah McNaughton's memoirs, and narratives such as Vera Brittain's autobiography of her experience as a Red Cross Voluntary Aid Detachment (VAD) nursing in France[40] 'challenge the definition that equates women with "home" they still continue to support the combatant/noncombatants'[41] division. Perhaps more importantly these women are still doing fundamentally domestic and caring roles to support men, some of them intimate caring roles. Vera Brittain, recalling her work as a VAD, noted that 'Towards the men I came to feel an almost adoring gratitude for their simple and natural acceptance of my ministrations. Short of actually going to bed with them, there was hardly an intimate service that I did not perform for one or another in the course of four years.'[42] Caring for the wounded was in many ways the apex of domestic femininity.

In such a cultural atmosphere, unsurprisingly, support for the Red Cross was ubiquitous; it raised £22 million during the war; its mission touched the spirit of the era, consequently its annual flag day was called 'Our day'. Amateur nursing was one opening for middle class women in wartime. For the majority of women who had neither funds, knowledge nor the freedom from domestic responsibilities to become a VAD, there were other possibilities, such as rolling bandages or assisting in local convalescence hospitals. A leading article in the *Worcester Herald* at the outbreak of the war explained:

Women who have not been trained as nurses would not be much good at the front, even if they were able to go, but there are few women who could not give efficient help in a sick room or a ward of a hospital under the supervision of a good trained head. Most, perhaps all, of the members of the Red Cross Society have been through an ambulance course and many have had instruction in nursing and although this does not imply sufficient knowledge to take sole charge it does mean that a woman is much better equipped than she would have been without instruction.[43]

Convalescence hospitals sprung up in larger houses, approximately 30 in Worcestershire alone. One of the first was in Evesham Manor, which the owner, Mrs Rudge, had ready to receive patients by 24 September 1914. Her example was followed by others including the Bishop's Palace at Hartlebury Castle, which became a VAD hospital in 1915. Soldiers' entries in the autograph book written to the commandant and staff at Hartlebury hospital emphasised it has been to them a 'home from home'. One inmate explained, 'I can honestly say you could not wish for a better staff that what is here. They are very kind to all of us and I can sincerely say they are doing all they possibly can for me.' Appreciation of the kindness, caring and nurturing appears in almost all the entries. 'I spent a most happy month at the above convalesce home, for which I am most grateful I found the nurses always very kind and anxious to help me when I was sick.'[44]

Caring for the wounded extended beyond those who nursed or volunteered in hospitals; local communities and indeed the whole country became involved in the National Egg Collection for the Wounded Soldiers, a scheme with Queen Alexandra as the patron. Over 2000 collection points were organised by volunteers throughout the country, from where eggs were packed into boxes with straw and shipped to hospitals in France and Britain. Poultry keeping was a predominantly female and domestic area of agriculture but in urban areas women were expected to utilise less eggs in their cooking contributing those saved to the campaign. In places ranging from Harrods to Much Wenlock in Shropshire, where women set up a stall in front of the Market Hall (see front cover) contributions were made to the approximately one million eggs required each month. Local communities were also involved in caring for the wounded more directly. Farmers donated food to Evesham Manor Hospital, local residents organised outings for the wounded soldiers, and women provided accommodation for wives and mothers when they visited their husbands and sons in the hospital. Indeed, one element of charitable work was that it enabled many women to undertake domestic and caring roles.

Wealthier wives or mothers often went to the Front to bring back injured or deceased relatives, although their interference near the battlefields was often unwelcome. For those without such funds visiting a sick relative could be facilitated by financial support from the Young Men's Christian Association (YMCA), as was extended, for example, to a woman whose son had been gassed when serving in the Shropshire Light Infantry. After a 20-mile walk to Hereford railway station, she was funded by the YMCA to travel by train and boat to France where she nursed her son for six weeks until he recovered. While she was away neighbours looked after her children.[45] Indeed, across the country a number of ad hoc and informal arrangements supported woman as wives and mothers to cope. For example, Mrs Stephens, the wife of a Colonel, who ran the Comforts Fund for the Second Battalion of the Rifle Brigade 'organised charitable collections for dependent mothers and subsequently she chased up their claims for the Separation Allowance',[46] whilst in the East End of London Sylvia Pankhurst recalled letters and visits from women asking for help in claiming their separation allowances.[47]

The patchwork of domestic caring by local and national charities played a significant role in meeting some of the social and emotional caring needs of wartime. However the level of concern and nurturing which can be lavished on someone in the unusual circumstances of war, when everyday life is 'touched by the lustre of the idealised nation',[48] cannot necessarily be maintained for long periods of time. An idealisation of domestic femininity as unswervingly caring and supportive is arguably incompatible with women's own emotional needs or the harsh reality of the domestic labour needed to maintain early twentieth century working class homes. Furthermore, as Adrian Gregory argues, as the war progressed concerns were expressed that not everyone was contributing equally,[49] a perennial problem when there is a high reliance on domestic and voluntary labour.

The unattainable ideal of home

For up to four years of war, home was lived and experienced in the imagination for many men, nurtured by parcels and letters, and punctuated by visits home. In such circumstances home was liable to be idealised, touched by nostalgia and sentimentality as in the postcard a young soldier from Shropshire sent to his parents with a picture of a cottage and the following poem:

> Home
> There is something that maketh a palace
> Out of four little walls and a prayer.
> A something seeth a garden
> In one little flower that is fair.
> That turneth two hearts to one purpose
> And maketh one heart out of two.
> That smiles when the sky is a grey one
> And smiles when the sky is blue.[50]

The rural home, as Alun Howkins has suggested, was the home that existed in the imagination of many soldiers.[51] A recruitment poster depicted a British soldier exclaiming to the public 'Isn't this worth fighting for' as he pointed towards rolling countryside, a dairy herd and, most importantly, a thatched cottage;[52] all emblems of Englishness and the ideal of the nation to be protected. The urban working class communities that many soldiers came from bore little resemblance to these idealised images or indeed to the convalescence hospitals in which men recuperated from injury. The Ministry of Reconstruction had identified the need for mass house building in 1917 but this was never realised and the housing crisis remained acute after the war.

Nevertheless 'whatever home meant, and however different it was from army life, men imagined it in their dreams, on sentry duty and at mealtimes, not just when writing home'.[53] Whilst Eric Leed's suggestion that these 'imaginings were nothing more than a kind of false consciousness'[54] could be described as too dismissive, it would perhaps be difficult for the everyday life to live up to the ideal for which men had risked their lives[55] – an idealisation perhaps maintained by the hesitancy of wives or mothers to fill their letters with their own everyday trials and tribulations which could be seen as trivial. Mrs Peel, for example, condemned 'girl clerks' from the Admiralty, who were in hysterics during an air raid, 'my sympathies are with the men who have to bear this kind of thing day after day and night after night.'[56]

However not all men had spent their war on the Western Front, not all women had had to cope with air raids or financial hardship. Once systems were established to pay separation allowances, war initially improved the standard of living for George Hewins' family in Stratford-upon-Avon. He had eight children and the regular payments for his wife and each of his eight children compared well to his pre-war pay. The home his wife was able to move into, that he visited when on leave, surpassed anything he had previously experienced:

> It was really modern, three bedrooms and two rooms downstairs – a nice front room and a kitchen. The coalhouse was inside and the toilet was in the yard, but it was a good toilet you didn't have to share! The missus loved it...One thing was certain she was better off with me in the army! She had money coming in regular, now, for the first time.[57]

This was the home that men and women wanted at the end of the war when as Bourke argues, 'Married men returned to their familiar beds; unmarried men sought companions. For these men, home was the ultimate retreat from the disciplines of military society.'[58] As both the Director of the Ministry of Pensions and *The Times* acknowledged, home was where soldiers wanted to return.[59] Historians' discussion of post-war gender roles has perhaps placed too much emphasis on women being pushed out of wartime jobs into the home when some occupations, such as munitions work, ended with the war. Furthermore, for men in the armed forces and many housewives who had struggled with an increasing workload caused by wartime shortages and the expansion of their domestic roles, there was also the pull towards their ideal – the domestic life of home. Thus the 1918 slogan: 'Homes Fit for Heroes' captured the structure of the feeling[60] of the moment. However for George Hewins' injury, problems with his pension and employment were to make domestic life in the inter-war years difficult. He was not alone, many disabled ex-servicemen struggled to re-adjust to domestic life as did those who had not maintained their bonds with home and family.[61] In some households the men did not return, but many of those who did were physically and emotionally injured and received very limited pension provision. There were increasing difficulties finding work as the economic recession of the inter-war years took hold and the domestic idyll that had been fought for proved elusive for many.

Conclusion

In many areas of voluntary work wartime gave women the opportunity to develop a range of new experiences, skills and confidence. Nevertheless in the main, women remained predominantly concerned with caring for or supporting men; domesticity expanded and was reworked to include care for men away from home and a range of domestic and caring tasks for others outside the parameters of the home. These created perhaps unrealistic ideals about women and domesticity and did little to fundamentally challenge gender roles or the status of women. In the post-war era 'women, far from being liberated found that traditional gender roles remained not only intact but in many cases reinforced'[62] and there was an increasing emphasis on the cult of domesticity.[63]

Notes

My thanks go in writing this chapter to Layla Byron who, when a student at the University of Worcester, looked at soldiers' relationship to their homes and in doing so identified some of the references used here.

1. M. Pugh (1992) *Women and the Women's Movement*, pp 19–21.
2. S. Gilbert and S. Gubar (1994) *No Man's Land*, p 262.
3. J. Giles (2004) *The Parlour and the Suburb*.
4. K. Hunt (2000) 'Negotiating the Boundaries', pp 389–410.

5. Men of Essex Regiment, Essex Regiment Poster (IWM PROC 286) reproduced in IWM (2012) *Fit Men Wanted: Original Posters from the Home Front* (London: Thames and Hudson).
6. Parliamentary Recruiting Committee 1915, IWM PST 5119 http://vads.ahds.ac.uk/large.php?uid=26884&sos=1
7. A. Freedman (2004) 'Zeppelins, Fiction and the Home Front', pp 47–62.
8. S. Pankhurst (1987[1932]) *Home Front*, p 77.
9. Mrs C. Peel quoted in J. Marlow (2009[1999]) *The Virago Book of Women*, p 201.
10. N. Huston (1983) 'Tales of War, Tears of Women', p 275.
11. J. Bourke (1996) *Dismembering the Male*, p 170.
12. See for example D. Todman (2008) *The Great War*; A. Gregory (2005) *The Last Great War*; and M. Roper (2009) *The Secret Battle*.
13. A. Gregory (2005) *The Last Great War*, p 134.
14. A. Tapert (1984) *Despatches from the Heart*, p 10.
15. M. Roper (2009) *The Secret Battle*, p 49.
16. Letters of *William John Brown to his Mother during the Great War*, private collection of Sean Brown.
17. S. Fowler (1999) 'War Charity Begins at Home', pp 17–23.
18. C. Acton (1999) 'Writing and Waiting', pp 54–83, p 62.
19. C. Acton (1999) 'Writing and Waiting', p 62.
20. C. Acton (1999) 'Writing and Waiting', p 80.
21. J. Hodgkins (2008) 'Hearts and Minds and Bodies', pp 9–19.
22. Letters of William Brown.
23. Letters of William Brown.
24. M. Roper (2009) *The Secret Battle*, p 9.
25. W. Owen (1985) 'W. Owen to Mother', p 236.
26. R. Duffett (2011), 'Beyond the Ration', pp 453–473, p 460.
27. Staffordshire Record Office SRO 5778/1/21.
28. E. Hobsbawn (1995) *The Age of Extremes*, p 25.
29. M. Roper (2009) *The Secret Battle*, p 48.
30. Manchester Evening News April 1915, extract reproduced in *Daily Mail*, 28 October 2013 accessed online http://www.dailymail.co.uk/news/article-2477985/Lonely-soldiers-proposed-women-sent-letters-trenches-First-World-War.html 12 February 2014.
31. S. Fowler (1999) 'War Charity Begins at Home', p 18.
32. C. Playne (1931) *Society at War*, p 94.
33. *Worcester Herald*, 8 August 1914.
34. P. Ward (2001) 'Women of Britain Say Go', pp 23–15.
35. P. Ward (2001) 'Women of Britain Say Go'.
36. M. Andrews (1997) *The Acceptable Face of Feminism*.
37. J. Marlow (1999) *The Virago Book of Women*, p 58.
38. Plaque on the corner of St Chad's Place and Tipping Street, facing Tipping Street in Stafford, Staffordshire.
39. S. MacNaughton in J. Marlow (1999) *The Virago Book of Women*, p 58.
40. V. Brittain (2010[1933]) *Testament of Youth*.
41. C. Acton (1999) 'Writing and Waiting', p 56.
42. V. Brittain (2010[1933]) *Testament of Youth*, p 143.
43. *Worcester Herald*, 8 August 1914 p 1.

44. Hartlebury Castle, Voluntary Aided Detachment, hospital at Autograph albums of soldiers who were at the hospital 1915–18, Worcestershire Archives and Archaeological Service Accession number 11662 ref 899:1114.
45. http://www.bbc.co.uk/programmes/p01p345j
46. M. Roper (2009) *The Secret Battle*, pp 215–216.
47. S. Pankhurst (1987[1932]) *The Home Front*, pp 77–84.
48. A. Heller (1984) *Everyday Life*, p 4.
49. A. Gregory (2005) *The Last Great War*, p 110.
50. www.bbc.co.uk/programmes/p01p350n
51. A. Howkins (1986) 'The Discovery of Rural England'.
52. Parliamentary Recruiting Committee 1915, The University Library Special Collections Leeds http://library.leeds.ac.uk/special-collections-exhibitions-war-propaganda#activate-image7
53. M. Roper (2009) *The Secret Battle*, p 72.
54. E. Leed (1981), *No Man's Land*, p 72.
55. J. Bourke (1996) *Dismembering the Male*, p 163.
56. S. Peel (1929) *How We Lived Then: 1914–1918: A Sketch of Social and Domestic Life During the War*, quoted in P. Ward 'Women of Britain say Go', p 35.
57. A. Hewins (1981) *The Dillen*, p 138.
58. J. Bourke (1996) *Dismembering the Male*, p 168.
59. J. Bourke (1996) *Dismembering the Male*, p 168.
60. R. Williams (1961) *The Long Revolution*.
61. J. Bourke (1996) *Dismembering the Male*.
62. P. Ward (2001) 'Women of Britain Say Go'.
63. See, for example J. Giles (2004) *The Parlour and the Suburb*; M. Andrews (2012) *Domesticating the Airwaves*; and A. Light (1991) *Forever England*.

References

Acton. C (1999) 'Writing and Waiting: The First World War Correspondence between Vera Brittain and Roland Leighton', *Gender and History*, 11, 1, April, pp 54–83.
Andrews. M (1997) *The Acceptable Face of Feminism: The Women's Institute as a Social Movement* (London: Lawrence and Wishart).
Andrews. M (2012) *Domesticating the Airwaves* (London: Continuum).
Bourke. J (1996) *Dismembering the Male: Britain, Men's Bodies and the Great War* (London: Reaktion Books).
Brittain. V (1933 reprinted 2010) *Testament of Youth* (London: Virago).
Duffett. R (2011) 'Beyond the Ration: Sharing and Scrounging on the Western Front', *Twentieth Century British History*, 22, 4, pp 453–473.
Freedman. A (2004) 'Zeppelins, Fiction and the Home Front', *Journal of Modern Literature*, 27, 3, Winter, pp 47–62.
Fowler. S (1999) 'War Charity Begins at Home', *History Today*, September, pp 17–23.
Gilbert. S and Gubar. S (1994) *No Man's Land: The Place of the Woman Writer in the Twentieth Century, Vol 3: Sexchanges* (London: Yale University Press).
Giles. J (2004) *The Parlour and the Suburb: Domestic Identities, Class, Femininity and Modernity* (Oxford: Berg).

Gregory. A (2005) *The Last Great War: British Society and the First World War* (Cambridge: Cambridge University Press).

Heller. A (1984) *Everyday Life* (Oxford: Routledge and Kegan Paul).

Hobsbawn. E (1995) *The Age of Extremes* (London: Abacus).

Hewins. A (1981) *The Dillen* (London: Elm Tree Books).

Hodgkins. J (2008) 'Hearts and Minds and Bodies: Reconsidering the Cinematic Language of *The Battle of the Somme*', in *Film & History: An Interdisciplinary Journal of Film and Television Studies*, pp 9–19.

Howkins. A (1986) 'The Discovery of Rural England', in *Englishness, Politics and Culture 1880–1920* by R. Colls and P. Dodd (eds) (London: Croom Helm) pp 78–92.

Huston. N (1983) 'Tales of War, Tears of Women', *Women's Studies International Forum 5*, pp 271–282.

Hunt. K (2000) 'Negotiating the Boundaries of the Domestic: British Socialist Women and the Politics of Consumption, *Women's History Review*, 9, 2, pp 389–410.

Leed. E (1981) *No Man's Land: Combat and Identity in World War One* (Cambridge: Cambridge University Press) cited in M Roper (2009) *The Secret Battle Emotional Survival in the Great War* (Manchester: Manchester University Press).

Light. A (1991) *Forever England: Femininity, Literature and Conservatism Between the Wars* (Oxford: Routledge).

Marlow. J (1999) *The Virago Book of Women and the Great War* (London: Virago).

Owen. W (1985) '"W. Owen to Mother" 6th April 1917', in J. Bell (ed.) *Wilfred Owen, Selected Letters* (Oxford: Oxford University Press).

Pankhurst. S (1987) *The Home Front*, orig. 1932 (London: Cresset Library).

Peel. Mrs C quoted in J. Marlow (1999 reprinted 2009) *The Virago Book of Women and the Great War* (London: Virago).

Playne. C (1931) *Society at War* (London: George Allen and Unwin).

Pugh. M (1992) *Women and the Women's Movement in Britain 1914–1959* (Basingstoke: Macmillan) pp 19–21.

Roper. M (2009) *The Secret Battle: Emotional Survival in the Great War* (Manchester: Manchester University Press.

Tapert. A (1984) *Despatches from the Heart: An Anthology of Letters from the Front* (London: Hamish Hamilton).

Todman. D (2008) *The Great War and Myth and Memory* (London: Hambledon).

Ward. P (2001) 'Women of Britain Say Go: Women's Patriotism in the First World War', *Twentieth Century British History*, 12, 1, pp 23–45.

Williams. R (1961) *The Long Revolution* (Harmondsworth: Pelican Books).

2

A Personal Account of the Home Front

Angela Clare Smith

Introduction

This chapter is based on a collection of letters between Jack and Gert Adam dating from the First World War. Unlike popular representations of women able to 'do their bit' during wartime, this story is one example of the many thousands of women whose role was raising children and maintaining their home. John Gill Simpson Adam, known as Jack, and Gertrude, known as Gert were both born in Doncaster; (Jack on 30 July 1883 and Gert on 22 October 1882). Jack worked for a time in Doncaster but once married, they moved down to Highbury in North London where Jack was a teacher at Drayton Park School. The couple had three children – John William Marshall, also known as Jack, born in 1909, followed by Peggy in 1910 and Madge in 1912. In March 1915 he volunteered to join the British Army. Many families have kept soldier's letters home and many museum archives contain thousands of such letters, but letters sent to soldiers are often lost, leaving fewer accounts of home life. However, this collection offers insights into life at home as Jack sometimes wrote on the reverse of his letters from Gert and many letters from Gert were returned to her. There are even letters between the children and their father. These letters provide an insight into not only Gert's experiences on the Home Front, coping without her husband and the grief of separation, but also into the lives of the many forgotten but remarkable women, whose personal memories add to the diversity of experiences from this period.[1] For arguably, it is through reading an individual's letters and individual stories rather than statistics of numbers killed, families divided, women widowed and children left fatherless, that an understanding can be gleaned of how families' everyday lives were affected by separation, anxiety and grief in wartime.

Jack and Gert's eloquent and heartfelt letters vividly capture their experiences and emotions; Jack's desire was for life on the Home Front to remain unchanged, and a recognisable home maintained for his return, making the separation seem just temporary; Gert at home with the three young children, wrote to Jack at every opportunity and encouraged the children to write to their father, knowing how much their letters would mean to him; Jack, huddled in his cold quarters, machine gun fire in the distance, wrote merrily of his 'adventures' and longed to get home. Gert described sitting by the window waiting for the post delivery, anxious as always for news; and Jack 'sitting on top of a shell-hole wounded in the knee',[2] wondering whether he would ever see his loved ones again. In the final months of the war Gert's letters to Jack were returned unopened and he was reported as missing in action. The collection reveals her anguish as she waited news and her endeavours to find out exactly what had happened to her husband. Jack did not return from the war and Gert was not told officially that he was killed until much later; leaving her alone to raise their three children.

Of course, using letters as a source has its weaknesses; they can be fragmentary and both writers' thoughts were perhaps self-censored as each writer wanted to reassure the other and selected what to share. Furthermore, although their experiences would have been shared by many, using just one family's account should not be used to make generalisations. Nevertheless, they add another example of the experiences of ordinary families in wartime, narratives that have been previously overlooked, forgotten and nearly lost.[3] The letters have a remarkable story as they were mislaid when the Adam family left their home, found much later by a subsequent owner and purchased by the Royal Armouries Museum in 2006, where they were used to create a play performed at the museum. After one particular performance it transpired that two of the couples' grandchildren were still living in the area and were delighted the letters had been found and their grandparents' story was being shared. They were able to fill in some of the gaps in the story and tell what happened to the family after the war. In 2009, the family discovered more letters which were added to the collection.

Surviving separation

Jack's background as a teacher meant his first role in the army was as a physical training instructor with the 12th Battalion of the London Regiment training new recruits in England. He rose very quickly through the ranks beginning with a promotion to Corporal within two or three days and in May 1915 he was made Sergeant. By August he was promoted to Company Sergeant Major and a later reference on his military career noted 'His experience in teachers' organisations at home made him a very valuable asset to the whole battalion and in any re-shuffling of companies and commanders there was always competition to get in Jack's company.[4] Initially whilst stationed in the south of England, it seems that Jack was able to make regular visits home and his family were able to visit him, but then Gert and the children moved back up to Doncaster to stay with her parents whilst he was away. However after spending much of the war in England, in January 1918 Jack was posted to France. The first letter, which Gert would have no doubt read anxiously, told of his journey across the Channel and is full of reassurances and cheerfulness.

My dear Gert,

Well, we went from Farnborough on Thursday and got aboard at 4.30pm. We started later, racing across at what seemed a terrible rate for a ship, and landed at our destination early in the morning. It was interesting to see our escort and the various tricks and dodges to get safely across. It was a very clear night, quite the worst for our purpose. The decks were strewn and packed with men.

I've met quite a number of my old boys.

We sleep in a tent tonight but it's a great adventure and very novel and interesting at present.

Give my love to the kiddies. For yourself I have nothing left. You have everything but my actual presence and that, I trust, you will have for all time shortly.

Well, Goodbye Darling. Your own Jack.

PS. Keep all my letters and I will tell you more when I see you.[5]

With Jack now in France, letters were sent back and forth almost daily between the couple and Gert kept these letters and many of his letters to the children.

From Daddy Adam. To my three Darlings: Jack, Peg, and Madge.

Still in the same place. Had a look around the town tonight. It's funny when you want something and can't ask for it. Everybody says S'il vous plait every time, which means If you Please.

We had to take our tent down this morning and just where I'd been sleeping was a ball of bits of paper and in the middle were three baby mice without any hair on. They are dead now.

Well, goodbye. I am going on a French train today and they are not half so nice as the English.

Ta ta. Dad.[6]

Although Jack nearly always maintains his cheery tone and optimism to reassure Gert back home, his reflections on events reveal his longing for home. 'We went down to Le Havre again yesterday. Boys keep coming in and going out. It made me nearly cry to see so many marching in the other day. I could see England from the shore'.[7] As well as hearing of Jack's experiences, letters from Gert show how she kept Jack up to date with her life with the children back at home.

I am sitting in front of the fire with Madge on my knee. She is much better but still not up to concert pitch. Just been reading Tennyson's Dora to Peg and Madge. Now Peg has got the hymn book (Just gone over to give Jack's back a pat while he is coughing). Now they are wanting tea, so will go and get it ready. Peg just remarked this is the 'baddest' writing I have done – and no wonder.[8]

A letter on 9 March suggests both her longing for him and her anxiety: 'My dear Jack, I could only make guesses at the place you have been in. I sincerely hope you are moving back. The nearer you are to England the better will suit me.'[9] Jack remains positive and reassures Gert that he will manage to get home on leave. 'My chum's wife wrote to say that married soldiers are to have leave every 6 months and in that case I shall be home for my birthday. I hope so.'[10] On his birthday, 30 July, Jack kept things light and told Gert about the letters his men were sending home. 'Dear mother, This war is a b_ _ r send me some humbugs.' Another one, 'Dear Wife, Please send 10/- and the "Christian Herald". Don't forget the "Christian Herald". Things go on charmingly and we laugh and joke the whole day through. There's no place like Blighty though. More later, Jack.'[11]

By August 1916, some 1.1 million letters were sent to the Western Front each day and it is perhaps inevitable difficulties with correspondence were a source of much frustration and some confusion. On 11 February, Jack wrote 'Still no letter arrives. I have had the one from Elsie. I am getting quite anxious that no other has arrived. Of course there may not have been time for you to have written since I gave you my new address.'[12] When he received word from Gert five days later he replied 'Well at last we are in touch and I have now received your letter written on Sunday last 10th.'[13] On 23 February, Jack again has not heard from Gert and wrote 'Sweetheart, I am somewhat at a loss about your letters; they have suddenly ceased to arrive. I don't think I have had one since Tuesday at least. I had one from Mother yesterday.'[14] He hears from her again on 26 February, 'I had your letter yesterday in which you are so pleased we have got into communication. I am awaiting your long letter, which you promise. I think you have all my letters haven't you. All I am missing are those you sent at first.'[15] The postal service was a lifeline for both those serving overseas and those at home. Awaiting the daily delivery at home or in the field would have been anxious, days at a time spent with no news. As van Emden suggests, 'If anything, it was easier not to receive a letter on a regular basis as a lengthy silence was not then misinterpreted as something ominous.'[16] Gert reveals how desperate she was to hear from Jack and the couples' anxiety would have been shared by many at the time and it would no doubt affect everyday life and functionality when nothing was heard. On 21 February, Gert had written the following to Jack:

> Oh Jack how glad I am we have got in touch at last – made one begin to feel desperate.
>
> Yes I think it takes about four days for your letters to reach me.
>
> This one was written on the 16th, got here this morning 21st.
>
> Busy morning boy so will write after dinner and send by this even post.
>
> Can't wait till afternoon – feel I must just let a little steam off. I heard too that leave is to be every six months for married soldiers, nine for single men. Oh boy it's too intoxicating to think of! It is so lovely to think you will really get my letters now; it puts some heart into me.
>
> Jack, I've written and written – smiles and tears, but I feel jubilant this morning.
>
> Mother is very glad you are getting plenty of food. She has been busy preparing pickles for when you come home. We get what we need. The worst is the standing for it. Mother was an hour and a half getting suet this morning. She is always thinking about you.
>
> You will know by Jack's letters he is in good spirits and going to school. Peg too is merry and bright. I think she has a daily practise on the trapezes at the Shakespeare drinking fountain. She does seem strong. She was taking the market men off last night. You would have rocked with laughter to hear her. Then she was Jack's horse. It was a wet night and they had to give vent to their energy indoors. I have

a fire every day in the front room and they play nicely there, or knit or draw.

I will send the Diary off tomorrow

Good bye till then

Your Own Darling.[17]

Jack's reply attempts to reassure her and indicated he is aware of the growing difficulties of everyday life on the Home Front, including the food queues.

I get your letters and they will follow me now.

Nothing to get desperate about, I can carry on my present job for duration. Yes, the leave is nice, but I am afraid 'military contingencies' will not allow it when the time comes. Let's hope they will. Bravo! for the pickles. Yes you've 'written and written' and incidentally I have not done bad have I? I don't see any necessity for tears, should be all smiles, it is with me.

I am sorry about the standing for food. I don't like that, and am very sorry for Mother. Give her my love.

Tell Peg Dad used to swing on the same bar when he was a boy and I should very much like to have heard her taking off the market men.

It's a good idea to take them in the room. All you want there is a piano.

I am expecting a diary and a long letter today.

I think there is nothing else darling.

God bless you all

Your Sweetheart.[18]

Gert's letters often shared her and her mother's concern over food. Voluntary rationing was introduced in some areas in 1917 and added to the strain of the mother with children to feed. On 16 February, Jack tells her 'yes you can manage with vegetables, the French in all the parts I have seen live on nothing else. The difficulty of looking after the allotment will be the worst.'[19] Again on 19 February he refers to food saying: 'I think the rationing will be better. We are alright and want nothing. I am sorry you are all so short of food. That is to say as things go. There is plenty of fresh butter here; I wish I could get it across. Here we are alright. I have my food today in sufficiency.' Aware from Gert's letter that the children had been unwell he added: 'Sorry about the kiddies' earache. They seem to have it pretty frequently.'[20] His continuing concern for her welfare is emphasised when, on 23 February, Jack provides instructions for Gert on the separation allowance she was entitled to.[21] As well as matters of food, money and the children, three letters hint at the longing for the intimacy of married life. In one letter Jack suggests that when he gets home 'I think we shall have another honeymoon'. In another he teases 'Frisky? I like that at your age. Why you're an old married woman; at least your husband's an old married man.' In a third and final letter Jack writes: 'I wish I could give it to you. Well we shall someday and it will be nice, but I am getting too old for sweet hearting you know.'[22]

During the first four months Jack was in France Gert was clearly worried, especially as he moved nearer to danger. Although Jack had remained safely in England during most of the war when he was posted overseas he and Gert were, to some extent, aware of the high death toll from newspapers, letters home, photography and film. They may have feared another 'big push' to break the stalemate on the Western Front, with Jack in the middle of it; in June 1918 Jack wrote home from the front line trying to reassure Gert. 'I wish your spirit was as good as mine. The danger is small unless you go over, and I am not likely to do that. Don't worry.'[23] However Jack's proximity to danger was evident in Field Service Postcards sent home in July. November 1914 had seen the first print run of one million copies of Field Service Postcards, designed to be sent by soldiers on the move or on the front line; a quick way to reassure those at home. 'The implicit optimism of the post card is worth noting.'[24] It can only be filled in with a name, date and one option of either the optimistic 'I am quite well' or 'been admitted to hospital'. There was no room for anything in between. 'I am quite well' was all Gert, and many thousands of wives and families were ever informed.[25] After hearing regular news from Jack, to suddenly received field service postcards and inconsistent letters must have made Gert anxious.

Things are going nicely here. This is a good dug-out but very low.

I hear leave will start again in 1919. My chum says that as the birth-rate is declining, soldiers are to be allowed home every Saturday night. What hopes.

I want you very hard sometimes but not in that sense. Lately in fact I forget sometimes I am married.

Yes, I remember you calling on the way upstairs. I wish I could hear you now.

Goodbye. Your darling.[26]

The collection of letters for this time is quite fragmented, but they remained in contact and Gert's letters, such as this one written on 25 July, refer to letters from Jack in July.

Dear Jack,

I've just got your long letter written last Sunday 21st.

I have not stopped to digest it because I want to post this early in the hopes of your getting it on your birthday.

We hoped once there would be no need to write, but one does not dare to hope too much for leave. I try not to think about it; except in a remote sort of way. Are there any hopes – say anywhere near? But I expect one has to wait ones turn. Well, at least if you cannot get home I hope you will get a long rest far away from the line.

Darling I do wish 'Many Happy Returns' and a long Return, and all my love

Ever Your Gert.[27]

Uncertainty: missing in action and waiting for news

In August 1918, Gert's letters to Jack began to be returned to her unopened. Her letter written to him on his birthday, 30 July 1918, a day which they had hoped he would spend at home with his family, came back stamped 'present location unknown'. She had written, 'It's your birthday night, 10.30, and from a weather point of view it has been a lovely day. I will get your paper off tomorrow and this letter. I've had a very busy day today.' Then, as she had not heard from Jack for a while, 'Well, I hope your day has been as happy as possible. I got your field card of the 24th, so by now you may be out. I hope so. Well, goodnight Jack. Your Darling.' Jack was not at this point Gert's only concern; she also mentioned her mother's health in the same letter, 'Mother has been very poorly and had to go to bed at last – has had pains, but I'm hoping a rest in bed will set her up.'[28] When another letter dated 1 August 1918 was also returned to her, Gert acknowledges her growing anxiety in the next letter. 'Dear Jack I'm here and almost ready for dropping off to sleep but I wonder where you are? Perhaps I shall hear something in the morning. I hope you are still going well.' She speaks of an end to the war which was in discussion at this stage. 'The war news continues to be good and I think the big strike is settled up in some way. Some people think the war is nearing the end. It's just dreadful for people to keep on being slaughtered, but I suppose it will probably be ended by other means than fighting.' She ends by saying 'Shall wait for the post before sending. She has just passed. Hope I'll hear something this afternoon. Best Love.'[29]

Gert finally hears news on 9 August but not from Jack himself; several letters had been returned to her and she had received nothing since the field post card on the 25 July. The letter Gert received telling her Jack had been injured was not part of the collection, but the letter she wrote immediately to Jack was, and provides an insight into the suffering of wives on the Home Front: 'My Dear Jack, I am sending this in the hope and prayer that you will be able to read and answer it. I heard this morning you had been wounded and Darling it has been one of the black days of my life. If it's only a scrawl in answer I will thank God for it. Your most anxious Gert.' Not knowing if Jack would receive this she wrote in the margin, 'I have no particulars should be very grateful for information from anyone.'[30] The letter was again later returned unopened and stamped 'Present Location Uncertain'. With no news as to his whereabouts Gert continued to hope and wrote to Jack each day although her anxiety and suffering when faced with the uncertainty is palpable.

Sat. Aug. 10th

My Dear Jack

I feel I must keep writing. I trust you will get the letters.

If I just get a word I'll be most thankful.

I think I must still have a hope that all is well or I don't know how I should bear it.

I have my information that you are wounded from the hospital

Your batman says he missed you 'after the scrap' but was told by some other fellows you were wounded in the knee.

My heart feels almost broken and I pray for just a word of assurance

Ever your Darling

The Kiddies are all well. They are like I am – wanting Daddie very badly.[31]

A letter from Jack Junior posted on 24 July was also returned unopened. Nine-year-old Jack had written, 'Dear Daddy, It is a long time since I wrote to you last. I am sending you a map of England. I have drawn it all myself. I get on very well at school. I can do the sums all right. How are you getting on? I hope you are all right.'[32] Gert now, like many mothers, was charged with reassuring the children that Daddy was safe whilst not knowing herself. From a later history of the Post Office Rifles 8th Battalion, City of London Regiment,[33] and correspondence between Gert and other soldiers in his regiment, it transpired that Jack's regiment had been involved in a daylight raid on the 25 July,[34] five days before his birthday. Jack did not return from the raid and for a considerable time there was such disarray that no one could account for his whereabouts. He was known to have been wounded, which Gert was informed of, but no one could say exactly what happened next.

The uncertainty continued and finding out exactly what happened to their loved ones was, for many wives and families, a significant strain as the remainder of the letters in the collection reveal. After hearing Jack was injured, Gert wrote to the War Office seeking information; she continued to write to Jack, hoping he was injured or taken prisoner and the letters would eventually find him. Sadly, she was only ever to hear ever more discouraging reports about that fateful daylight raid on July 25, from which Jack would never return. A Post Office telegraph dated '31 Aug 18' simply reads 'Regret Sergt Major Adam reported missing since 25.7.18 forward authority for report of death quote casualties 702557 War Office'[35]. On 27 August, Gert had written to the Secretary of the Queen Victoria Jubilee Fund Association for information. Her understated 'I am very troubled' masked a whirlwind of emotions.

> Dear Sir,
>
> I should be very grateful for any information you could give me regarding my husband No.388027 Rank Coy. Sgt. Maj., Name J. G. S. Adam. London Regt A. Coy. I have had no news from him since a field card dated July 24th. He was seen sitting on the top of a shell-hole wounded in the knee and then lost sight of. He has been officially reported 'missing'.
>
> I am very troubled. I should be so thankful if I could know he was a prisoner of war.
>
> Thanking you in anticipation. I am Yours Truly. G. Adam.[36]

However, this letter was returned nearly a month later, unopened, stamped in Geneva, 7 September 1918 and London, 23 September 1918.

Gert did get a reply from Geneva on the 13 September though. 'In reply to your enquiry concerning: Adam Sgt. M. 388027 London Rgt. we herewith beg to inform you that his name has not yet appeared on the Lists of Prisoners, received from Germany. When it does so, we shall let you know as soon as possible.' The letter also stated 'As we find that many enquirers forward us photographs of their missing relatives or friends, we would mention that these are of no use to us in our investigations.'[37] This blunt reflection provides evidence of families' desperation for news and the sheer size of the job keeping track of prisoners and locating missing men.

Gert also corresponded with members of Jack's Regiment trying to find out what had happened, but received only piecemeal evidence. Several letters arrived between September to December 1918, often dashing her hopes of his return. A letter from the Commanding Officer of the 8th London Regiment made it clear that Gert received no final answers as to what had happened to Jack, and perhaps gave her false hopes as well as indicating that communication was sometimes problematic.

Dear Mrs. Adam,

Your registered letter dated Sept 9th duly received yesterday – I regret no trace can be found of your former letter. I regret very much that I cannot give you any definite information about your husband. Every enquiry has been made and I am afraid it is more than probable that he was killed – but no one actually saw him killed nor was his body found, and as some prisoners were captured it is quite possible that he was amongst them. All the information we have been able to collect has been too uncertain to say definitely that he was killed – so I hope that you may shortly hear he is a prisoner in Germany. It takes a long time to get a letter through and it is more than possible you would not have heard yet. You have my sincerest sympathy in this matter and I much regret not being able to help you more.[38]

On 4 October she received the following:

We regret to say that we have received another very discouraging report about your husband from Private MacPhail 48818, who states that he saw your husband lying severely wounded in the leg in an enemy trench to the north of Albert on July 25th. He states that he heard Captain Poulton ask him if he could get back and your husband replied that he would try, but Private MacPhail does not know what became of him subsequently. We greatly fear that your husband met with some further disaster after he was seen by Private MacPhail, but we are continuing our enquiries in every direction on your behalf.[39]

Another account, this time from the Regiment's Chaplain, was unable to provide any further information, but at least shared a memory of Jack whilst again revealing the chaos at the front when dealing with heavy death tolls.

> I may add that I saw your husband only a few moments before he went over and that I marvelled at the cheerfulness and confidence which prevailed generally in spite of the coming ordeal.
>
> You have the sincere sympathy of all out here in this very trying time – even though we are too occupied to write much – our casualties have been so numerous in the last few months that it has been impossible to deal with each one as we should have liked to do – and in many cases there has been a complete absence of any information whatsoever.[40]

When the armistice was signed in November 1918, Gert still did not know the fate of her husband. She had the responsibility of explaining to her children, aged nine, eight and six, that the fighting had ceased but she did not know when or whether their father would return. The grief of wives and families whose loved ones would not return added a bitter twist to the celebrations. Many solders remained overseas long after November 1918, but the feeling of relief now they were out of danger would have provided some comfort. Knowing a husband had been killed lent pity and support to women, but not knowing for sure, Gert was caught between possible relief, that he may well be on his way back to her and the children, and fear that she would never see him again. Every knock at the door could be a letter of good news or bad, or even Jack himself returned. It was not until 2 December that Gert received a letter from the War Office stating that as Jack was missing since 25 July 'and that, as no further information concerning him has since been received, it has been presumed for official purposes that he died on or since that date and is presumed dead.'[41] Unwilling to accept the presumption, Gert continued her enquiries, but each came back with a similar response that presumed he had been killed. However in January 1919, nearly six months after she had first heard Jack was missing, Gert received the following letter which seemed more definitive than those previous received and hopefully gave some consolation.

I will now give you some information which has long been on my mind. Your husband was wounded in the knee. Well, after we had finished the raid, the Battalion came out for rest and were relieved by another Battalion. During my stay in hospital I ran across some of these fellows. While they were out on patrol, they came across a Sgt Major dead in a shell hole and on enquiring as to his description I am sorry to say that he answered to the description of your husband and from the position they described it was just where I saw him sitting when he was wounded.

I assure you that it upsets me very much to tell you this but I felt it my duty to and it must be a big suspense on your mind but I can assure you that your husband was a soldier and a gentleman and loved by all the boys who came under his command. He will be sadly missed by all of us.

Trusting this letter will find you all well. May God help you bear the misfortune that has befallen you.

Yours sincerely, A.J. Bick.[42]

Jack's body was never found and Gert was widowed aged 36 with three young children.

Widowhood

In 2009, Gert's grandchildren found an additional selection of letters and it seems that Gert had selected her most personal of the letters from Jack and kept these separately from the rest. This new selection included a letter in an envelope simply marked 'In case, G Adam'. The letter had been written by Jack in February 1918, in case the worse was to happen. This letter must have been some comfort to Gert and she had shared it with their three children.[43]

Darling,

It's somewhat difficult to imagine that one has gone under and write from the other side. Still in view of the possibility I ought to write something.

I may say if I am knocked out I shall be surprised. The casualties among my rank are very few.

Well as far as life is concerned I have no complaints to make. Except that I was not able to provide for you quite as I should have wished but the 3 children who caused the inconvenience will now repay for it. It would have been a great pity had I left no one behind to comfort you.

For ourselves I have not a single regret or fault to find.

You are darling exactly all that a woman should be and to me perfect. Would I had been so good as yourself.

I love you if I may make myself equal to you but I more worship. You are more an object of worship than love.

I think ours was a perfect match. I had the common sense of the average man and you the goodness and love of the best little woman in the world.

Greater things I believe were in store for us had I remained with you but when our country is in need I have no hesitation in making the final sacrifice.

Much more I think darling but you can realise the difficulty of the expression. My love story has been equal to anyone in the world and leaves nothing to be desired.[44]

In 1922 Gert received the British War Medal, Victory Medal and commemorative plaque issued by the War Office. These were in the original box of letters, all still in their postal envelopes; opened, but not displayed. The collection also contained details of memorial services held in Doncaster, an image of the memorial in Pozieres British Cemetery in France where Jack's name was inscribed and a letter about a Teacher's Memorial in London County Hall, unveiled in October 1924. It is not known if Gert attended any memorial services. As Nicholson notes in her study of post-war life, although the war was over, 'Formal occasions of remembrance designed to comfort often produced the reverse effect.'[45] The decision in 1915 that no corpses would be returned home, along with the sheer number of those who were unidentifiable and not found, and the lack of evidence of death, gave rise in many an inability to believe in death. Gert's passport, issued on 27 July 1937, showed two visits to France – Dieppe 2 August 1937 – 14 August 1937 and Saint-Malo, Normandy 14 August 1938 – 20 August 1938.[46] The couples' grandchildren informed us that Gert spent lots of her time continuing to write letters asking for information about Jack, and her two visits to France, taking young Jack Junior with her, were spent visiting hospitals in the hope of finding Jack. She never gave up hope that he might still be alive, and never re-married.

Jack advised Gert in his 'in case of death' letter that 'Financially you should be sound to the end.[47] For many war widows the 'Pensions were always miserly',[48] and depended on variables such as the rank of the deceased, age of widow and number of children. In some ways, Gert was one of the lucky ones. Because of Jack's rank as a Sergeant Major, she would have received at least three times that of a private soldier's widow, on top of his teacher's pension. For many women the pension was simply not enough and they had to return to work or take up new employment. Gert was also living with her parents and would not have to worry about rent or finding accommodation, in addition they provided some support for her. However, Gert had lost forever the life she had imagined she would return to after the war. Her life in London as mistress of her own house was gone. As her parents got older it is probable that their care also rested with her. The impact of Jack's death on Gert, his family, friends and three young children can only be imagined. Despite losing their father, Gert's children did well. In his 'in case of death' letter, Jack had advised her to keep a firm hand with Jack Junior and echoed his concerns for his son expressed in his other letters. He need not have worried though, both Jack Junior and Madge, his youngest daughter, gained firsts at Oxford University and Jack Junior went on to become honorary canon of Blackburn Cathedral. Madge was the first woman to get a first in Physics at Oxford and was later elected the first female fellow of the Royal Astronomical Society.[49] Peggy, the middle child, married a curate at Balby Church, which was often mentioned in her parents' letters. Peggy's husband also became a canon, this time at York Minster and their son followed suit.

Afterword

The correspondence between Gert and Jack serves as a reminder of the impact of the First World War on the lives of so many individuals and families throughout the country, in particular the many thousands of wives and children left behind. Whilst their lives may not have been directly involved in the war or war work, they were forever altered. In some ways Gert and Jack's story is one of the more fortunate ones. Their separation, although permanent, was only for the last year of the war and Jack also went willingly as a volunteer. Jack's rank meant Gert was provided for with a good separation allowance and later widow's allowance and she was able to reside with her parents and did not need to work. As explored elsewhere in this volume, for many this was not the case. It has been noted that children in work increased considerably during and after the war, again revealing the shortfall faced by families with husbands and fathers overseas and if they were killed.[50] But what is universal from this case study, is the anxiety of waiting for news and the impact on family life caused by separation and in this case, the loss of a husband and father.

Notes

1. See I. Beckett (2006) *Home Front*; and S. Humphries and R. van Emden (2004) *All Quiet on the Home Front*.
2. Royal Armouries Collection, Gert Adam to the Queen Victoria Jubilee Fund Association, 27 August 1918.
3. Roper interestingly looks at soldiers' letters written to family and friends and also the importance of correspondence for soldiers' and families' well-being; M. Roper (2010) *The Secret Battle*.
4. Royal Armouries, Reference by Mr Brown, Late Col. Sgt. 12th London Regiment, about Jack Adam. Undated, but written after his death in 1918.
5. Royal Armouries, Jack Adam to Gert Adam, 26 January 1918.
6. Royal Armouries, Jack Adam to Jack, Peg and Madge Adam, 27 January 1918.
7. Royal Armouries, Jack Adam to Gert Adam, 13 March 1918.
8. Royal Armouries, Gert Adam to Jack Adam, 21 January 1918.
9. Royal Armouries, Gert Adam to Jack Adam, 9 March 1918.
10. Royal Armouries, Jack Adam to Gert Adam, 16 February 1918.
11. Royal Armouries, Jack Adam to Gert Adam, 28 January 1918.
12. Royal Armouries, Jack Adam to Gert Adam, 11 February 1918.
13. Royal Armouries, Jack Adam to Gert Adam, 16 February 1918.
14. Royal Armouries, Jack Adam to Gert Adam, 23 February 1918.
15. Royal Armouries, Jack Adam to Gert Adam, 27 February 1918.
16. R. van Emden (2011) *The Quick and the Dead*, p 36.
17. Royal Armouries, Gert Adam to Jack Adam, 21 February 1918.
18. Royal Armouries, Jack Adam to Gert Adam, 27 February 1918.
19. Royal Armouries, Jack Adam to Gert Adam, 16 February 1918.
20. Royal Armouries, Jack Adam to Gert Adam, 19 February 1918.
21. Royal Armouries, Jack Adam to Gert Adam, 23 February 1918.
22. Royal Armouries, Jack Adam to Gert Adam, 21 March 1918.
23. Royal Armouries, Jack Adam to Gert Adam, 9 June 1918.
24. P. Fussell (1975) *The Great War and Modern Memory*, p 185.
25. Field Service Postcards from Jack Adam to Gert Adam, dated 3, 4, 7, 9, 10, 11, 17 and 18 July 1918. All simply with his name, date and 'I am quite well' left unscratched out.
26. Royal Armouries, Jack Adam to Gert Adam, 23 June 1918.
27. Royal Armouries, Gert Adam to Jack Adam 25 July 1918.
28. Royal Armouries, Gert Adam to Jack Adam, 30 July 1918.
29. Royal Armouries, Gert Adam to Jack Adam, 1 August 1918.
30. Royal Armouries, Gert Adam to Jack Adam, 9 August 1918.
31. Royal Armouries, Gert Adam to Jack Adam, 10 August 1918.
32. Royal Armouries, Jack Adam Junior to Jack Adam, 23 July 1918.

33. Jack originally served in France as CSM with the 1/6th London Regiment, then for a short time with the 1/12th and later the 1/8th Battalion, Post Office Rifles, 8th Battalion, City of London Regiment.
34. Imperial War Museum (1997) History *of the Post Office Rifles, 8th Battalion City of London Regiment 1914–1918* (London: Imperial War Museum).
35. Royal Armouries, Post Office Telegraph from the War Office to Gert Adam, 31 August 1918.
36. Royal Armouries, Gert Adam to the Queen Victoria Jubilee Fund Association, 27 August 1918.
37. Royal Armouries, Comite International De La Croix-Rouge: Agence Internationale Des Prisoners De Guerre to Gert Adam, 13 September 1918.
38. Royal Armouries, Commanding Officer of the 8th London Regiment [signature illegible] to Gert Adam, 17 September 1918.
39. Royal Armouries, K. Robson, British Red Cross and Order of St. John to Gert Adam, 4 October 1918.
40. Royal Armouries, Howard James, Chaplain, 8th London Regiment to Gert Adam, 4 October 1918.
41. Royal Armouries, The War Office to Gert Adam, 2 December 1918.
42. Royal Armouries, A. J. Bick to Gert Adam, date is unclear but he references a letter from Gert dated 23 August 1918 so most likely from August to September 1918.
43. In the second selection of letters found in 2009, they were all inside a leather wallet with a note which read 'J. P. & M. read any of these you like'. These letters were kindly donated by the family to be kept with the rest at the Royal Armouries.
44. Royal Armouries, Jack Adam to Gert Adam, dated 4 February 1918, carried on his person and returned to Gert after his death in July 1918.
45. J. Nicholson (2009) *The Great Silence*, p 5.
46. Royal Armouries, Passport of Gert Adam, issued 27 July 1937.
47. Royal Armouries, Jack Adam to Gert Adam, 4 February 1918.
48. R. van Emden (2011) *The Quick and the Dead*, p 214.
49. K. Williams, 'Madge Adam: Solar Physicist Acclaimed for her work on Sunspots and Magnetic Fields', in *The Guardian*, 10 September 2001, p 16. Also C. Haines (2001) *International Women in Science: A Biographical Dictionary to 1950* (California: ABC-CLIO Inc.). Additional information provided by the family.
50. R. van Emden (2011) *The Quick and the Dead*, pp 217–226.

References

Beckett. I (2006) *Home Front 1914–1918: How Britain Survived the Great War* (Surrey: The National Archives).

Emden. R van (2011) *The Quick and the Dead: Fallen Soldiers and Their Families in the Great War* (London: Bloomsbury).

Fussell. P (1975) *The Great War and Modern Memory* (Oxford: Oxford University Press).

Humphries. S and van Emden. R (2004) *All Quiet on the Home Front: An Oral History of Life in Britain During the First World War* (London: Headline).

Imperial War Museum (1997) *History of the Post Office Rifles, 8th Battalion City of London Regiment 1914–1918* (London: Imperial War Museum).

Nicholson. J (2009) *The Great Silence 1918–1920: Living in the Shadow of the Great War* (London: John Murray).

Roper. M (2010) *The Secret Battle: Emotional Survival in the Great War* (Manchester: Manchester University Press).

3
Soldiering On: War Widows in First World War Britain

Janis Lomas

Introduction

Before the First World War there was very little financial help for the vast majority of widows of soldiers. This began to change in the first two years of the war, as financial provision for war widows gradually moved from charitable support underpinned by a tiny amount of state provision to a fully regulated system. This was provided by an entirely new government department: the Ministry of Pensions. Founded in December 1916, the Ministry was created specifically to deal with claims for war disability and war widows' pensions. This represented a fundamental change and recognition that the scale of this war needed new solutions and structures. The introduction of a government funded system of separation allowances and war pensions, gave working-class soldiers' widows a safety net and an alternative to charity or the workhouse that was long overdue. However, a close examination of their treatment provides evidence of both continuity as well as change, as social class and patriarchy continued to define and confine them.

This chapter draws on a wide variety of sources. Official documents such as the Ministry of Pensions' Annual Reports, *Hansard*, and papers held in the National Archives give valuable insights into government thinking, as does the published work of other historians, but access to letters from war widows themselves through the War Widows Archive[1] has also provided a personal perspective which considerably enhances that gained from official materials and government reports. Although the introduction of the war widows' pension represented one of the first gendered provisions in favour of women, a striking feature in the treatment of working-class war widows was the persistence of judgemental attitudes which defined them as either 'deserving' of help or 'undeserving'. This ideology, which had governed both the Victorian Poor Law and the manner in which charities had operated, became enshrined in state legislation and continued to govern the lives of these widows for decades to come. It was to make retention of their pension dependent on their good behaviour and respectability. In addition, the war widows' pension was hedged with restrictions. For example, any woman who married a soldier who had already been invalided out of the army as unfit for further duties would not receive a war widows' pension if he subsequently died as a result of those injuries. This stipulation may have been designed to prevent women marrying war-disabled men to gain a pension. This and many other rules were to make it increasingly difficult for war widows to qualify for a pension after the war was over.

Background

At the beginning of the war the relatively small number of widows of soldiers fell into two distinct categories and their treatment was dependent upon the category into which they fell. They were either 'on the strength' and therefore part of the 'regimental family' or 'off the strength' and did not exist as far as the regiment was concerned. To be accepted as 'on the strength' your soldier husband had to have been given permission to marry; permission which was only given as a reward for long service or an exemplary record. In many regiments only six per cent of soldiers were allowed to marry. If their soldier husbands died, widows 'on the strength' could expect a tiny army pension of 5s (25p) a week and perhaps a menial job to allow them to remain within army barracks. However, soldiers continued to marry without permission, these wives were 'off the strength' and for these women the regiment accepted no responsibility. As far as the army was concerned they did not exist. They were not allowed to live in army barracks and if their husbands died they were not given any financial assistance by the army. For these widows the only help available was the Poor Law or service charities.

The main charities which provided for the widows of soldiers were the Royal Patriotic Fund Corporation (RPFC) and the Soldiers' and Sailors' Families Association (SSFA). Financial assistance from these charities was dependent on the widow's respectability. The RPFC and the SSFA instigated a system of visiting the widows' homes and investigating their behaviour and conduct to judge whether they were deserving of financial help. In this regard these charities were following the principles of the Charity Organisation Society (COS). This extremely influential organisation, founded in 1869, laid down principles and co-ordinated the administration of charities. The COS believed that the indiscriminate giving of help undermined the ability of an individual to help themselves. It advocated visiting and reporting on families to enable caseworkers to distinguish between the deserving or undeserving and to offer education and advice in household management. It insisted that relief should be a charitable matter and that the involvement of the state should be extremely limited. In order for the widow of a soldier to receive financial assistance her respectability and intent to help herself, her abilities as a mother, her good housekeeping and temperance all needed to be investigated. To this end a system of visits was instigated and largely carried out by middle-class women, who visited homes, asked questions around the neighbourhood, and ensured that the house was clean and that the children were well kept. If a widow did not live up to these ideals her pension could be ended or administered by the charity as they considered appropriate. Although by 1914 the doctrine of the COS was no longer being practiced by all charities, service charities were still following these general principles.

Wives and widows at the outbreak of the First World War

When war was declared in August 1914 the class composition and marital status of the British army began to change quite quickly. Three days after the declaration of war Kitchener appealed for volunteers to join the colours and huge numbers of men flocked to recruiting offices. There were sometimes queues a mile in length and by the end of September 1914, 750,000 men had volunteered.[2] It appears that it was expected that the vast majority of volunteers would be single men, however this was not the case, Jack Adam, in Chapter 2 of this book, was only one of many thousands of married men who volunteered to join the colours in the early years of the war. There was a rapid recognition that these men came from various strata of society, not just the lowly socio-economic group from which the private soldier had traditionally been recruited. As the journalist, Rowland Kenney, wrote at the time: 'In the past we had recruited the regular army from the flotsam and jetsam of industrialisation...but when it came to millions being required, other sources needed to be tapped.'[3] In addition to an acknowledgement of the varied class position of these new volunteers there was also a recognition that military service was not going to be a career for these men. They had enlisted 'for the duration' only, and most expected the war to be over fairly quickly. Their army service was therefore considered to be just a short break from civilian life. There was immediate pressure from union leaders and Labour and Liberal politicians for the government to promise that adequate provision would be forthcoming for the families left behind.

On 10 August 1914, only six days after the outbreak of war, Prime Minister Herbert Asquith, bowed to pressure and announced that the minimal level of separation allowances already being paid to naval widows and the small number of 'on the strength' army widows, would now be extended to the wives of all volunteers. Separation allowance was an amount deducted from the pay of a serviceman and allocated to a dependant at home, usually a wife, but it could also be a parent, or a sibling, providing the soldier had contributed towards their upkeep before their enlistment. Asquith's announcement was the first attempt at a systematic state organisation for payments to families while the serviceman was stationed abroad. In addition to separation allowances, war widows' pensions were also introduced on 10 August. The pension that Asquith introduced paid just five shillings (25p) a week to the war widow of a private soldier. This was a totally inadequate amount. In 1913, Maud Pember Reeves had published her groundbreaking study detailing the terrible struggle families were enduring while trying to survive on *Round about a Pound a Week*. In the early years of the century the pioneering studies of poverty undertaken by Seebohm Rowntree and Charles Booth had suggested 25/- (£1.25) and 30/- (£1.50) respectively as being the minimum needed to support a family but Pember Reeves argued that by 1913, 30/- was not enough to provide adequate nutrition for families with children.[4] As the war continued, wartime inflation was to increase the hardship. As Karen Hunt in Chapter 5 demonstrates, families struggled to survive during the war years.

Charities such as the SSFA and the RPFC were therefore desperately needed to top up these miniscule state pensions and allowances. Furthermore the government had acted quickly in announcing financial recompense without the logistical support being in place. This was to have repercussions for much of the war. The army paymasters were totally overwhelmed. As they had refused to recognise 'off the strength' army wives and widows they had no record of them. In addition, they were also faced with validating claims from many thousands more families of volunteers than they had expected (see Figure 3.1). Consequently, there were often delays of weeks or even months before war pensions and separation allowances were being regularly paid; soldiers' families were often left without any means of survival. In the first weeks and months of the war the delays caused terrible hardship. Many servicemen's wives and widows were forced to sell their possessions, move into cheaper rooms and to apply to the Poor Law.[5] The scandal of families becoming destitute because their husbands had responded to the call to fight for King and Country caused great disquiet. Government were only too well aware that this could discourage volunteers for which there was an ever-increasing need.

Voluntary organisations stepped into the void left by the lack of adequate state organisation, particularly the SSFA. By 1915, the SSFA had established 900 branches staffed by some 50,000 voluntary workers.[6] The SSFA now began to administer and validate claims for both separation allowances and pensions on behalf of the War Office. Under the system the SSFA instigated, the amounts given to top up separation allowances and pensions were unregulated and differed from one area of the country to another. It left servicemen's families dependent on the personal judgement of volunteers. In George Hewins' autobiography *The Dillen*, George describes how his wife Emma went to register for separation allowance after George was conscripted into the army. He writes:

> A bloke sat on a stool and gave the allowance out. Well, this bloke starts umming and fussing about handing it over – you'd have thought it was *his* money! He gives the missus a nasty look and he says: 'EIGHT children! Was they all born in wedlock, missus?' She felt herself going red. She said: 'What do you think I am?' And she dropped him one on the jaw. She knocked him out! She knocked him out in one![7]

Sylvia Pankhurst, living and working in the East End of London, was also very scathing about the methods used by some of the SSFA's visitors. She noted:

> From all over the country, not least from my own district, came complaints that officials of the Soldiers' and Sailors' Families Association were telling the women whose men were at the war to move into one room, and to sell pianos, gramophones, even furniture, before applying anywhere for aid. The notion that the women were entitled to separation allowance as a right, not as a charitable act of grace, seemed difficult for the Association's officials to assimilate. In Newcastle soldiers' wives were given food tickets instead of the money due to them, and were permitted to obtain household commodities only from a prescribed list, which comprised the cheap, inferior qualities of food.[8]

For widows the payments SSFA and the RPFC made were needed to supplement their meagre pension and the additional amounts these organisations paid out varied from 7/- (35p) to 9/- (45p) per week according to age and 'the station in life of the beneficiaries'[9]. The charities had other agendas beyond economic survival. In 1915, Helen Anstey, one of the SSFA's lady volunteers, wrote that the system of visiting presented 'an excellent opportunity for educating them [soldiers' wives] in true patriotism and loyalty to their country.' Validating claims involved combining 'searching enquiries' with a system of 'friendly visiting'. Payments were made conditional on the widow's good behaviour and reputation and 'always with the idea of inculcating self-help rather than reliance.' The SSFA volunteers were convinced that 'a link of sympathy has been forged between class and class' and through the tactful efforts of the visitors, 'numberless homes have become better, happier, cleaner', resulting in the husband returning to find 'a real home, money in the bank and a sober, affectionate wife – all through the influence of the SSFA.'[10] This rosy picture was very different to the way the administration of war pensions was viewed in many other quarters.

Despite a doubling of the minimum war widows' pension in November 1915, the pension levels were still terribly low. The new amount still only allowed the widow (aged under 35 years) of a private soldier, 10/- (50p) a week, a hopelessly inadequate amount on which to live. It was inevitable that change should be advocated both inside and outside of government. An example of this is the meeting which took place at the Westminster Palace Hotel, London, in June 1916. This meeting was attended by the Mayors and Town Clerks of 41 major towns and cities throughout England, Wales and Scotland. Organised by Sir Archibald Salvidge, the Conservative MP for Liverpool, the meeting unanimously supported a resolution that the payment of war pensions, grants and allowances should be borne by the Exchequer. Also, that the attempt being made to combine statutory with benevolent provision was 'fundamentally unsound and that Parliament should bear its responsibilities and not shelve what was a national duty unto private philanthropy or charity.'[11]

It gradually became clear that the numbers of volunteers coming forward were not going to be sufficient to fight a war on such a huge scale and that sooner or later conscription was going to have to be introduced. There was great resistance to the introduction of conscription as Britain had always prided itself on having a volunteer army. However by the middle of 1915, 75,000 men had already been killed[12] and the initial enthusiasm for volunteering was beginning to fade. The Military

Service Bill which introduced conscription was finally passed through Parliament in January 1916. At first it applied only to single men but by May 1916 it had been amended and extended to all men aged between 18 and 41 years. In 1918 this was again amended to include all men up to 51 years. The introduction of conscription increased the unease about the involvement of charities in validating claims for war pensions. The numbers of casualties on the Somme in 1916 – 58,000 British soldiers died on 1 July 1916, the first day of the offensive – escalated the war to a whole new level of horror and at long last there was a recognition that a state system of administration was going to be needed to deal with the scale of these casualties. This led directly to the founding, in December 1916, of the Ministry of Pensions.

The state steps in: the Ministry of Pensions and the Special Grants Committee

The establishment of the Ministry of Pensions brought separation allowances, disability pensions and widows' pensions fully under the control of the state and eliminated the involvement of the voluntary sector in topping up inadequate payments. The amounts given were dependent on the rank of the combatant. 80 per cent of all war widows' pensions were for the lowest rank, that of Private. For much of the war, separation allowances remained higher than the war widows' pension. The Treasury justified this by the fact that a pension might be for life while a separation allowance was of limited duration. They also insisted that widows' expenses were less; their reasoning was that wives had to keep the home going for their husband's return, while widows were told they could move to somewhere cheaper. As Sir Charles Harris, Permanent Under-Secretary at the War Office, explained to Parliament : 'The man who goes to fight is entitled to expect that his home or cottage, or whatever it is, shall be kept together as long as he is alive ... When the man is dead it is in all ranks of society customary for the widow to move into a smaller house.'[13] Moving to a smaller house was not really a feasible proposition to a war widow living in a couple of rooms with several children but the suggestion that they should, serves to illustrate the gulf in experience between politicians and working-class war widows.

The service charities' system of insisting that a war widow had to be 'deserving' of help by their good behaviour and respectability did not cease with the founding of the Ministry of Pensions, in fact it became enshrined in law and was systematically enforced through a committee within the Ministry of Pensions. This was the innocuously sounding

Special Grants Committee. Any grants awarded by this committee were almost entirely for the families of deceased officers. These families could apply for education grants for children to attend a 'good school' and for higher pension allowances. In addition, the committee could allocate additional weekly amounts. These were called the 'alternative pension' and were specifically designed for those war widows who could show that they had enjoyed a much higher standard of living before their husbands' war service began. In Chapter 2, it can be seen that the financial recompense received by an officer's widow, Gertrude Adam, may well have helped her to remain at home to care for her children and probably to also obtain grants to help finance the secondary and university education of her children. The Special Grants Committee could also allow lump sum payments in cases of hardship and arrange fostering and adoptions for children in need of new homes. However, a great deal of the work of the committee was not concerned with the awarding of grants. It was instead concerned with the forfeiture of pensions to those women deemed undeserving.

The Special Grants Committee had some very high profile members. It was chaired by Sir Matthew Nathan, a distinguished soldier, civil servant and Colonial Governor, who was the Secretary to the Ministry of Pensions, and one of the committee members was Pamela McKenna. She was the wife of Reginald McKenna, who had been both Home Secretary and Chancellor of the Exchequer in Asquith's government. Pamela McKenna held some rather disturbing views of women from the lowest end of the social scale as can be discerned from this letter written in 1918. Sir Matthew Nathan had asked her opinion on the proposed bill for the Endowment of Mothers to which Mrs McKenna replied:

> ... there is one type of unmarried mother to whom, in no circumstances, should pension be payable. I mean the mentally deficient woman, not sufficiently feeble-minded to be placed under control, who drifts from one workhouse to another, burdening the community with a succession of feebler minded children. *It would be better for her to be exterminated than endowed* [my emphasis].[14]

Of the 15 committee members there were several who were also representatives of both the SSFA and the RPFC. It is hardly surprising therefore that the Special Grants Committee continued to decide to terminate or to administer in trust both separation allowances and war widows' pensions, using the same methodology and with similar criteria to those of the service charities, which it had replaced. It is possible to discern a continuum of ideas concerning working-class women from the 1834 Poor Law Amendment Act onwards. The Special Grants Committee made decisions of a similar nature, and in a similar manner to that of both the Poor Law Commissioners, and of charitable bodies, and people with comparable value systems and from analogous backgrounds administered the various systems. The Committee operated without any right of appeal and had wide-ranging powers. The legislation formalised firm guidelines for the removal of war widows' pensions.

In the first year of its operation between March 1918 and March 1919 no fewer than 939 war widows forfeited their pensions. These cases were to continue to be heard throughout the inter-war years. During those years 5,607 widows had their pensions administered in trust and a further 8,768 women forfeited their war widows' pension entirely.[15] The legislation governing the Ministry of Pensions also enshrined in law the service charities' practice of administration in trust. This may have meant that the widow's rent and other bills would be paid for her to teach her good housekeeping and money management and she might receive food stamps rather than a cash payment. In some cases allowances were paid for the upkeep of the children, but she herself received no money. This was felt to teach her not to squander her pension on frivolous expenditure or on alcohol. It also administered the pension of any war widow whose payment 'should not be forfeited for a single lapse into misconduct, providing that the misconduct had ceased.'[16] As Braybon and Summerfield wrote of the view of working-class women without men in this period: 'By and large they were held in need of moral education and guardianship, like servants, they needed "watching".'[17] The committee also had the power to remove children from their mother's care and place them under the control of the Ministry of Pensions. By 1924, there were 3181 children whose mothers were alive who were in the care of the department, of these 668 had been committed into care by the Special Grants Committee using their powers under the 1908 Children Act.[18] This legislation was to continue to adjudicate on First World War widows and their children until it was finally disbanded in May 1972.

The case of Annie A. serves to demonstrate the effect that these rules could have.[19] The papers on the case span over 12 years. The allegations against her stem from a couple called Mr and Mrs Abbott who had rooms in the same house as the widow. In the first instance Mrs Abbott reported Annie A. to the local War Pensions' Committee, alleging that Annie A. frequently went out for a drink with a widower called Wiggins. On this 'evidence' Annie A. had her pension administered in trust. There was clearly ill feeling between the Abbotts and Annie A. as a few months later there was a serious altercation which resulted in Annie A. having her leg fractured and Mr Abbott being charged with causing the injury. However, despite the possibility that the original complaint was malicious, reports and investigations were to continue year after year. Frequent visits were made to the house, police reports were instigated, an 'inquiry agent' was employed and neighbours were interviewed to attempt to prove cohabitation between Wiggins and Annie A. Five years after the first correspondence a report states that: 'the widow sees Wiggins occasionally, they have a drink together but he never enters the house.' This is followed by the bald statement: 'Decision: Continue in trust.'

Eleven years after the first investigation began an Inquiry Officer's report states that her neighbour has told him that: 'as far as she was aware Wiggins had never slept away from his own house...that he had been ill and absent from work for several months...he had visited Mrs A.'s house three or four times a week and taken her to the pictures or for a drink.' In the same report Mrs A. was described as having 'gone off on a long day's charing and that she is more or less regularly employed in that way.' This information seemed to point to Annie A. being a hard working woman who was not living with Mr Wiggins, but despite this the Chairman of the War Pensions' Committee decided to refer her case to the Special Grants Committee. The Special Grants Committee then decided that she was to forfeit her pension.

She called at the office to protest. Her eldest son wrote begging them to reconsider, writing that: 'Wiggins was a friend of his father and mother prior to the war and has continued to be a friend of the family. The association between them is only friendship and the children often go out with them.' He goes on to say that he and his brothers and sisters are willing to appear before the Committee to vouch for their mother's respectability. Finally, there is a request from the British Legion asking for further reconsideration of the case. Tantalisingly, twelve years after the investigation into her began, the papers end with the question 'Are the committee prepared to reconsider?' Unfortunately, the response to the question is missing. We will therefore never know if the intervention by the British Legion had any effect or not.

The papers that have survived clearly show that the decision to firstly administer and then forfeit her pension condemned her and her children to great financial hardship. Despite the lack of any firm evidence of cohabitation the moral agenda that governed the lives of these women deemed her not respectable enough to be deserving of a pension. Although the grounds for the pension being forfeited are not stated in the case documents, if, as seems likely, the Special Grants Committee removed her pension for cohabitation, it was impossible that her pension could ever be restored to her. Before 1961, the rule was that a pension lost for cohabitation could never be reinstated.[20] These women were left entirely to their own resources and were not allowed to claim from any alternative source, as the Ministry of Pensions rules stated: 'A pension to a widow is the replacement of support which her husband would have given, and that if she by her actions would have forfeited her claim on her husband, the community should not be called on to support her.'[21]

The experiences of war widows

The rising prices during the war meant that receipt of a war widows' pension only alleviated the most basic want; it certainly did not mean the end of poverty.[22] Before the First World War, the average woman's wage was 13s. 6d. (67½p) a week[23] but by 1915, when a war widow was expected to live on 10/- (50p) a week, a bus conductress was earning £2. 5s. (£2.25p) and a munitions worker in the National Shell Factories up to £3. 4s. 2d.(£3.21p).[24] As the levels of pension provision were so low, war widowed mothers still needed to find work to subsidise their pension as this letter demonstrates.

> I lost my Father in the Royal Marines, after he had done 21 years he came out. 1914 called up for war service and died in 1915, leaving my late Mother with six children and none of them old enough to carry on the business my Father had saved up for. I was only 12 and 5 brothers under me. My Mother used to work in the Royal Marine Barracks doing men's washing, as the war pension was very low at the time.[25]

Traces of the Victorian regiments' paternalistic attitude towards 'on the strength' widows can be perceived in this letter. The widow was 'looked after' by being found work within the barracks, although it was work of the most menial sort, washing being one of the lowest ranking in the status hierarchy of women's work.[26]

Another war widow had her first baby only six weeks after her husband was killed in 1914, but her experiences of work and poverty were shared by many others. Her letter not only graphically illustrates the paucity of pension provision, but also the indomitable spirit which helped her to survive these experiences:

> When I first lost my husband I had 18/6 old money for myself and two children, one child from my husband's first marriage, she lived

with her grandparents, so of course 5/- a week I gave to them, and had 13/6 for myself and my child. But after a year I got back to work and after ups and downs, have got through, scrubbing floors, white washing cellars and ceilings, going out washing for 2/6 a day, from 8am to 8pm. I worked on Leeds market up to being 84 and then fell and smashed the elbow in my left arm ... Thank God after the first year I have had good health and although I am now 90, don't do so badly, I do my own washing and most of my own cleaning, I live alone but never feel lonely.[27]

The cheerful tone of this extract belies the grinding poverty she must have experienced while existing for a year on just 13/6d (67½p) a week.

Much of the service charities rules and ideology continued under the Ministry of Pensions. For instance, service charities had coined the phrase 'unmarried wives' to differentiate any woman who was living with a soldier to whom she was not married from a legitimately married woman. When the Ministry was established this practice was to continue. In 1917 the amount given to 'unmarried wives' was set at one third lower than the war widows' pension; any 'unmarried wife' was only entitled to payments during the war and for 12 months after unless they had his dependent children to support. There had to be evidence that the soldier had accepted paternity of the children and the widow had to have been in receipt of a separation allowance before the man's death for a pension to be paid. These high levels of proof proved insurmountable for most 'unmarried wives'. Out of a total of war widows' pensions numbering 192,698, by March 1919 only 2,645 'unmarried wives' pensions had been paid.

Apart from these women, widows of men who had committed suicide were refused a pension until March 1917.[28] Widows of those who had been killed on the battlefield or had contracted a fatal disease and died while on active service could also be refused a pension if 'the man's death from either disease or injury was due, or partly due, to his own fault or negligence.' It is difficult to see how a death from disease could be his own fault or negligence and perhaps the authorities eventually realised this, for by 1917 the rules had been slightly amended and these cases were said to be 'more liberally dealt with'. There was a narrow definition of a war widow and any woman who married a man who was already war disabled or diseased was not granted a war widows' pension if he later died from his injuries. Any marriage that took place after the war ended or any child born after the war was also not eligible for war pension support. This letter written by a war widow many years later describes the lifetime of menial, low-paid work that this meant for her and her children.

> He died in 1934, Army paid all his funeral expenses. I was left with 5 children, the youngest 1 year. I was informed as we were married after his discharge I was not eligible for a pension. I took in knitting, 4/6 for knitting a jumper, then I got a job sewing £3 a week, I was taxed on that – the workroom was an old loft, [I worked] 9 till 6. Then we had army camps nearby, I took in washing for the troops, it was hard work, camp left, so then I went out working in a house, washing, scrubbing and cleaning, £2.10s a week. Did that long as I was able then took out-work from a factory folding handkerchiefs. 35/- [£1.75] for 200 dozen, 2,400 items and carried them to the factory.[29]

There was also a seven-year rule in place. If a soldier lived seven years or more after his war injury occurred, his death was judged as not being attributable to his war service and therefore once again, the war widow would not be granted a pension. In addition, many of the widows of the 343 men and three officers[30] who were shot by their own side for cowardice or desertion during or shortly after the First World War,[31] were also refused a war widows' pension. One of these men was Harry Farr. After a court martial lasting just twenty minutes, he was shot for cowardice. This was despite him having just been returned to the front after spending five months in hospital for shell shock. His wife, Gertrude, spoke, aged 98, on a Radio 4 programme where she graphically described receiving a telegram telling her that her husband had died:

> They just sent me a letter from the war office and all it said was: 'Dear Madam we regret to inform you that your husband has died. He was sentenced for cowardice and was shot at dawn on 16th October.' They were the exact words, that was all I got.[32]

She then described pushing the letter into her blouse petrified that someone would see it. She hid the circumstances of Harry's death from everyone because of the stigma she felt. Her pension was then stopped and she had to tell her mother and mother-in-law the truth. As Harry had been executed Gertrude, was no longer entitled to receive any money from the army, she and their daughter were destitute. The three women kept the circumstances of Harry Farr's death a guilty secret from other family members as Gertrude Farr struggled to support herself and her baby daughter. During 1917, the press publicised the fact that this was happening to families and on 21 November 1917, the War Cabinet decided that in future these women were to be told their husbands had died on active service. The Ministry of Pensions then had no choice but to allow claims from these women, which it did from 4 January 1918. However, the Ministry would not have sought out those women who had already been refused a pension, the onus of any claim was on the claimant. If she did not know these claims were now being met, she would not have been informed of it; hence Gertrude Farr did not know for decades that she could have received her war widows' pension.

Afterword

Although these allowances and pensions paid during the First World War represented one of the first gendered welfare provisions in favour of women, the rules of entitlement were drawn so narrowly that many thousands of widows of dead servicemen were refused a war widows' pension. For those who were able to claim a pension, clear distinctions were made between the widows of officers and those of the rank-and-file. The system of war pensions reproduced the hierarchical system of military service with rank determining the value of a man's life. While working-class women, were given minimal pensions, had their behaviour scrutinised and their morals questioned and judged, every attempt was made to help officers' families maintain the class position they would have had if their father had lived. Officers' children were often sent to private boarding schools with the help of grants from the Special Grants Committee. Additionally, officers' widows could be awarded an alternative pension. This was much higher than the war widows' pension and could be as much as £5.77 a week for a war widow with three children.[33]

The distinctions between war widows did not lessen after the war ended. Rank continued to determine treatment and the amount received. During the inter-war years it was to become increasingly difficult to prove entitlement to a war widows' pension. As described earlier, the seven-year rule meant that a woman was only entitled to a pension 'if the soldier died of wounds, injuries or disease within seven years of his removal from duty.'[34] Also any woman who married a soldier after the war ended was not entitled to a war widows' pension if he subsequently died, even if his death was due to his war service. Furthermore, any child born after the man's discharge was not entitled to state support. It was also up to the widow to prove that their husband had died as a result of his injuries and even if he had been receiving a 100 per cent disability pension their claims were frequently rejected. For all these women their financial situation after their husbands' death was extremely difficult and often left widows unable to support themselves and their children. It has proved impossible to prove conclusively but unlike the relatively small number of regular soldiers who were married before the war, it has been estimated that between 40–65 per cent of the soldiers in the First World War were married men.[35] If the lower figure is taken the numbers of war widows who were refused a pension still consists of tens of thousands. It may well be that the introduction of the much less generous widows' pension in 1926, may have been partly to avoid large numbers of these ineligible soldiers' widows and their children, having to resort to the Poor Law for support.

In 1939 the new rates for Second World War widows were introduced at a lower rate than the amount already being paid to the widows of the First World War. The rates were equalised by 1944 but by that time wartime inflation had eroded the worth of the war widows' pension to the extent that all war widows without a separate income were impoverished. This set the pattern and after the Second World War many war widows were in desperate need and forced to claim National Assistance. They were also treated substantially worse than male war pensioners.[36] This position remained until 1990 when, after a nineteen-year campaign war widows finally achieved a much increased pension and many of the anomalies in their treatment were finally addressed.

Notes

1. *The War Widows' Archive: The Iris Strange Collection*, contains almost 8,000 items and is held at the university library of Staffordshire University. The majority of the letters are from Second World War widows but there are also three hundred letters from widows of the First World War. See J. Lomas (1994) 'So I Married Again': Letters from British Widows of the First and Second World Wars', in *History Workshop Journal* 38, pp 218–227.
2. R. Rees (2001) *Poverty and Public Health*, p 36.
3. R. Kenney (1914) 'Soldiers' Dependents', *The English Review*, 19, pp 112–118.
4. M. Pember Reeves (1979) *Round About a Pound a Week*, p 217.
5. A telling comment on the stigma which the Poor Law attracted is the lengths to which the government went to remove these women from Poor Law registers. The government issued a circular to all Local Authorities insisting that these women had their names removed from the Roll of Paupers and the money they had been given was repaid to parishes by the National Relief Fund.
6. S. Pedersen (1990) 'Gender, Welfare', p 992.
7. A. Hewins (1981) *The Dillen*, p 138.
8. E. S. Pankhurst (1987[1932]) *The Home Front*, p 25.

9. Parliamentary Papers: Cd. 8333 (1916) *Report of the Royal Patriotic Fund Corporation* 61, App. xxxii; 23 and App. iii. (London: HMSO).
10. H. Anstey (1915), The Home-side of War Time, *Contemporary Review* 1915, Vol.108 pp 237–243.
11. *Liverpool Echo* (1916) Friday 23 June 23 p 1.
12. G. Braybon and P. Summerfield (eds) (1987) *Out of the Cage*, p 34.
13. *Reports from the Select Committee on Naval and Military Services (Pensions and Grants)* (1915) *1914–1916* (53, 196, 328), iv, evidence of Sir Charles Harris, para 13 (London: HMSO).
14. *National Archives* (1918): PIN 15/405, Mrs. McKenna to Matthew Nathan, 25 February 1918. (London: HMSO).
15. *Ministry of Pensions' Second Annual Report, 31 March 1918–31 March 1919*, p 39, para 126 (London: HMSO).
16. *Ministry of Pensions' First Annual Report, 31 March.1917–31 March 1918*, p 69 (London: HMSO).
17. G. Braybon and P. Summerfield (1987) *Out of the Cage*, p 107.
18. J. Lomas (1997) Unpublished PhD thesis. *War Widows in British Society 1914–1990*, Staffordshire University, Appendix A, Table 2, p 267.
19. *National Archives* (1923) PIN 84/2 Document: S.G.P.F. 18656 (London: HMSO).
20. From an unpublished War Pensions' Agency document, entitled: *A Short History of War Pensions*, para. 81 (date unknown).
21. J. Lomas (1997) *War Widows*, p 90.
22. Provision was increased in early 1920 to the more realistic figure of 26/8 (£1.33) and remained at this level until 1939 despite the cost of living index falling by a third in this period.
23. G. Braybon and P. Summerfield (1987) *Out of the Cage*, p 51.
24. R. Adam (1974) *A Woman's Place*, p 49.
25. *War Widows' Archive*, Box 1.
26. J. Lewis (1984) *Women in England 1870–1950* (Hemel Hempstead: Wheatsheaf) p 60.
27. *War Widows' Archive*, Box 1.
28. G. Thomas (1981), *State Maintenance of Women During the First World War*, Unpublished PhD Thesis, Sussex p 139.
29. *War Widows' Archive*, Box 1
30. There were only three officers executed, one of whom was convicted of murder. Most officers were quietly sent home as 'inefficient' if their nerves failed them; W. Moore (1974) *The Thin Yellow Line*, p 92.
31. A mass pardon of the 306 British soldiers was finally given the Royal Assent on 8th November 2006 after many years of campaigning by the family of Harry Farr and others.
32. BBC Radio 4, 16 September 1993, *It is with Very Great Regret*, Producer: Matt Thompson. Interviewer: Julian Putkowski.
33. J. Lomas (1997) *War Widows*, p 86.
34. *MoP Second Annual Report*, p 64.
35. W. Hayes-Fisher MP told the Council of the RPFC in 1915 that he had been told that '65% of what is called "Kitchener's Army" are married men'; D. Blomfield-Smith (1992) *Heritage of Help*, p 117. However, Susan Pedersen quotes a much lower figure, stating by 1917, 40% were married; S. Pedersen (1990) 'Gender, Welfare', p 989.

36. J. Lomas (1997) *War Widows* and J. Lomas (2011) '"They took my husband, they took the money and just left me": War Widows and Remembrance after the Second World War'; Andrews. M with Bagot-Jewitt. C and Hunt. N. (2011) *Lest We Forget*, pp 193–196.

References

Adam. R (1975) *A Woman's Place* (London: Chatto & Windus).

Andrews. M with Bagot-Jewitt. C and Hunt. N. (eds) (2011) *Lest We Forget: Remembrance and Commemoration* (Stroud: The History Press).

Anstey. H (1915) 'The Home-side of Wartime', *Contemporary Review*, 108, August, pp 240–245.

Babbington. A (1983) *For The Sake of Example: Capital Courts Martial 1914–20* (London: Secker and Warburg).

Bamfield. V (1974) *On The Strength: The Story of the British Army Wife* (London: Charles Knight).

Blomfield-Smith. D (1992) *Heritage of Help: The Story of the Royal Patriotic Fund* (London: Robert Hale).

Bock. G and Thane. P (1991) *Maternity and Gender Policies: Women and the Rise of the European Welfare States 1880s–1950s* (London: Routledge).

Braybon. G and Summerfield. P (1987) *Out of The Cage: Women's Experiences in Two World Wars* (London: Pandora Press).

Compton. P (1970) *Colonel's Lady and Camp Follower* (London: Robert Hale).

Gildea. Colonel Sir J (1916) *Historical Record of the Work of the Soldiers' and Sailors' Families Association from 1885 to 1916* (London: Eyre and Spottiswoode).

Gregory. A (1994) *The Silence of Memory, Armistice Day 1919–1946* (Oxford: Berg).

Hewins. A (1981) *The Dillen* (London: Hamish Hamilton).

Higonnet M, Jenson. J, Michel. S and Weitz. M. (1987) *Behind The Lines: Gender and the Two World Wars* (New Haven: Yale University Press).

Kent. S K (1993) *Making Peace: The Reconstruction of Gender in Interwar Britain* (Princeton: Princeton University Press).

Koven. S and Michel. S (1993) *Mothers of a New World: Maternalist Policies and the Origins of Welfare States* (London: Routledge).

Levine. P (1994) 'Walking the Streets in a Way No Decent Woman Should: Women Police in World War', *Journal of Modern History*, 66, 1, March, pp 34–78.

Lewis. J (1980) *The Politics of Motherhood* (Beckenham: Croom Helm).

Lewis. J (ed.) (1986) *Labour and Love: Women's Experience of Home and Family 1850–1940* (Oxford: Blackwell).

Marris. P (1958) *Widows and Their Families* (London: Routledge and Kegan Paul).

Moore. W (1974) *The Thin Yellow Line* (London: Leo Cooper).

Pankhurst. S (1987[1932]) *The Home Front* (London: Hutchinson).

Pedersen. S (1990) 'Gender, Welfare, and Citizenship in Britain during the Great War', *American History Review*, 95, pp 983–1006.

Pedersen. S (1993) *Family, Dependence, and the Origins of the Welfare State: Britain and France, 1914–1945* (Cambridge: Cambridge University Press).

Pember-Reeves. M (1979[1913]) *Round About a Pound a Week* (London: Virago).

Pope. R (1991) *War and Society in Britain 1899–1948* (London: Longman).

Prochaska. F K (1980) *Women and Philanthropy in 19th Century England* (Oxford: Oxford University Press).

Rees. R (2001) *Poverty and Public Health 1815–1949* (London: Heinemann).

Reese. P (1992) *Homecoming Heroes: An Account of the Reassimilation of British Military Personnel into Civilian Life* (London: Leo Cooper).

Richardson. A (1984) *Widows' Benefits* (London: Policy Studies Institute).

Roberts. Robert (1973) *The Classic Slum: Salford Life in the First Quarter of the Century* (London: Pelican).

Silverman. P R (1981) *Helping Women Cope With Grief* (London: SAGE).

Simkins. P (1988) *Kitchener's Army: The Raising of the New Armies, 1914–16* (Manchester: Manchester University Press).

Thane. P (1982) *The Foundations of the Welfare State* (London: Longman).

Trustram. M (1984) *Women of the Regiment* (Cambridge: Cambridge University Press).

Turner. J (ed.) (1988) *Britain and the First World War* (London: Unwin Hyman).

Wall. R and Winter. J (1988) *The Upheaval of War* (Cambridge: Cambridge University Press).

Wilson. T (1986) *The Myriad Faces of War: Britain and the Great War 1914–1918* (London: Polity Press).

4
Mortality or Morality? Keeping Workers Safe in the First World War

Anne Spurgeon

Introduction

In February 1915, Home Office pathologist, Dr Bernard Spilsbury, conducted a post-mortem on the body of a man who had been poisoned while employed in the manufacture of the explosive, trinitrotoluene (TNT). Dr Thomas Legge, Medical Inspector of Factories, who was present at the post-mortem, concurred with Spilsbury's conclusion that the man's death was due to a form of toxic jaundice, liver disease caused by exposure to TNT.[1] Most contact with this substance however took place, not in the manufacture of TNT, but in munitions factories, where large numbers of women were employed in filling explosive shells. Legge began investigating whether similar cases of liver disease had occurred amongst these workers and by the summer of that year had identified 46 such cases, including two deaths.[2] Toxic jaundice was immediately designated a notifiable disease, requiring cases to be officially reported to the Home Office. By the end of 1918 a further 430 cases, of which 111 were fatal, had been recorded.[3]

Female munition workers have occupied a prominent position in the historical picture of the Home Front during the First world War.[4] The image of the so-called 'canaries' who emerged from the factory each day with hands and faces stained a lurid yellow by TNT dust, has come to epitomise the hazardous and unpleasant conditions faced by those who rallied to support the war effort. And yet this emphasis on munition workers, or more specifically on shell fillers, may sometimes distort our broader understanding of industrial labour during the war. For these women represented only one part of a much larger working population[5] and their experiences were, in many ways, untypical of the majority. The Ministry of Munitions, mindful of the need to recruit women into armaments production, was particularly attentive to the needs of its labour force. It produced a series of reports on the subject between 1915 and 1918[6] and invested considerable resources in the development and maintenance of health and safety provision in filling factories. The result was a notable decline in TNT poisoning such that the total figure for the duration of the war masks a significant reduction in cases from a peak of 206 (57 deaths) in 1916, to 35 (ten deaths) in 1918.[7] This occurred despite a large increase in the workforce over the same period.

Elsewhere in industry the government approach to health and safety was rather less focussed. There were, for example, 1190 cases of lead poisoning between 1915 and 1918, with 74 deaths, the majority in male workers.[8] Much of the rest of the population was engaged in the manufacture of an extensive range of other goods, equally essential for the prosecution of the war.[9] Everything from mercury thermometers and bronzed field glasses to soldiers' boots and horses' nosebags was manufactured under government contract in factories and small workshops classified as 'government-controlled'.[10] By 1916 there were just over 3,000 such establishments employing approximately 1.25 million people of whom about one fifth were women. Most of the rest were men considered too old or unfit for military service, and boys below conscription age.[11] Some of these workers were completely new to employment, while others had been forced to transfer to unfamiliar trades as existing industries closed down or adapted their production to wartime needs. As early as 1914, for example, tailors in Leeds moved to the mass production of army uniforms, canvas knapsacks and mattress covers; a Bradford carpet maker adapted his machinery to weave army blankets; and a Birmingham pen maker began producing surgical instruments. Meanwhile, in Scotland, the requisition of the Aberdeen herring fleet meant that women skilled in gutting and packing fish, moved to the jute works of Dundee.[12]

As a result of the rapid recruitment of thousands of inexperienced workers, and the imperative for enormous levels of production,[13] the risk of industrial accidents and disease increased significantly. Outside the large armaments factories, however, the problem appears to have attracted little government attention. Given the heavy demands on national finances and the spectacle of unprecedented slaughter on the battlefields, this neglect of industrial health and safety on the Home Front was perhaps unsurprising. However, the simultaneous diversion of significant resources into other, seemingly less urgent elements of the working environment, namely welfare facilities, is more difficult to explain. The welfare system established during the war focussed largely on the general well-being of the workforce, providing facilities such as canteens, lavatories, cloakrooms and living accommodation and its development raises interesting questions about the nature of national priorities during the period and how these came to be determined. This chapter, therefore, will consider the general state of industrial health and safety during the war and will, in addition, discuss the attitudes and assumptions which underpinned the simultaneous development of welfare provision. An examination of the relationship between these different aspects of working conditions suggests that the welfare policy, in terms of the way it was conceived, delivered and enforced, tended to further undermine an already depleted health and safety system.

Health and safety

When TNT was first identified as an industrial poison in 1915, the Factory Department already possessed many of the tools required to address the problem. In the preceding two decades there had been considerable advances in the prevention of industrial disease, a product of new medical and scientific knowledge and increasingly interventionist government policies.[14] The concept of a notifiable industrial disease had been established under the Factory Act of 1901[15] and required not only the notification of each case to the Home Office but also the introduction of measures to protect those at risk. In the case of toxic jaundice these measures included improvements in filling equipment, changes in work practices, the provision of protective clothing and washing facilities, and the separation of working and eating areas in each factory.[16] In addition, the government introduced comprehensive health surveillance of the workforce, a process overseen by specially appointed factory doctors. Meanwhile, members of the welfare department, who were considered competent to identify early symptoms of poisoning, carried out routine medical inspections of workers. Welfare officers were further expected to ensure that workers did not bring metal items into the workplace which might trigger an explosion, to maintain records of absence from work and its causes, to organise the separation of working and eating places, to design appropriate protective clothing and to supervise its use. In national armaments factories, therefore, the welfare system developed initially as one arm of an integrated industrial health and safety system designed to address a specific occupational risk.

In other factories and workshops, however, the introduction of welfare provision followed a rather different path, such that it often became separated from, and even conflicted with, the practice of health and safety. Principal Woman Factory Inspector, Adelaide Anderson, feared that it had become 'a graft or a veneer on poor or bad conditions'.[17] Part of the problem was a failure to recognise the diverse nature of workplaces, not only in terms of the nature of their production activity but also in terms of the nature and severity of the hazards they contained. In contrast to the plethora of reports concerned with armaments factories, details of conditions elsewhere in industry are very limited, a vacuum which itself reflects a general neglect of the subject. The Annual Reports of the Chief Inspector of Factories and Workshops, the usual source of this information, were much reduced in size and scope between 1914 and 1918 and the inclusion of information about industrial hazards, as well as the compilation of detailed statistics delineating the cause, nature and number of industrial accidents and cases of industrial disease was largely discontinued. Much of our knowledge of employment conditions outside the armaments factories thus relies on retrospective assessments provided by individual factory inspectors in their reports for 1919.[18] These unsystematic observations, together with records of other notifiable diseases, maintained throughout the war,[19] offer us a brief glimpse of wartime health and safety. Together they indicate a rise in the number of cases of industrial disease and fatal accidents during the war. Men, who continued to dominate employment in the most dangerous industries, were the main victims, but there was also a shift in gender distribution in that cases in women were noticeably increased.[20] None of this is surprising for many of those now employed were inexperienced, poorly trained and operating under conditions of extreme pressure. Overwhelmed by the need for training, the government elected to leave the responsibility for this with employers as 'the persons best equipped for this task',[21] an approach which contrasted sharply with the official training courses and instruction manuals offered to new recruits to the armaments industry.[22] When viewed from the perspective of health and safety, the substitution or dilution[23] of a skilled male workforce with unskilled, often female labour, was not always particularly successful. There was a sharp rise in 'fatal accidents involving machinery'[24] during the war, something that Chief Factory Inspector Robert Graves attributed to a resumption of unsafe practices and a failure to use machinery guarding and other safety devices. The Inspector for the North Western Division, for example, reported that 33 female crane operators suffered 'serious injuries involving bone fractures, lacerations or crushing of parts of the body.'[25]

Meanwhile the Factory Department was severely depleted. By the end of 1914, 30 male factory inspectors out of a total of 195 had enlisted in the army, while a further 35 had been seconded to other departments for war-related work.[26] The number of government clerks, whose job it was to compile statistics on industrial accidents and diseases, was similarly reduced by the demands of army recruitment. In all, 62 inspectors and 41 clerks saw active service between 1914 and 1918.[27] The separate Women's Factory Inspectorate, established in 1893, had developed into a competent and experienced organisation but it remained extremely small, numbering just 19 inspectors in 1914. Throughout the war the government was reluctant to invest in more inspectors, finally conceding the appointment of just three extra women inspectors in 1916 and a further six in 1917.[28] However, four of these were voluntary, unpaid appointments and all were regarded as temporary. The overall picture, therefore, is of an under-resourced, over-stretched Factory Department, a vulnerable workforce and a consequential decline in health and safety standards. It was against this background that the government elected to extend its armament workers' welfare system into a nationwide scheme.

Welfare

The nature of welfare provision was defined by the Factory Act of 1916, which enshrined in law the requirement for 'special provision to be made at the factory or workshop for securing the welfare of the workers or any class of workers employed'.[29] The content of this provision was defined by Welfare Orders issued to specific industries, and included the following: 'Arrangements for preparing, or heating, and taking meals, the supply of drinking water; the supply of protective clothing; ambulance and first aid arrangements; the supply and use of seats in workrooms; facilities for washing; accommodation for clothing; arrangements for supervision of workers.[30] Although not explicitly stated, these provisions were, in practice, concerned with making factories fit places to work for one particular 'class of workers', namely women. The terms of the Act had been drawn up following an extensive government survey of existing facilities, carried out during the second year of the war in almost 1400 factories across the country.[31] The fact that an already overworked women's factory inspectorate was detailed to conduct this survey conveyed two important messages, first that the subject was sufficiently important to justify the diversion of scarce resources away from more traditional areas of health and safety, and second, that welfare provision was the business of women, both in terms of its recipients and those charged with its enforcement. From 1915 a primary duty of women factory inspectors was to assess workplaces in terms of welfare needs and to issue official Welfare Orders. Principal Woman Factory Inspector, Adelaide Anderson's response to these developments suggests that, initially at least, inspectors greeted these requirements with a degree of satisfaction.

> A question arises, like the riddle of Samson, why has the manufacture of the munitions of war on a terrible scale led at last to the systematic introduction of hygienic safeguards that Factory Inspectors have advocated for many years, such as the supervision of women by women in factories, the provision of means of personal cleanliness, proper meal and rest rooms, and qualified nurses?[32]

The women's factory inspectorate had been founded on the premise that women required special protection in the workplace. Women lacked representation both at a political level and in terms of their membership of well-organised unions and, it was argued, factory legislation often failed to take account of the particular risks associated with female employment. Over the previous decade women inspectors had attempted to draw attention to these risks and had, in addition, called repeatedly for the introduction of practical measures that would render the workplace a more suitable environment for women. High on their list were women's lavatories (often absent in early twentieth century factories), washrooms and canteens. They also wished to see the introduction of female supervisors. Women, it was argued, would feel more able to confide their worries to other women, an important justification for the original appointment of women factory inspectors and powerfully supported by the increasing number of concerns submitted to women inspectors by female workers over the years since 1893.[33] Women inspectors were thus natural allies of the industrial welfare programme at the beginning of the war, viewing it as an important element of wider health and safety policy. By 1918, however, they appeared to have considerable misgivings about the way the system had developed. Welfare had, according to Anderson, 'failed...as a merely superimposed factor on unreformed factory life'.[34] In many workplaces, it seems, health, safety and welfare had ceased to be complementary elements of a single system. In peacetime there had been a degree of synergy between these different elements, but the wartime welfare system was driven by rather different objectives to those that had underpinned the pre-war requirement for industrial health and safety. Most obviously there was now an urgent need to maximise production, a requirement addressed largely y the implementation of new systems of scientific management.[35] tandardisation of procedures and the allocation of each worker to one outine task with carefully timed work and rest periods would, it was rgued, increase performance and minimise the need for high levels of ndividual skill. Meanwhile human comfort, engendered by an agreeable vorking environment, would energise and motivate workers, mitigating he effects of boredom and routine which threatened to slow produc- ion and increase errors. As one advocate declared, 'it is only when high pirits and enthusiasm enter the human machine that, like a well-oiled ngine, all parts work smoothly and produce the greatest effort with the ast friction.'[36] In large armaments factories, therefore, the combination f scientific management and industrial welfare seemed to offer a solu- ion to the immediate problem of extracting a high level of production om a large, inexperienced and unskilled workforce. However, many mployers, engaged in other forms of production in smaller factories nd workshops, remained unconvinced of these advantages, viewing he compulsory investment in canteens and women's lavatories as an nnecessary burden at a time of national crisis.

Of equal importance was the need to attract women and girls into ndustry and, perhaps more importantly, to reassure their parents. The ppointment of Seebohm Rowntree as the first Director of Welfare ervices, an employer dedicated to paternalistic control as the basis for vell-ordered industrial communities, was a strong indicator of the model he government had in mind.[37] In 1915 the Ministry of Munitions issued uidance to employers about the necessity of providing 'such supervi- ion as may be necessary to ensure in the factories a standard of behav- our such as would not offend an employee coming from a respectable ome.'[38] Amongst certain sections of the population there was growing nxiety that mass female employment, especially when it involved the eographical displacement of young, unsupervised and well paid young irls, might constitute a serious moral threat to the nation. Some of these oncerns were reminiscent of earlier debates about the damage wrought n the national health and character when women neglected their tradi- onal roles of child bearing and child rearing in favour of paid work.[39] he resurgence of similar anxieties now extended to include unmarried irls. A lack of parental guidance and any sense of mature responsibility, was argued, placed them, and by implication the nation as a whole, 1 serious moral danger.[40] The remedy for these ills appeared to lie in ne specific clause of the 1916 Act which referred to the 'supervision f workers'. Thus supervision of housing would 'prevent women and ds from lodging with disreputable people'[41] and 'supervision outside the factory may be necessary to ensure that girls and boys living away from home are not demoralised during their free time'.[42] Such risks were considered to be exacerbated in times of war when fatalistic attitudes fostered carefree, and careless, behaviour.

In practice, therefore, 'supervision of workers' meant 'supervision of women', and involved the requirement of employers to appoint female welfare supervisors, mandatory in large factories but also strongly encouraged elsewhere.[43] In addition to their practical functions as outlined by the Act, these women were also encouraged to provide recreational and educational activities for employees outside working hours. Such activities presumably offered a diversion from other less desirable pursuits. It is not difficult to see how the performance of these duties might shade over into the moral supervision and instruction of the workforce. Largely untrained and drawn from the middle classes many supervisors seem to have over-interpreted their role, extending their gaze to include the private lives of workers, censuring their behaviour, personal appearance and other aspects of their general lifestyle.[44] Whilst the establishment of canteens and lavatories was undoubtedly appreciated, many welfare supervisors, it seems, were not. Writing in the Chief Factory Inspector's Report for 1918, Superintendent Inspector, Isabel Taylor, observed that 'it has become no uncommon thing to hear of some stupid act of petty tyranny quoted as an example of "welfare".'[45] Moreover the frequent ignorance and incompetence of welfare supervisors in matters of health and safety engendered a mistrust and lack of respect. Lady Peggy Hamilton, a middle-class veteran of several factories and workshops who had, rather unusually, chosen industrial employment, was forthright in her criticisms. She noted that welfare officers invariably had no working experience and no knowledge of industrial hazards. The protective clothing they designed could be uncomfortable and largely useless while their response to sickness was often uninformed. Hamilton cited an incident where a young girl had experienced breathing difficulties after exposure to gas escaping from a furnace. The welfare officer, it seems, regarded the girl's symptoms as 'purely psychological'.[46]

Welfare supervisors, themselves, were often aware of the resentment their presence provoked and felt helpless in the face of it. Guidance from the Ministry of Munitions, primarily intended to emphasise their independence from Trade Union activity, effectively rendered their position untenable. Charged with caring for the workers' well-being they were nevertheless instructed to consider themselves as part of the management of the factory and not as workers' representatives.[47] This tended to undermine their function as a channel for workers' concerns

The welfare supervisor at Armstrong-Whitworth's munitions factory in Newcastle upon Tyne remarked that they 'appeared to the workers in the light of spies who were going to watch and report to management ... or as goody-goody people who were going to poke their noses into the workers' private affairs'.[48] Anderson's deputy, Rose Squire, noted that the high level of responsibility placed on welfare officers was coupled with a relatively low status within the management hierarchy. And their lack of legal backing, she argued, made it impossible for them to stand their ground when faced with autocratic employers.[49] Undoubtedly some welfare supervisors seem to have successfully negotiated the awkward boundary between workers and employers,[50] but many others found themselves caught between an unsympathetic employer and a hostile, unco-operative workforce.

Factory inspection

The primary agents of enforcement of the welfare system were the women factory inspectors. Policing the scheme seems to have occupied large swathes of their time despite the additional need, as Anderson noted pointedly, to overcome a prevailing but erroneous belief that other existing factory regulations were 'in abeyance'.[51] The women inspectors were further required to assess the conditions under which employers might be granted an Emergency Order, a temporary modification of factory regulations during times of national emergency. This facility, established under the Factory Act of 1901,[52] was, in practice, usually concerned with the suspension of the normal prohibition on female night work to enable employers to maintain continuous production. Early in 1914, Anderson reported on the 'breathless endeavour, to watch over the application of the incessantly flowing Emergency Orders.'[53] The implementation of such Orders often ran counter to the protective principle which informed much of the welfare system, for the original exclusion of women from night work had been influenced as much by moral concerns as by those of health and safety.[54] Thus Emergency Orders granted during the war could only be issued under a particular set of conditions. An essential prerequisite was the presence of a 'responsible woman', (an undefined designation), to supervise and protect female employees during the night. The reports of individual women factory inspectors provide ample evidence that it was the enforcement of this requirement, as well as the ascertainment of suitable eating areas, cloakrooms and lavatories, that occupied most of their time throughout the war. Issues more directly associated with health and safety hazards, meanwhile, were often relegated to the periphery of their reports. Thus in February 1915, Superintendent Inspector Hilda Martindale visited the premises of Joseph & Jesse Siddons Ltd, a Staffordshire foundry engaged in the production of soldiers' mess tins. Observing that three young women under the age of twenty years were employed during the night alongside four men, she reported that 'None of the girls could be considered a responsible woman'.[55] Rejecting the owners' protestations that the men were long-serving and entirely trustworthy employees, she required the women be removed from the night shift and replaced by young boys.

The incident at Siddons foundry, typical of many repeated throughout the country, underlines the centrality of moral issues in the factory inspection process during this period and the apparently disproportionate amount of time and energy devoted to such concerns. Martindale made only passing reference in her report to what might be considered traditional health and safety issues, noting simply that the manufacturing process contained no lead and thus did not constitute a danger to health. She made no mention of the well-established risks associated with foundry work, as evidenced by official accident statistics for 1914. There were, for example, over seven thousand reported accidents in foundries that year of which 27 were fatal.[56] Moreover, the inspection of welfare provision, itself, seems to have been severely under-resourced. As late as September 1917, inspector Mary Buckley recorded that there were 536 government-controlled factories in the Birmingham area of which 81 had still not been visited. Of those already inspected, welfare conditions in 129 were either bad or very bad, requiring further quarterly visits. In 145, where conditions were somewhat better, six-monthly visits were recommended. Conditions in some other factories and workshops were described as 'not good' but, as Buckley concluded rather hopelessly, future visits were 'inappropriate since little improvement can be effected.'[57]

The increasing antipathy of the women inspectors towards the welfare system reflected not only their professional reservations but also their personal resentment at the apparent downgrading of their own role. Before the war the Annual Report of the Principal Lady Factory Inspector had been replete with statistics on industrial accidents and disease, as well as anecdotal observations on specific concerns related to women's employment and recommendations for action. This form of report disappeared after 1914, to be replaced with a section dedicated largely to the progress of welfare provision, formally cataloguing the number of canteens, cloakrooms and lavatories now available in various workplaces, as well as the number and type of Welfare and Emergency Orders issued.[58] In 1918 Anderson observed, with barely concealed annoyance, the large staff that had been allocated to the welfare department, while the number of factory inspectors had remained largely unchanged.[59] The most explicit condemnation of the situation, however, came from Squire, who, in 1917, was reluctantly transferred to the role of Co-Director of Welfare Services. Here she joined Dr Edgar Collis, one of only two medical inspectors of factories, who had been similarly seconded a year earlier. Underlining the primacy of the welfare operation, and perhaps also the good reputation accorded to the staff of the Factory Department, both moves had been ordered by Winston Churchill, Minister of Munitions, in an attempt to salvage what seems to have been an increasingly dysfunctional situation. On arrival Squire observed 'a staff of over 100 ... an inharmonious crowd, beset by jealousies and gossip, disintegrating forces, and difficulties of mushroom growth.'[60] Noting the numerous failings of the system she added that she 'doubted whether anyone could put right what ... was due to the fundamental mistake of setting up a separate organisation to deal with industrial conditions.'[61] It is here that a major source of resentment lay, for the provision of welfare, a long held aspiration of the women factory inspectors, had effectively been taken out of their hands and allocated to a new department, generously staffed by inexperienced and seemingly incompetent women. Their own position, meanwhile, had been reduced to something resembling a moral police force, simultaneously rendering ineffective their hard won professional skills as health and safety inspectors.

Afterword

There is little doubt that in most workplaces health and safety declined during the First World War and the steady improvements observed during the early years of the twentieth century came to a temporary halt. Ironically it was in the armaments factories, generally perceived as emblematic of hazardous working conditions, that most was done to protect the workforce and where most success was achieved. Elsewhere, however, workers were largely neglected, a situation compounded, it seems, by the diversion of significant resources into an industrial welfare system which prioritised moral well-being over accident and disease prevention. The war appears to have represented the high point of state-regulated industrial welfare. Long resisted by the government, its introduction was only conceded when women's employment became central to the war effort. Any doubts that welfare was primarily a female concern were dispelled by the indecent haste with which its administrative structure was dismantled when hostilities ceased. Within weeks of the Armistice, in November 1918, the Welfare Department had effectively been closed down, absorbed into the Department of Demobilization and Resettlement.

In 1919 the government appointed a Women's Employment Committee to consider the future of 'industrial welfare'.[62] Members noted that the concept had become tarnished during the war. It had acquired 'an unpleasant significance'[63] in labour circles because it had involved 'excursions into the field of private home life normally outside factory administration.'[64] The Secretary of the National Federation of Women Workers, Mary Macarthur, was more direct in her condemnation, declaring at a Federation conference in 1918 that, among women workers, there was 'no word in the English language more hated than welfare'.[65] The welfare system had long been regarded by trade unionists as an attempt to undermine their representation in factories and hence weaken workers' ability to negotiate their own employment conditions. Workers' criticisms during the war had added considerable grist to this particular mill. Meanwhile the Committee, which included a significant contingent of women factory inspectors, remained convinced that welfare could be made to work for the benefit of the labour force. It recommended the continuance of industrial welfare provision as a State requirement, urging a return to original notions of practical comfort and well-being as an integral part of a wider health and safety system. It recommended proper training for welfare supervisors, and a special role for factory inspectors as workplace advisors, with legal powers to require employers to make the necessary provisions.[66]

However, official attitudes towards welfare, now freed from the imperative to encourage and accommodate female employment, were already moving in a different direction. The Health of Munitions Workers Committee had transmuted into the Industrial Health Research Board after the war, developing a programme of research to investigate the effects on performance of factors such as repetitive work, lighting, noise, temperature and various other physical and ergonomic aspects of the working environment.[67] In 1921, an organisation with similar scientific interests, the National Institute of Industrial Psychology, was formed with support from industrial sponsors.[68] The recommendations that flowed from these two institutions, directed at the workforce as a whole and unashamedly aimed at production maximisation, were largely uncontaminated by the moral tone which had undermined much of the wartime system. This new form of welfare held considerably more appeal for employers who were increasingly inclined to adopt measures on a voluntary basis. By contrast, the State began to retreat from welfare provision. For the women factory inspectors this undoubted disappointment was to be followed by a further blow, for their strong identification with the wartime welfare agenda had considerably undermined their own pre-war role as health and safety professionals. After 1918 they were unable to re-establish their former position as the explicit protectors of women at work. Their separate Annual Report did not reappear in 1919, and the concerns of women workers were subsequently distributed across other sections organised by subject rather than by gender. In 1921 this new approach was formalised, in the amalgamation of the men's and women's factory inspectorates, into a single organisation, effectively abolishing the need to deal separately with the risks and needs of women in the industrial workplace. Meanwhile, during the inter-war years, much of industrial welfare moved outside the State-regulated health and safety system and entered the realm of private, employer-initiated provision.[69]

Notes

1. T. M. Legge 'Trintrotoluene Poisoning', in *Annual Report of the Chief Inspector of Factories and Workshops for the Year 1917*, (1918) Cd. 9108 (London: HMSO) pp. 21–24.
2. T. M. Legge (1917) 'Trintrotoluene Poisoning'.
3. A. M. Anderson (1922) *Women in the Factory*, pp 306–307.
4. A. Ineson and D. Thom (1985) 'T.N.T Poisoning', pp 89–107; G. Braybon (1989) *Women Workers*; A. Woollacott (1994) *On Her Their Lives Depend*; D. Thom (1998) *Nice Girls and Rude Girls*.
5. M. Pugh (2000) *Women and the Women's Movement*, pp 18–21; Woollacott (1994) *On Her Their Lives Depend*, p 25.
6. TNA, MUN5/94/346/5.
7. T. M. Legge 'Industrial Poisoning', in *Annual Report of the Chief Inspector of Factories and Workshops for the Year 1918*, (1919) Cmd. 340 (London: HMSO) Chapter VIII.
8. A. M. Anderson, (1922) *Women in the Factory*, Appendix II.
9. G. Holloway (2005) *Women and Work*, pp 130–143.
10. A designation applied when at least 75 per cent of output was produced under government contract for wartime supplies.
11. TNA, MUN5/70/324/17.
12. A. M. Anderson 'Women and Girls in Industry', in *Annual Report of the Chief Inspector of Factories and Workshops for the Year 1914*, (1915) Cd. 8051 (London: HMSO) Chapter IV.
13. A. Woollacott (1994) *On Her Their Lives Depend*, pp. 24–30.
14. P. W. J. Bartrip (2002) *The Home Office*, p 267–289.

15. Factory and Workshop Act 1901 (1 Edw VII c.22).
16. Health of Munition Workers Committee, *Memorandum No. 8, Special Industrial Diseases,* (1916) Cd. 8214 (London: HMSO).
17. *Annual Report of the Chief Inspector of Factories and Workshops for the Year 1918,* (1919), Cmd. 340 (London: HMSO) p 43.
18. *Annual Report of the Chief Inspector of Factories and Workshops for the Year 1919,* (1920), Cmd. 941 (London: HMSO) Chapter II, Chapter III.
19. Registers of cases of poisoning by lead, arsenic, mercury and phosphorus, and cases of ankylostomiasis and anthrax were maintained, but not made public until after the war. TNA LAB 56/20.
20. A. M. Anderson (1922) *Women in the Factory,* Appendix II.
21. TNA, MUN 5/77/325/102.
22. TNA, MUN 5/77/325/102; Imperial War Museum, PST 5471.
23. Dilution was the process whereby skilled workers were replaced by unskilled workers to perform unskilled or semi-skilled tasks. Substitution was the process whereby male workers were replaced by female workers. Since women substitutes were often unskilled, substitution was often a form of dilution.
24. *Annual Report of the Chief Inspector for the Year 1919,* p 3, p 15.
25. *Annual Report of the Chief Inspector for the Year 1919,* p 20.
26. *Annual Report of the Chief Inspector for the Year 1914,* p iv.
27. *Annual Report of the Chief Inspector for the Year 1918,* p vii.
28. TNA, HO45/10790/300791.
29. Police, Factories (Miscellaneous Provisions) Act 1916, (6 & 7 Geo V c.31), Part 11, Factories and Workshops.
30. Police, Factories (Miscellaneous Provisions) Act 1916.
31. A. M. Anderson (1922) *Women in the Factory,* Appendix II.
32. *Annual Report of the Chief Inspector of Factories and Workshops for the Year 1915,* (1916) Cd. 8276 (London: HMSO) p 15.
33. Complaints about working conditions submitted to women inspectors increased from approximately 300 in 1896 to over 2000 in 1913. *Annual Report of the Chief Inspector of Factories and Workshops to HM Principal Secretary of State for the Home Office, for the year 1896,* (1897) Cd. 8561 (London: HMSO) p 57; *Annual Report of the Chief Inspector of Factories and Workshops for the Year 1913,* (1914) Cd. 7491 (London: HMSO) p 74.
34. *Annual Report of the Chief Inspector for the Year 1918,* p 43.
35. S. Kreis (1995) 'Early Experiments in British Scientific Management: The Health of Munition Workers' Committee, 1915–1920', *Journal of Management History,* 1, 2, pp 65–78.
36. B. Meakin (1905) *Model Factories,* p 203.
37. B. Harrison, 'Rowntree, (Benjamin) Seebohm (1871–1954)', *Oxford Dictionary of National Biography,* Oxford University Press (2004) [online edn, January 2008, accessed 2 December 2013].
38. TNA, MUN5/93/346/101.
39. A. Davin (1978) 'Imperialism and Motherhood', pp 9–65.
40. Middle-class anxieties were well-illustrated in Madeline Ida Bedford's popular poem 'Munitions Wages' published in 1917, where Bedford assumes the persona of a munition worker to express their presumed careless attitudes towards life and morality. M. I. Bedford (1917) 'Munition Wages', in C. Reilly (ed.) (1997) *The Virago Book of Women's War Poetry and Verse* (London: Virago) p 7.

41. TNA, MUN5/93/346/131.
42. 'Demoralised' in the sense of 'corrupted'. National Archives, MUN5/93/346/118.
43. R. Squire (1927) *Thirty Years in Public Service*, p 180.
44. P. Hamilton (1978) *Three Years or the Duration*, p 75.
45. *Annual Report of the Chief Inspector for the Year 1918*, p 43.
46. P. Hamilton (1978) *Three Years or the Duration*, p 75.
47. Cited in: A. Ineson and D. Thom (1985) 'T.N.T. Poisoning', p 98.
48. E. B. Jayne (no date) 'A Resumé of Women's Welfare Work at Sir W. G. Armstrong-Whitworth & Co. Ltd. 1916–1919', pp 1–5. IWM, Mun 24/15.
49. R. Squire (1927) *Thirty Years in Public Service*, p 181.
50. Welfare Supervisor Margaret Dibbin at Howe Bridge Cotton Spinning Company, Lancashire, was popular and effective, maintaining a warm correspondence with both employer and workers following her departure to join the Factory Inspectorate in 1917. Personal communication, Anderson family papers.
51. *Annual Report of the Chief Inspector for the Year 1914*, p 39.
52. Factory and Workshop Act 1901.
53. *Annual Report of the Chief Inspector for the Year 1914*, p 39.
54. Originally established by the Factory Act, 1847 (10 & 11 Vict c.29). This was reinforced by the Berne Convention of 1905; B. E. Lowe (1921) *The International Protection of Labor*, p 174.
55. TNA, HO45/10790 300791.
56. *Annual Report of the Chief Inspector for the Year 1914*, Table 9, p 129.
57. TNA, MUN 5/93/346/128.
58. *Annual Report of the Chief Inspector for the Year 1918*, Chapter IV.
59. *Annual Report of the Chief Inspector for the Year 1918*, p 31.
60. R. Squire (1927) *Thirty Years in Public Service*, p 180.
61. R. Squire (1927) *Thirty Years in Public Service*, p 178.
62. *Report of the Women's Employment Committee*, (1919), Cmd. 9239 (London: HMSO).
63. *Report of the Women's Employment Committee*, p 39.
64. *Report of the Women's Employment Committee*, p 39.
65. Cited in D. Thom (1998) *Nice Girls and Rude Girls*, p 132.
66. *Report of the Women's Employment Committee*, p 39.
67. Established in 1918 as the Industrial Fatigue Board. Renamed the Industrial Health Research Board in 1921 to reflect the wider scope of its investigations.
68. S. Shimmin and D. Wallis (1994) *Fifty Years of Occupational Psychology*, p 4.
69. H. Jones (1983) 'Employers' Welfare Schemes and Industrial Relations in Inter-War Britain', *Business History*, 25, 1, pp 61–75.

References

Anderson. A M (1922) *Women in the Factory. An Administrative Adventure* (London: John Murray).
Bartrip. P W J (2002) *The Home Office and the Dangerous Trades. Regulating Occupational Disease in Victorian and Edwardian Britain* (Amsterdam New York: Rodopi).

Braybon. G (1989) *Women Workers in the First World War: The British Experience*. (London: Routledge).

Davin. A (1978) 'Imperialism and Motherhood', *History Workshop*, 5, Spring, pp 9–65.

Hamilton. P (1978) *Three Years or the Duration. The Memoirs of a Munition Worker* (London: Peter Owen).

Holloway. G (2005) *Women and Work in Britain since 1840* (London and New York: Routledge).

Ineson. A and Thom. D (1985) 'T.N.T. Poisoning and the Employment of Women Workers in the First World War', in P Weindling (ed.) *The Social History of Occupational Health* (London: Croom Helm) pp 89–107.

Lowe. B E (1921) *The International Protection of Labor. History and Law* (New York: MacMillan).

Meakin. B (1905) *Model Factories and Villages: Ideal Conditions of Labour and Housing* (Philadelphia: George W Jacobs).

Pugh. M (2000) *Women and the Women's Movement in Britain, 1914–1999* (Basingstoke: MacMillan).

Shimmin. S and Wallis. D (1994) *Fifty Years of Occupational Psychology in Britain* (Leicester: British Psychological Society).

Squire. R (1927) *Thirty Years in Public Service. An Industrial Retrospect* (London: Nisbet & Co).

Thom. D (1998) *Nice Girls and Rude Girls: Women Workers in World War 1* (London: I B Tauris & Co Ltd).

Woollacott. A (1994) *On Her Their Lives Depend. Munitions Workers in the Great War* (London: University of California Press).

5

A Heroine at Home: The Housewife on the First World War Home Front

Karen Hunt

Introduction

When we visualise women on the First World War Home Front we tend to think of women munition workers rather than women in food queues. The first group are remembered as young, energetic and patriotically 'doing their bit', while the others, if they are there at all, are older, greyer and passive. Yet, of course, many of these women were the same people dealing with different aspects of ensuring their own and their family's survival in the new phenomenon of 'total war'. The purpose of this chapter is to bring the women in the food queue back into focus thereby raising questions more broadly about how we understand the Home Front, particularly what the war meant for everyday life in Britain as the nature of the crisis deepened from 1914 to 1918. Ironically we actually know more about how this was experienced in other belligerent nations, such as Germany and Austria, than we do about Britain.[1] That in itself says something about how the Home Front has figured in the British historiography of First World War and how these debates have in turn affected the representation of the civilian experience of the war in popular culture, within heritage sites and as part of the memorialisation of the war. We seem to have difficulty in populating the heterogeneous British Home Front in our collective imagination – with men as well as women; with the young and the old, as well as those of working/ army age; and with those who were dependent on others as well as paid workers. This chapter asks what difference it makes to our understanding of the Home Front if we put the housewives back into the stories we tell of the First World War.

Why the housewife?

The recognition of the First World War as the first 'total war' which mobilised the civilian population as an essential part of the war machine brought women into the story of the war as more than the mothers, wives, sisters and girlfriends of fighting men. From the beginning there was a sense that this was a new kind of war and women would have a different role, no longer just waiting for news. Already a sexual division of 'total war' was emerging, as a women's column published in October 1914 made clear:

> For, to-day, a woman must play her part in this the greatest international struggle as surely as if she were in the thick of the fighting line, and to carry out the work allotted to her she must sink all thought of self ... There is no hero at the front who has not a heroine at home paying her share of this ... The fact that men are fighting at the front and the women are in the background is not a matter for comparison, provided we are everyone in the place where our country needs us, doing the work most suitable to each of us for the benefit of the greatest number.[2]

But were there different ways of being 'a heroine at home'?

Although we have a simplistic image of how women did their bit in the First World War, dressed in the distinctive uniforms of a munitionette, a Voluntary Aid Detachment (VAD) or a member of the Women's Land Army, actually women's war work was more varied than this and only some of it was waged.[3] Nor was this picture a consistent one for the war as a whole. Women did not immediately replace the men who had 'gone to the colours', and it took time to set in place the industry-specific arrangements for the 'dilution' of skilled jobs only 'for the duration' of the war, in the language of the time. These trade union brokered agreements protected the jobs of skilled men so that the labour process could be broken down during the war and substitutes made from unskilled men, boys and women. The strict understanding was that after the war industries would return to their pre-war forms with a clear gendered division of labour. The story of women's war work in First World War was not a simple one and, like many narratives of the war, depended on the opportunities and constraints of particular localities as well as the circumstances of individual women. As importantly, the statistics of the time remind us that there are other stories to tell.

The number that mesmerises us is the Board of Trade's estimate that in the United Kingdom, 1,659,000 women entered the labour-force between July 1914 and July 1918.[4] Clearly this is a significant number and represents major changes in individual lives and households across the war years. However there are some other statistics that have been neglected and should give us pause for thought. Despite its limitations as a source for women, Census data from either side of the war can be used to bring another group of women into focus.[5] For England and Wales, in 1911, 14,357,113 women were over 10 years old and thus a good proportion of these were potential workers but actually only 4,830,734 were in paid work, that is 33.65 per cent (See Table 5.1).

In 1921, 5,065,332 of females over 12 years old were recorded as in paid work which is 32.26 per cent of female potential workers. A sizeable group of women were therefore not in paid employment and many of them were housewives, that is they had the responsibility for the running of their household however substantial or inadequate the income brought in by their husbands or children. Obviously not every woman lived in a family household but whether she was a lodger, lived alone or in a shared female household, it was almost always a woman who undertook the responsibilities of a housewife. So how many women are we talking about and how do they compare to the number of women in the wartime labour-force? Martin Pugh has estimated that the numbers of women workers expanded by about a quarter over the war to about 6.19 million.[6] He suggests that the majority of women remained in the home. Again using Census figures from before and after the war we can create an estimate of the number of housewives on the First World War Home Front (see Table 5.2).

By adding together the numbers of non-working females over 10/12 years of age with the numbers of married and widowed women

Table 5.1 Women and waged work (figures from the Census in England and Wales)

	Total Population	Total Females	Women over 10 years	Women in paid work	Married women workers	Widowed women workers
1911	36,070,492	18,624,884	14,357,113	4,830,734	680,191	411,011
1921	37,886,699	19,811,460	15,699,805	5,065,332	693,034	425,981

Source: Information extracted from Marwick (1977) *Women at War*, p. 166, table 1.

Table 5.2 Finding the housewives (figures from the Census in England and Wales)

	A	B	C	A + B + C
	Non-working women over 10/12 years (over 10/12 minus occupied)	Married women workers	Widowed women workers	Housewives?
1911	9,526,379	680,191	411,011	10,617,581
1921	10,634,473	693,034	425,981	11,753,488

Source: Information extracted from Marwick, (1977) *Women at War*, p. 166, table 1.

workers, both of whom would have had to run their households as well as working, produces the figure of about 10.62 million possible housewives in England and Wales for 1911 and 11.75 million by 1921. Even deducting the numbers of women who officially entered the workforce for the duration of the war, there were certainly considerably more housewives than women war workers and, of course, even single women workers had to feed themselves and attend to domestic labour or find someone to do it for them, hence the importance of hostels for newly-recruited munitionettes.[7] Although these figures are only indicative, there was clearly a significant group of women who were not officially engaged in paid work, many of whom were housewives and termed themselves as such. What happens if we try to put them back into the stories of First World War?

Although historians have recorded evidence that might help to create a history of the wartime housewife, few dwell on these women's experiences or how housewives were seen and saw themselves collectively, and how this affected their individual identity and agency within their daily lives. The housewife had the principal responsibility in most households for translating the family's income into meals on the table. During the war the context for this daily task was one of food shortages, unequal distribution of food and fuel, long food queues and hardship which affected the Home Fronts of all combatant nations. What had been seen as a domestic matter for women was now a public and state concern. Beyond Britain one response to these conditions was violent cost-of-living protests that erupted across the world in 1917 and 1918. Their most striking feature was the significant involvement of unorganised working-class housewives. Yet there were no comparable violent mass actions in wartime Britain despite significant food shortages and profiteering. On the British Home Front the housewife remains hidden behind her more visible sisters, the munitionettes and the VADs, and her voice is much more muted. Why?

It is striking that in the various approaches taken by historians to the British Home Front, very little attention has been given to individual civilian agency, particularly that of ordinary women in their everyday lives.[8] The housewife and the challenges of daily life are marginalised in the optimistic narrative of women's participation in the First World War which focusses on the freedoms and opportunities that war brought to (some) women, a narrative begun by Arthur Marwick and still very powerful in popular histories such as Kate Adie's *Fighting on the Home Front*.[9] Historians who give equal space to the Home Front (such as Trevor Wilson) or who concentrate upon it (such as Gerard deGroot or Adrian Gregory) include material from which one might begin to create a view of everyday life on the Home Front from the perspective of the housewife.[10] Although Gregory acknowledges that wars are 'intensely gendered and gendering events' this is not central to his analysis because he claims it 'is not the only thing about civilian life during the war'.[11] Indeed, the housewife is rarely mentioned, except for a section which focusses on the diary of a middle-class housewife, Ethel Bilsborough.[12] She is quoted as complaining of being defined as a housewife in the Universal Registration Act of 1915: 'I have no use for the silly thing, and why did they put "household duties" as my principle occupation in life when they certainly constitute the least.'[13] Nevertheless her diary shows how increasingly the war impinged on her daily domestic life.

As for histories of the housewife, there is a popular history but the First World War does not feature in it. Its focus is on the practices of housewifery rather than the experience of the housewife.[14] More academic studies tend to focus on the period up to the war but do not include the many challenges it brought. For example, Joanna Bourke explores housework in the context of work more generally for Ireland from 1890–1914.[15] In her feminist argument about the nature and extent of unpaid domestic labour, she terms domestic labourers 'houseworkers' rather than housewives. Language, both then and now, remains crucial to understanding the everyday lives of these women, how they were seen and how they saw themselves. Studies like Bourke's of largely rural communities remind us of the range of experiences that may hide under the term 'housewife' during First World War.

The studies of women more generally in First World War Britain tend to focus on paid work.[16] Most of these were published in the 1980s and were framed by feminist arguments about the patriarchal nature of the labour market. More recently the shift in emphasis has been to the ways in which dominant discourses shaped women's identity. Susan Grayzel's comparative study of French and British women's wartime identities focusses on motherhood. She argues that 'the war from its outset, paradoxically both expanded the range of possibilities for women and curtailed them by, among other things, heightening the emphasis on motherhood as women's primary patriotic role and the core of their national identity.'[17] In keeping with studies that focus on maternalism, Grayzel's view is that 'the maintenance of gender order in society via an appropriate maternity became a fundamental tactic of war.'[18] So although women were, as she says, continually reminded that what happened at 'home' was pivotal to what happened in the theatre of war, this study is not about the women who sustained households by their daily domestic labour, except inasmuch as some, but by no means all, were mothers too. Moreover this is also a history which is more concerned with discourse than everyday life or even how one framed the other. It is not the intention of Grayzel's study to give voice to the First World War housewife, and her agency is incidental to the related but different story she tells. However, of course, important studies of gender on the Home Front, such as Grayzel's, set a context for what is argued in this chapter.

In fact it is examples from beyond Britain which are most stimulating when it comes to recovering the British First World War housewife. These are the studies of women and everyday life on the Home Fronts of other belligerent nations, such as Belinda Davis's on Berlin and Maureen Healy's on Vienna, as well as particular explorations of housewives' riots across the world.[19] I have used these to think through why the British example seems to be different and what that says about women's politics in and beyond the First World War.[20] Moreover, explicitly comparative history such as Tammy Proctor's *Civilians in a World at War, 1914–18*, can also help to reframe national and even local studies. Proctor includes an exploration of the construction of Home Fronts across the world which is suggestive of where one might dig deeper within individual national examples, although it is striking that the word 'housewife' is rarely mentioned.[21] A detailed study of British housewives on the First World War Home Front has yet to be written but there are examples from elsewhere in the world of what this might offer to our understanding of the British Home Front more generally. Meanwhile, the housewife herself remains opaque in the histories of First World War Britain.

Who was the housewife?

The housewife is a slippery identity where the use of language can be an important indicator of ambivalences. The term can be used to construct an audience but can also be adopted as an individual or collective identity. It is class, in particular, which affects how people use the term about women and whether women choose to self-identify in this way. The First World War was a particular moment when 'the housewife', as distinct from a wife or mother, emerged into public discourse but also into public spaces. She was addressed by the national and the local state, by politicians and a whole range of pressure groups; she was spoken on behalf of by political organisations, women's groups, and individual female public figures; and she spoke for herself. The housewife also took action: she went shopping and attended to domestic chores, but she also queued and may have lobbied, engaged in consumer boycotts and even rioted.

However, discerning who the housewife was remains complex.[22] In Britain limits were placed on the self-organisation of housewives by the ambiguous understanding of who constituted a consumer and thus who could speak for the ordinary housewife as she battled the food queues. Unlike in Germany and Austria, there was no agreement in Britain that the ordinary consumer and the housewife were synonymous. The term 'housewife' was little used in the mainstream, socialist, labour or women's press or in local and national government publications. It was only later, during and after Second World War, that 'the housewife' became a rallying point for a certain sort of women's politics – middle class and often quite right wing.[23] Language was important. So, for example, the National Women's Council (NWC), whose food campaign in the early years of the war focussed on the working-class housewife, used the language of housekeepers and 'chancellors of the exchequer'.[24] Self-styled housewives leagues or groups existed in Austria and America but are much less visible in Britain. Rugby Housewives Committee was rare and seems to have lasted from 1913 to 1920. It concerned itself with the wartime shortage, cost and distribution of food and was one of the local groups which successfully lobbied to get better representation of women on the Rugby Food Control Committee.[25] Occasionally other organisations used the term housewife, such as a United Suffragists' meeting in early 1915, which demanded that, 'the Housewives of the Nation shall help to decide the Price of Food'.[26] As the war progressed when and how the term 'housewife' was used about women and by women was indicative of the degree to which the politics of food became central to the sustainability of the Home Front.

In the wartime local and national press, the housewife is an enigmatic figure as she moves in and out of view. In the *Daily Mail*, there are examples of housewives being addressed, as with regular compilations of food prices in London and other markets, and of correspondents styling themselves as housewives or speaking on behalf of what they see as shared concerns. Thus, 'As a housewife – and I speak for many other housewives – I would give a glad welcome to compulsory stoppage of waste.'[27] However, in this case, the class of the unnamed correspondent becomes clear as, using the language of the Home Front, she claimed, 'The only results for the poor housewife who battles in her home are surliness from her tradesmen and sulkiness and deliberate waste from her servants.' This housewife may have claimed to speak for housewives more generally but her material circumstances were very different from the women that the NWC sought to galvanise or those who formed the deputation of housewives to the Food Controller in 1917. The latter was organised by the Women's Party and consisted of women from across the country who defined themselves as housewives and who spoke from experience of the terrible effect of the food queues. One said, 'If the people are refused food, and know it is there, they will get it. There will be another revolution, and it will not take long.'[28] However, the *Daily Mail* also reported experiences from the food queues, noting for example in Portsmouth that 'women of all classes are among those waiting, some going from shop to shop.'[29] Despite its conservative social attitudes, it too was urging in its editorials by the end of 1917 that: 'The problem is not so much profiteering as scarcity, and the only remedy for it is an equitable system of distribution on a basis of compulsory rations.'[30] Yet their housewife readers might have slightly different anxieties about the new systems of food control than their poorer sisters: 'In the old days a housewife who laid up stores of food for emergency was commended for her prudence: now, if she has more than a limited quantity in the house, she is liable to fine and imprisonment.'[31]

So the housewife was definitely present on the First World War Home Front but she is an ambiguous figure, sometimes a sort of 'everywoman' but more often with an assumed or stated class position. Yet increasingly a shared set of challenges faced the housewife and, it was noted, lessons were being drawn across class boundaries. The *Manchester Guardian* recorded in 1915 that 'The open-air markets have long been the favourite shopping places of the poor, but in the last few weeks many middle-class housewives have discovered their existence, and are learning to apply something of the same skill in discrimination and buying which every middle-class woman in France or Germany or Switzerland knows how to use.'[32] A piece in the *Daily Mail* by 'A Housewife' entitled 'Heroines at Home. War Drudgery Without Excitement' provides a description of the housewife (in 1916) which seems to reach out to other women's experience yet actually underlines class differences: 'Tired out by heavy work to which she is not used, worn by anxieties as to her absent husband or sons, no wonder those women who have stopped in their homes since August 1914 and have bravely tried to keep things going are now in a state of nervous despair and are inclined to "let the whole thing go".... the weary drudge of everyday economy falls on the stay-at-home woman with children to care for.' She predicted of housewives that 'some day they will turn when one more brave than others says: "Government controlled food and provision stores at fair prices, and unjust profits were forbidden since they arise out of the necessities of life."'[33] But how were the voices of housewives to be heard as the challenges of the Home Front became more demanding?

How do we find the housewife?

The Ministry of Food wanted to reach the housewife in its propaganda campaigns for food economy as in the now much-reproduced poster 'The Kitchen is the Key to Victory. Eat Less Bread'.[34] By 1917 this was becoming urgent, as the Ministry's Director of Women's Services, Mrs Pember-Reeves explained to a women's meeting at Stockport Town Hall on 'How Women May Do Their Bit':

> If there was any question that would be settled by the people it was the food question, because they all had to have it. ... This was largely a woman's question. The war had turned it into the hands of the women, and it was for the women to do the trick. It is now their job, and if they choose to do it, they could confound the Prussians.[35]

But reaching the ordinary housewife was not so easy. This meeting was the culmination of 84 meetings held over a week in the town by Stockport Food Economy Committee with the specific aim of reaching the working classes. New tactics were adopted such as sending speakers to local picture houses to try to engage more reluctant audiences. But how did women respond to these pleas for economy? It was suggested that 'housewives, who have never wasted, ... are a little intolerant of the long columns written in the daily paper for their exclusive benefit. ...

[T]he exhortation to save is a seed which could find more soil to thrive in if it were directed to the lovers of luxury, the wasters and the thriftless.'[36] Where were the spaces in which housewives themselves might voice their experiences and move from the targets of food economy and food control to agents within the debates about how to solve the wartime food question?

One way to establish who speaks for the housewife and the housewives' experiences on the Home Front is to look at the different spaces in which the housewife might speak. Only then can we determine whether this was a homogenous voice or a series of different voices, inflected by class (principally) and location (rural or urban) or a series of ventriloquist performances by various individuals or groups speaking on behalf of the housewife. At the national level, there were some new opportunities in which the housewife or her experience might be represented. The labour movement created a wartime co-ordinating body, the War Emergency: Workers' National Committee (WEWNC), to safeguard working-class interests. It claimed to speak on behalf of the entire working class and also included in its definition of 'the public' the lower middle class, bringing, it is estimated, some 90 per cent of the population under its aegis.[37] Although it was nominally a representative body, Royden Harrison's research suggests 'it could not claim to speak authoritatively on behalf of women workers or working-class consumers.'[38] Its large and predominantly male Committee contained women like Marion Phillips and Margaret Bondfield, who by now were in effect career Labour Women employed within the movement and based firmly within London, attending committee after committee. They were neither ordinary housewives, former housewives nor directly connected with the daily struggles of women on local Home Fronts across the country. However, they were sympathetic to the challenges faced by the housewife as the crisis deepened but theirs was not the voice of the housewife. The voluminous papers of the WEWNC do however give us access to some of the local groups and individual voices of those facing the everyday realities of the food crisis. Another national space where the housewife might be heard was formed in 1918 by the Ministry of Food. This was the Consumers' Council which brought together representatives of the labour movement, the co-operative movement and a set of interests termed 'the unorganised consumer'. Although the latter sounds like a description of 'the housewife', the three people chosen to represent these interests (Lord Rathcreedan, the Countess of Selbourne and Sir William Ashley) were unlikely to be mistaken for housewives. They were described at the time as 'ludicrous choices'.[39] Nobody in authority seemed to know how to reach the voices of the unorganised consumer or ordinary housewife.

The local rather than the national might be a more welcoming space for the housewife. From the outset of the war new structures were hurriedly erected to address the effect of the emergency on ordinary people. These were the Citizen Committees and local committees of the Prince of Wales National Relief Fund. Although women were not yet recognised as citizens, at least in terms of the national franchise, these local committees could provide for some women the possibility of active engagement in the development of local practice around the food supply. However, many of those women would have agreed with Sylvia Pankhurst's account of such a committee: 'Everything was dominated by the city fathers; we others were but extras imported to satisfy the Cabinet Committee's regulations, designed to please the public, by giving a suggestion of breadth and impartiality to the scheme.'[40] As the radical newspaper the *Herald* commented, 'We do not belittle any of the work women are doing, but we are certain that the most effective work for the poor is to work with them rather than for them, because by doing so you really enable them to help themselves.'[41] The same could be said for housewives of whatever class, and of the various relief committees (including those run by suffragists such as the Women's Suffrage National Aid Corps) which in the end seemed to speak for, rather than as, housewives.

The Food Control Committees (FCC) set up by local authorities in the summer of 1917 at the request of the Food Controller, seemed to offer a better prospect for the housewife and her daily concerns. Set up to safeguard the interests of consumers as the food crisis worsened, particularly because of the effect of the U-boat blockade, these committees had to have a representative of labour and a woman among their 12 members. Many authorities were unimaginative when it came to selecting their one FCC woman –occasionally there were more. They looked to a woman councillor if they had one, wives of councillors or other well-connected women. Others turned to women's organisations such as the Women's Cooperative Guild or to the National Union of Women Workers. The latter was, despite its name, a middle-class philanthropic organisation whose members' presence on the York FCC, prompted the local Trades Council to comment that this 'left the working class organisations unrepresented as far as a lady was concerned.'[42] There were many protests that FCCs, which every local authority was obliged to appoint, were too often dominated by retailers and farmers but also that women were poorly or inappropriately represented. In Wakefield, the complaint was that the FCC should include at least one woman who 'has a knowledge, from actual experience, of the conditions prevailing in a Yorkshire working class household.'[43] Most of the women who sat on FCCs were selected rather than representatives – a survey in 1919 showed that FCCs consisted of 17.8 per cent women of which only 2.75 per cent were nominated by organisations.[44] The issue was therefore about who these women were as well as their number. They were rarely the women in the food queues which came to dominate the urban landscape from the late autumn of 1917.

If formal organisations offered more opportunities for those who spoke on behalf of the housewife, there were a range of informal and even spontaneous activities across the war where her presence was noted. At the outbreak of the war Margaretta Hicks sought to link together socialist women like herself with unorganised working-class housewives through the NWC's local meetings on the food supply and by giving practical support to women who wanted to serve on local committees, for example by providing childcare.[45] The NWC worked with a wide range of other women's and labour groups, campaigning on issues such as milk depots, cost-price restaurants, meals for school children, rising prices and food production. However it only touched the working-class neighbourhoods of London, and only until November 1915.

For the country as a whole, the informal organisation in which housewives might share their experiences of the food crisis and voice their concerns were the Food Vigilance Committees (FVC), formed from 1917. FVCs drew on a wide range of working-class organisations from trade unions to churches as well as the unorganised. They sought to democratise food control and ensure a fair distribution of scarce resources. Many had women officers and surviving minutes from meetings of Willesden FVC show women driving the business of the committee forward.[46] In many ways FVCs were the spaces in which the ordinary housewife had the most prospect of translating broad concerns about her own and her family's well-being into a more self-consciously political demand. It is here that one becomes aware that most ordinary consumers were women who at this stage of the war faced a daily battle to provide an adequate diet for their households. As Lewisham FVC asked, 'Are you satisfied with the present high price of food and the conditions of shopping? ... Why should you stand in queues for your children? The Rich and Well-to-do do not do it! It is beneath their dignity! Should it not be beneath the dignity of the wives of the workers?'[47] FVCs were an important space in which a woman, including those who were housewives, could affect the politics of food and engage with the impact of the wartime economy on her neighbourhood and daily life. However, because these were informal organisations, they have left comparatively few traces. The full extent to which housewives chose to participate even in the most fleeting ways, in the activities and protests of the FVCs is still to be uncovered.

For some women it was in the few British housewives organisations and in spontaneous protests that they found a space to act. One example is the Edmonton Housewives League's campaign for a municipal milk depot which used the weapon of a consumer boycott: 'Housewives strike against the dairymen ... Refuse to have any milk tomorrow and leave it in their hands.'[48] It is in direct action over food shortages that the housewife finally becomes visible. However, although she forms the crowd, it is rarely her voice that is heard in the protests. The most spontaneous form of direct action was the food riot, although these were relatively few in Britain compared to Germany.[49] Shortages of potatoes prompted food riots by housewives in the market-places of rural Cumberland in early 1917.[50] 'Angry women' in Nottingham were reported to have 'invaded a chipped-potato shop and demanded the sale of all the potatoes in stock.'[51] There clearly were disturbances in Britain prompted by food shortages. Domestic food riots were certainly feared and probably under-reported while the press eagerly highlighted foreign riots in the propaganda battle over civilian morale.[52] Food riots are also 'remembered' in oral testimony, although Amelia Harris is unusual in having actually witnessed one: 'Crowds of people stormed the bread shops, they broke in, beat up the owners and took what they could. I saw that.'[53] Here was a possible space for action, although rarely one in which the voice of the housewife can be heard.

Individual voices of the housewife are most likely to be found in diaries and in letters. However, the ordinary housewife rarely had time to keep a diary and, unless she is remembered for other reasons, the result is unlikely to have found its way into the public domain. There is no equivalent of Mass Observation for the First World War. Some personal material has survived, such as the Ethel Bilsborough diary mentioned earlier.[54] Letters to the front recounting the effect of food shortages were a powerful influence on the government's decision to introduce rationing, as deteriorating civilian morale could have a disastrous effect on military morale.[55] However these letters are less likely to have survived as soldiers rarely had the means in the trenches to keep wives' or mothers' letters so their accounts of daily life are much rarer. Whether in diaries or letters, the banality of surviving on the Home Front is much less likely to be recorded than the exceptional event or the cheery anecdote.

Finally, there is another sort of public space in which the housewife might speak – the press. This included national newspapers, so for example Emily Mason from Salford asked the *Manchester Guardian*, 'May I give my actual experience as a housewife?'[56] There was also an extensive local press whose detailed reporting was less likely to be censored, as well as specialist magazines. These might be political spaces such as *Labour Woman*, which after the war had a column entitled 'The Housewife', or the apparently apolitical such as 'Tea Table Topics' by Gertrude Webb in the monthly *London and North Western Railway Gazette*. Hers is a thoughtful voice that reflects on the evolving experience during the war of women who used the railways and who might have worked for it as clerks. It is critical of middle-class complacency and sympathetic to the poor without being sentimental or taking an explicit political position. For all these spaces within the public sphere, the issue remained the same. Did the housewife speak for herself, seek to represent her views as shared or typical or was she being spoken on behalf of or appealed to as a silent audience for persuasion and even coercion?

Conclusion: what difference does it make if we put the housewife back into the First World War story?

However the First World War housewife is defined, it is clear that she was part of a sizeable group who have been far from visible in the stories told of the war, whether in academic or popular histories. It takes some effort to find her and to differentiate between how she was constructed as an audience for exhortations to economise and what were her actual experiences of managing the material and emotional survival of herself and her household. But putting her back into the First World War story does make a difference. The experience of the housewife was shaped by her class, or strictly speaking the class of her husband, if she had one. Her material position was also determined by what happened to the household income during the war: the mix of wages or salaries might change, and the household budget could be affected by wartime rates of pay and bonuses, and depleted through the loss of wage-earners and inadequate separation allowances.[57] It also mattered where she lived: congested urban neighbourhoods were different to provincial towns, rural villages and suburbia. Although it is still not fully recognised, place framed the experience of all on the Home Front to the point where it might be more appropriate to speak of local Home Fronts.[58] There were differences amongst First World War housewives, based on class and location but also age, size of household, the wartime experience of menfolk, and the degree to which connections were made with the experience of other housewives. But there were also many similarities, not least that they shared many of the same challenges and responses. The balance between these similarities and differences affected when and how women chose to identify as housewives and what consequence that had for them and their local communities.

So how is our understanding of the war enhanced by putting back the housewife, rather than the undifferentiated 'woman' or even the wife, mother, female worker or volunteer? It enables us to recognise the diversity of experiences on the Home Front and that the Home Front was not homogenous. Not only were civilians much more diverse than is commonly recognised, as photographs of street scenes from the war remind us, but the Home Front also evolved and changed over the duration of the war. This is particularly apparent from the close study of local newspapers which enable the mapping of how everyday life was sustained in a changing and unpredictable context. This was the first experience of 'total war' in Britain and at each level of society and in every mundane corner of life the war brought challenges for which people were unprepared and had to improvise solutions. Although the war economy was necessarily more centralised than its peacetime equivalent, the Home Front could only succeed if it was made to work in local communities and in daily life. The housewife was an important part of this. Highlighting the housewife within the First World War story underscores the importance of the Home Front to the prosecution of the war. Food was a weapon of war, wielded in everyday life not by national government but by housewives in their kitchens and in food queues, shops and market places. Germany and Britain's naval blockades were designed to break civilian morale as feeding a civilian population (including its armament workers) in addition to the army would stretch the wartime economy to breaking point. In 'total war' civilian morale could not be ignored. Food riots could bring down governments. Moreover, the extraordinary volume of post exchanged between home and war front, meant that military morale could be seriously threatened by news of hardship and even hunger in the family that the soldier believed himself to be fighting for.[59] The kitchen really was 'the Key to Victory.

Looking for the First World War housewife should also make us more critical about which voices we hear when we examine the 'Great War experience'. We privilege the government, the artist/writer, and now the soldier's voice and that of the VAD, but hearing the voices of ordinary women on the Home Front, particularly the housewife, is much more difficult. Yet the government worried that it was the cost of living and food in particular, rather than industrial protests, which would destabilise the British Home Front and endanger the war front.[60] Putting the housewife back into the stories of the First World War will help us to understand what the Home Front meant in everyday life and why the housewife and the preparation of daily meals was so central to the experience of this first 'total war' in Britain, as well as elsewhere. It will also broaden the range of who and what is remembered. A 'total war' is made and experienced by civilians as well as the military and government, yet we find that hard to memorialise. In relation to this first 'total war' could we envisage adding to the various First World War memorials, one to the 'unknown housewife' as representative of the heroines at home?

Notes

1. B. J. Davis (2000) *Home Fires Burning*; M. Healy (2004) *Vienna and the Fall of the Habsburg Empire*.
2. G. Webb, 'Heroism of the Hearth', *London and North Western Railway Gazette*, October 1914.
3. S. R. Grayzel (2002) *Women and the First World War*.
4. Board of Trade figures, quoted in M. Pugh (1992) *Women and the Women's Movement*, p 20. Pugh suggests that the actual figure was lower (about 1,259,000) because the Board of Trade neglected the dominant women's occupation of the time – domestic service – when they compiled the figures for 1914.
5. E. Higgs (1987) 'Women, occupations, and work', pp 59–80.
6. M. Pugh (1992) *Women and the Women's Movement*, p 20.
7. A. Woollacott (1994) *On Her Their Lives Depend*.
8. See J. Winter and A. Prost (2005) *The Great War in History*.
9. A. Marwick (1977) *Women at War*; K. Adie (2013) *Fighting on the Home Front*.
10. T. Wilson (1986) *The Myriad Faces of War*; G. J. DeGroot (1996) *Blighty*; A Gregory (2008) *The Last Great War*.
11. Gregory (2008) *The Last Great War*, p 7.
12. Gregory (2008) *The Last Great War*, pp 216–220.
13. Quoted in Gregory (2008) *The Last Great War*, p 217.
14. U. A. Robertson (1999) *The Illustrated History of the Housewife*.
15. J. Bourke (1993) *Husbandry to Housewifery*, pp 201–202. See also E. Ross (1993) *Love and Toil*.
16. G. Braybon (1981) *Women Workers*; D. Thom (1998) *Nice Girls and Rude Girls*; Woollacott (1994) *On Her Their Lives Depend*.
17. S. R. Grayzel (1999) *Women's Identities at War*, p 3.
18. S. R. Grayzel (1999) *Women's Identities at War*, p 3.
19. Davis (2000) *Home Fires Burning*; Healy (2004) *Vienna*; T. Kaplan (1987) 'Women and Communal Strikes'; J. Smart (1986) 'Feminists, Food and the Fair Price'; B. A. Engel (1997) 'Not By Bread Alone', pp 696–721.
20. K. Hunt (2010) 'The Politics of Food', pp 8–26.

21. T. M. Proctor (2010) *Civilians in a World at War*, p 101.
22. See K. Hunt (2000) 'Negotiating the Boundaries', pp 389–410; J. Hannam and K. Hunt (2002) *Socialist Women*, chapter 6.
23. See J. Hinton (1994) 'Militant Housewives', pp 129–156.
24. *Justice*, 5 November 1914.
25. *Justice*, 5 November 1914; *Rugby Advertiser*, 28 July 2008; *Coventry Evening Telegraph*, 12 September 1917.
26. *Herald*, 20 February 1915.
27. *Daily Mail*, 18 April 1916.
28. *The Times*, 5 December 1917.
29. *Daily Mail*, 21 December 1917.
30. *Daily Mail*, 31 December 1917.
31. *Daily Mail*, 16 January 1918.
32. *Manchester Guardian*, 27 January 1915.
33. *Daily Mail*, 11 April 1916.
34. http://www.iwm.org.uk/collections/item/object/28676.
35. *Stockport Advertiser*, 25 May 1917.
36. G. Webb, 'Domestic Economy and the War', LNWR Gazette, September 1915.
37. M. Barnett (1985) *British Food Policy*, p 31.
38. R. Harrison (1971) 'The War Emergency Workers', p 213.
39. Papers of the War Emergency: Workers' National Committee, Labour History Study and Archive Centre, Manchester (hereafter WNC), 10/1/121.
40. S. Pankhurst (1987[1932]) *The Home Front*, p 41.
41. *Herald*, 10 October 1914.
42. WNC 12/278.
43. WNC 10/3/54.
44. M. Hilton (2003) *Consumerism*, p 66.
45. *Justice*, 17 September 1914. For Hicks and the NWC, see Hunt (2000) 'Negotiating the Boundaries'.
46. WNC 10/1/85–95.
47. WNC 12/181.
48. WNC 10/4/8.
49. F. Trentmann (2001) 'Bread, Milk and Democracy', p 139.
50. A. J. Coles (1978) 'The Moral Economy', pp 157–176.
51. *Daily Mail*, 9 March 1917.
52. For example, see reports of food riots in Lisbon and Zurich (*Birmingham Daily Post*, 23 May 1917; *Liverpool Daily Post*, 11 September 1918).
53. R. van Emden and S. Humphries (2003) *All Quiet on the Home Front*, p 202.
54. See the collections of WW1 diaries and letters at the Imperial War Museum and the Peter Liddle Collection, Brotherton Library, Leeds.
55. For the government's awareness of soldiers' anxieties about food shortages on the Home Front, see B. Waites (1987) *A Class Society at War*, pp 230–231.
56. *Manchester Guardian*, 20 November 1917.
57. See the Janis Lomas chapter.
58. See, for example, K. Grieves (2004) *Sussex in the First World War*.
59. See M. Roper (2009) *The Secret Battle*, pp 103–106.
60. Commission of Enquiry into Industrial Unrest (1917) *Report* (London: HMSO), TNA CAB/24/23.

References

Adie. K (2013) *Fighting on the Home Front: The Legacy of Women in World War One* (London: Hodder & Stoughton).

Barnett. M (1985) *British Food Policy During the First World War* (London: Allen & Unwin).

Bourke. J (1993) *Husbandry to Housewifery. Women, Economic Change, and Housework in Ireland, 1890–1914* (Oxford: Clarendon).

Braybon. G (1981) *Women Workers in the First World War* (London: Croom Helm).

Coles. A J (1978) 'The Moral Economy of the Crowd: Some Twentieth-Century Food Riots', *The Journal of British Studies*, 18, 1, pp 157–176.

Davis. B J (2000) *Home Fires Burning: Food, Politics and Everyday Life in World War 1 Berlin* (Chapel Hill: University of North Carolina Press).

DeGroot. G J (1996) *Blighty. British Society in the Era of the Great War* (Harlow: Pearson).

Emden. R and Humphries. S (2003) *All Quiet on the Home Front: An Oral History of Life in Britain During the First World War* (London: Headline).

Engel. B A (1997) 'Not By Bread Alone: Subsistence Riots in Russia During World War I', *The Journal of Modern History*, 69, 4, pp 696–721.

Grayzel. S R (1999) *Women's Identities at War. Gender, Motherhood, and Politics in Britain and France During the First World War* (Chapel Hill: University of North Carolina Press).

Grayzel. S R (2002) *Women and the First World War* (Harlow: Pearson).

Gregory. A (2008) *The Last Great War. British Society and the First World War* (Cambridge: Cambridge University Press).

Grieves. K (2004) *Sussex in the First World War* (Lewes: Sussex Record Society).

Hannam. J and Hunt. K (2002) *Socialist Women. Britain, 1880s to 1920s* (London: Routledge).

Harrison. R (1971) 'The War Emergency Workers' National Committee, 1914–20'. in A Briggs. and J Saville. (eds), *Essays in Labour History, 1886–1923* (London: Macmillan).

Healy. M (2004) *Vienna and the Fall of the Habsburg Empire. Total War and Everyday Life in World War I* (Cambridge: Cambridge University Press).

Higgs. E (1987) 'Women, Occupations, and Work in the Nineteenth Century Censuses', *History Workshop Journal*, 23, pp 59–80.

Hilton. M (2003) *Consumerism in Twentieth Century Britain* (Cambridge: Cambridge University Press).

Hinton. J (1994) 'Militant Housewives: The British Housewives League and the Attlee Government', *History Workshop Journal*, 38, pp 129–156.

Hunt. K (2000) 'Negotiating the Boundaries of the Domestic: British Socialist Women and the Politics of Consumption', *Women's History Review*, 9, 2, pp 389–410.

Hunt. K (2010) 'The Politics of Food and Women's Neighbourhood Activism in First World War Britain', *International Labor and Working Class History*, 77, 1, pp 8–26.

Kaplan. T (1987) 'Women and Communal Strikes in the Crisis of 1917–22', in R. Bridenthal, S. Stuard, E. Merry and W. Hanks (eds), *Becoming Visible. Women in European History* (Boston: Houghton Mifflin) pp 429–447.

Marwick. A (1977) *Women at War 1914–1918* (London: Fontana).

Pankhurst. S (1987[1932]) *The Home Front* (London: Cresset).

Proctor. T M (2010) *Civilians in a World at War 1914–1918* (New York: New York University Press).

Pugh. M (1992) *Women and the Women's Movement in Britain 1914–59* (Basingstoke: Macmillan).

Robertson. U A (1999) *The Illustrated History of the Housewife, 1650–1950* (Stroud: Sutton).

Roper. M (2009) *The Secret Battle. Emotional Survival in the Great War* (Manchester: Manchester University Press).

Ross. E (1993) *Love and Toil: Motherhood in Outcast London, 1870–1918* (Oxford: Oxford University Press).

Smart. J (1986) 'Feminists, Food and the Fair Price: The Cost of Living Demonstrations in Melbourne, August–September 1917', *Labour History*, 50, pp 113–131.

Thom. D (1998) *Nice Girls and Rude Girls. Women Workers in World War I* (London: I B Tauris).

Trentmann. F (2001) 'Bread, Milk and Democracy: Consumption and Citizenship', in M Daunton. and M Hilton. (eds), *The Politics of Consumption* (Oxford: Berg) pp 129–163.

Waites. B (1987) *A Class Society at War. England 1914–1918* (Leamington Spa: Berg).

Wilson. T (1986) *The Myriad Faces of War. Britain and the Great War, 1914–1918* (Cambridge: Polity).

Winter. J and Prost. A (2005) *The Great War in History: Debates and Controversies, 1914 to the Present* (Cambridge: Cambridge University Press).

Woollacott. A (1994) *On Her Their Lives Depend. Munitions Workers in the Great War* (London: University of California Press).

6
Female Agricultural Workers in Wales in the First World War

Thomas George

Introduction

The countryside became an essential component of the 'Home Front' during the First world War, with the 'rural idyll' being held up as something worth defending and as strengthening the link with the front line. Yet a detailed account of female agricultural workers in Wales during the First World War has yet to emerge; studies focussing on the agricultural workforce in Wales at the end of the nineteenth and beginning of the twentieth century only make passive references to the role of women. Welsh society during the early twentieth century was underpinned by the gendered ideology of separate spheres. With an economy built on heavy industry, many women, especially in urban areas, were confined to the home or in domestic service.[3] But the idea of separate spheres did not fully represent women's experiences of work in Wales before 1914. Aside from various other trades including dressmaking and working in tinplate factories, they also formed an integral part of the agricultural workforce.

Many women employed in agriculture during the First world War were engaged in general farm work, including hoeing and tending to animals, others were trained in market gardening or loading bales of hay, undertaking timber cutting and felling trees. Between 1915 and December 1916, demand for additional female labour on farms was often intermittent and localised. Obstacles in recruiting and employing female labour were especially prevalent during this period in Wales and persisted throughout the war. Apathy amongst women themselves, unfavourable local labour conditions and conceptions of gender and femininity all contributed to such circumstances. With the increasing emphasis on food production at the beginning of 1917, there was a growing demand for female labour, trained in jobs previously only undertaken by men. Therefore, the female agricultural labour force comprised both experienced workers and wartime recruits from a wide variety of economic backgrounds including the land girls portrayed in propaganda. The female workforce was more than just a patriotic construct shaped by the war effort[4] which arguably restricts understanding of the female agricultural worker. Different groups of women from various social and economic backgrounds undertook a range of agricultural work, often dictated by wartime conditions and traditional working practices in local areas. This chapter explores the course of recruitment and training amongst women undertaking agricultural work throughout Wales. Although regionally specific, it seeks to broaden our understanding of the female agricultural worker, those involved in their organisation and recruitment alongside the importance of contemporary conceptions surrounding women's employment. With notions of gender and class informing ideas and experiences of women's work in agriculture, focussing on particular localities allows for a greater understanding of the female agricultural worker and the processes involved in their organisation. Furthermore aspects of identity including age, marital status and social background and the relationship between them, were integral to understanding women's work in agriculture during this period.[5]

The employment of rural women workers throughout the rest of Britain at the beginning of the twentieth century has been discussed, both in relation to different farming methods and the way in which male and female labour was used on farms. Farm labourers were often divided by the kind of farm they were employed on and the level of skill involved in their work. These factors very often determined wages and working conditions alongside how frequently they found employment. Male workers were generally paid higher wages and got more work, especially those who tended to animals.[6] Scholarship examining the role of women in agriculture throughout Britain during the war has shown the importance of regional variations in patterns of employment.[7]

Family Labour

In Wales, as in other areas of Britain, women were already employed in some kinds of farm work prior to 1914. This was emphasised in a report compiled by Silyn Roberts in October 1918, then acting as the Administrative Inspector for the Women's Branch of the Food Production Department, which found that proportionally there were more women in Wales undertaking agricultural work than in any other area of Britain by 1914.[8] Ascertaining the extent of women's work during the nineteenth century from the census returns is however hampered by under-recording and inconsistencies regarding classification, although the inclusion of female relatives in 1911 makes the situation clearer. Where pastoral farms and smallholdings dominated the rural landscape, farmers were heavily reliant on family relatives as a source of labour.[9] For example in the administrative county of Carmarthenshire, amongst the 4,003 women and girls recorded as 'Farmers, Graziers and Farm Workers', 2,733 were listed as relatives assisting farmers.[10] Prior to 1914, due to the size of the farms and the preference for using relatives, Wales was the only region in Britain to have a comparatively small number of hired male labourers.[11] Instead wives, daughters and female domestic servants were integral components of the farm structure, undertaking tasks including tending to poultry and cattle, cleaning out the stables, milking and making butter.

Female relatives of Welsh farmers continued to play an important role in maintaining the production of food and livestock during the war. Additional training, primarily further education about dairy work and the use of implements and machinery,[12] gave some the opportunity to enhance their knowledge and skills base. Courses were also provided for those with or without any practical knowledge or experience of farm work. In December 1915, the University College of South Wales and Monmouthshire in conjunction with the Glamorgan War Agricultural Committee began to organise a series of short 'special wartime' courses to instruct women in 'light' farm work. Such courses were often extensions of those previously in place for men.[13] A farm bailiff or foreman was often in charge of groups of women, and provided practical demonstrations in milking, dairying instruction and caring for animals. The content of the early courses reflected the gendered division of farm work, as women were not yet responsible for cultivation and general labouring.[14] The women who registered for courses came from a variety of backgrounds, for example, of the ten women who attended a course at St Fagans in November 1915, three were registered as 'collier's daughters living at home', whilst the rest were made up of shop assistants, a kitchen maid and a smallholder's daughter.[15]

During the harvest period especially local village women were also employed on a casual basis. They were generally classified as unskilled, and consequently undertook low paid work.[16] Nevertheless, with the onset of war, potential labour shortages in agriculture became a source of concern. In June 1915, the *Daily Chronicle* claimed that there was a shortage of male farm workers in south Wales and farmers' daughters attending the Women's College in Cardiff could be used instead.[17] During the previous month, recruiting officers were ordered to refuse skilled agricultural labourers who tried to volunteer, although workers categorised as less skilled were readily accepted.[18] By the summer of 1916, very few women had been placed to work on farms. Silyn Roberts, now acting as Women's Agricultural Organising Officer for Wales, found that

> those [farms] able to employ a number of labourers are comparatively few, and the number of women employed other than members of the family are fewer still ... and have in many districts taken part in the movement enrolling themselves on the local register.[19]

Throughout Wales, nearly 70 per cent of holdings had less than 50 acres of land. Combined with increasing mechanisation and the pastoral nature of agriculture in Wales, there was very little demand for general labourers or additional labour in certain districts.[20] Not all areas of Glamorganshire experienced a shortage in male labour, especially in areas where little arable land or dairy farming took place.[21]

The Women's War Agricultural Committees

By the autumn of 1915, a War Agricultural Committee (WAC) was formed in each county across Britain and the following February, the Board of Agriculture was encouraging all WACs to establish a Women's Farm Labour Committee. These later became known as Women's War Agricultural Committees (WWAC), working with a host of existing groups, including branches of the Women's Institute, to organise recruitment.[22] During the spring of 1916, WWACs in Wales recognised potential labour shortages by establishing where the main sources of female labour could be found. District committees alongside local representatives started to negotiate with farmers to try and encourage them to employ women.[23] Both local and central government officials suggested that women already working on the land needed to be supplemented by a larger skilled workforce that was trained and proficient in different varieties of farm work. But local recruiters encountered a number of interrelated social and economic factors that severely curtailed the organisation of female labour. To begin with there was little demand for additional female labour on farms as there was a plentiful supply of male labour from other industries that could be used instead. A report compiled by Miss Pritchard, the Organising Secretary of the County Committee for Anglesey, noted that

> there are the quarrymen available in many parts, the quarries shut down for weeks sometimes and the men go off to the farms, also they are getting supplies of soldier labour in places, so that with these resources to fall back on, and the fact that so few men comparatively have gone from Anglesey one can understand that the farmers are not very keen on employing women, nor the women see the point of volunteering for work.[24]

Similar conditions were apparent in the colliery district of Mynyddcerrig in Carmarthenshire. Mr Hugh Morgan reported in July 1916 that

> it would appear that no scarcity of labour exists in this immediate neighbourhood as colliers after their days work and those working night shifts together with the usual women's assistance is sufficient to meet the requirements of the farmers around and most of the young girls not required at home are helping in shops.[25]

The early recruitment campaigns were also hindered by the motivations of women themselves. Recruiters believed that outside of the farming community, there was a deep-seated assumption that farm work was degrading for women. This was especially the view amongst older women, who it was believed thought manual labour was 'beneath them'.[26] The increasing press coverage of local recruitment campaigns often revealed that the success of schemes depended on the level of support within the community.[27] In one instance in north Wales, it appeared not all village women were keen to undertake farm work. In April 1918, a reporter for the local press at a public meeting of the Women's War Agricultural Committee South Caernarfonshire, noted that one representative of the committee, J. P. Hall,

> was afraid that the village girls [living in localities surrounding the farm] of the district were thinking that it was an insult for them to work on the land. He had no doubt that the country girls [those living on farms] were working very hard on the land, but the committee ought to induce the village girls to do their share.[28]

According to a summary of reports compiled by the Board of Trade examining the activities of WWACs, by 1916 large numbers of women in Wales had refused to officially register with their local committee. This was particularly common in Pembrokeshire, where a government report noted 'there is a real prejudice against registering'.[29] According to the same report, in fact many women in Wales considered it to be an 'unnecessary fuss' and feared that by putting their names forward they risked being moved away from their local area[30] demonstrating that local ties were as strong as the desire to help the war effort.

This unwillingness to undertake farm work was also compounded by the expansion of other wartime occupations available to women. Before the outbreak of war, there had been a steady increase in women leaving the countryside. Many travelled to the coalfield areas of south Wales, as fathers and husbands found work at local collieries and steel factories.[31] A number of local agricultural committees in Wales alluded to this trend, suggesting that the munitions industry was recruiting the majority of female labour in some localities. In March 1916, at a meeting of the Carmarthenshire War Agricultural Committee when the issue of female labour was discussed, the presence of munitions factories and tinplate works in the south-west at Pembrey, Llanelli and Swansea was thought to have drained potential labour, especially younger women and girls, away from farm work in the area.[32] The north and west of the county relied heavily on female labour especially in dairy farming, which was the dominant economic activity. However for many young and single women in rural parts of Wales, moving to more urbanised areas gave them the opportunity to leave poor living conditions in the countryside and to escape the physical demands of farm work.[33] In the spring of 1916, the proximity of such factories was noted by the Agricultural Organiser for Carmarthenshire, who argued that women should be made aware of the importance of farm work because 'it was essential to enlist the sympathy of the women, and to point out to them that it was quite important to produce food, as it was to produce munitions.'[34] With the county of Carmarthenshire being primarily pastoral, combined with a fall in imports from abroad of dairy products and meat and output at home, there was an added incentive for recruiters to encourage women to participate in farm work within this area.

Increasing involvement of women in agriculture

The table below demonstrates there was a deficit in the number of women permanently employed on the land compared to the level found in July 1914. This corresponds with the establishment of munitions factories and the increasing availability of other occupations open to women.

Table 6.1   Percentage excess (+) or deficit (–) in numbers of females permanently employed in agriculture in Wales as compared with July 1914*

Date	April 1914	April 1915	April 1916	April 1917	April 1918
	–5.9	–5.5	–3.8	+4.2	–2.5

Note: *Numbers employed in July 1914 = 100

Source: LSE Beveridge Papers, 6/124–154, No. 129 Report on the state of employment in all occupations in the United Kingdom in April 1918, pp. 1–47. Information based on table XV: Employment Exchange Areas: The State of Employment among Workpeople Permanently Employed in Agriculture, pp 33–34.

For only a few months after the Women's Land Army (WLA) had been established in January 1917, there was a recorded excess in the figures.[35] It must however be borne in mind that these statistics only show those who had registered with labour exchanges and may not represent the entire Welsh female agricultural workforce. Attempts to compile an accurate figure for the number of women actually placed on a farm in each locality were beset by problems. Monthly returns compiled by the Village Registrar and District Representatives according to one report were often 'poor and confused' and it was 'therefore difficult to secure any accurate figures'.[36] Furthermore the rise in numbers between 1916 and 1917 may have possibly been due to the increasing numbers of women coming from England, or further afield, as part of the WLA.[37]

The foremost obstacle to placing female labour on farms was a shortage of accommodation. Known as the 'living-in' system, traditionally workers would lodge in farm outbuildings.[38] The introduction of land value duty in 1910, and five years later rent control, led to a sharp decline in the number of houses being built in rural areas of England and Wales.[39] Those that remained were deemed largely uninhabitable. Edgar Leyshon Chappell, a local government official investigating labour conditions in south Wales during the war, noted this accommodation could not be used because of the potential health risks.[40] Some accommodation was provided for land girls by philanthropic groups including the Young Women's Christian Association (YWCA) and the Girls Friendly Society (GFS). Only in areas where the local labour shortage was at its most critical, relying on workers from outside the county, was there some level of housing provision. In Cardiganshire, a YWCA depot and hostel were established in Aberystwyth during June 1918.[41] In the same year, the Glamorganshire Women's War Agricultural Committee attempted to counter the shortage of housing by establishing a hostel in Cadoxton, near Cardiff for new female recruits to be trained on neighbouring farms.[42]

Gendered conceptions of women's work reinforced the initial resistance amongst farmers and employers to the replacement of male workers exclusively by female labour. In Glamorganshire, a number of the War Agricultural Sub-committees came to the conclusion that the nature of the farming and its location would be too physically demanding for women, especially middle-class ladies from the towns. It was noted that 'many farms, especially scattered farms in the mining valleys, include a considerable proportion of mountain land, where the work and conditions are quite unsuitable for women.'[43] Public meetings organised by farmers throughout Wales, also voiced misgivings about whether women would be able to replace skilled male labourers after only a few months' training. Members of the WLA were in time issued with a uniform which attempted to establish a 'robust form' of femininity closely entwined with ideas of respectability and patriotism in order to underplay the degree of physicality and suitability for the work. This new 'masculine' uniform, which included breeches and puttees, was purposefully feminised in order to try and alleviate opposition to their appearance.[44] Many farmers and those from within rural communities, however, questioned women's modesty and decency for wearing such attire. Mrs Edith Lyttleton, the Deputy Director of the Women's Branch of the Ministry of Agriculture, in an address at a formal presentation of service ribbons in Caernarvon in 1919, suggested that 'on the Welsh hills there still lingered a prejudice against women on the land wearing uniforms'.[45] Back in Glamorganshire, farmers were accused of refusing to employ female labour and finding ways to keep their sons at home.[46] At Military Tribunals, farmers would often appeal for male farm relatives to be exempted from army service.[47]

In Cardiganshire, the University College Wales (UCW) organised gangs or 'squads' of female university students to undertake hoeing during their summer vacation. They primarily worked in the root fields adjoining the house of Sir George Stapledon and his wife Doris at Glanymor, Clarach in Aberystwyth. By the summer of 1916, 18 farmers had put in requests for the assistance of Stapledon's gang with field work and hay making.[48] Farmers and local representatives began to see the benefit of such schemes, especially with such an increasing shortage of both casual and permanent labour in the county.[49] At this time, George Stapledon was an advisory officer in agricultural botany at the university, whilst Doris was the Hon. Secretary of the Cardiganshire Women's War Agricultural Committee.[50]

WWACs were initially encouraged to recruit young, strong, healthy and educated women with a good moral character. It was believed that this kind of recruit would have no qualms about accepting the physically demanding work, receiving low pay or working long hours.[51] An 'educated' woman, primarily from a middle-class background, who had received some level of formal education, was believed to be the model land worker. This was partly due to the assumption that being well-read and therefore 'imaginative' made them more competent and self-reliant. She would also work on the basis of patriotism alone and would generally not be concerned with working conditions, including wages.[52] This was the impression of female recruits that organisers and recruiters wanted to convey to farmers, and those within rural communities who believed that middle-class women from urban areas would be unsuitable for farm work.[53] These early recruits were therefore carefully selected and given extensive training by local organisers.

Whereas in Carmarthenshire and Anglesey female labour was not in high demand by the summer of 1916, in some rural areas of Cardiganshire the labour shortage was more severe. Mrs Abel Jones, also from the Cardiganshire Women's War Agricultural Committee, noted how the Stapledon gang was needed by one farmer because he had lost six sons to the army.[54] Farmers also relied on these women to control the spread of weeds in order to maintain the growth of crops. However, it was not just agricultural students who were formed into such units.

Local village women were also organised in this way. The formation of these gangs involved gathering information on the women and girls who had volunteered. This occurred in the district of Hay and Talgarth in the county of Breconshire, with the express purpose of ascertaining to what extent these women were available to work and whether additional training was needed. The data compiled reveals a diverse workforce, with women and girls from a variety of different age groups and varying levels of knowledge in farm work. In this case, the vast majority of women were middle-aged, married or widowed with little or no degree of experience. This was also found amongst young, unmarried girls who had volunteered.[55] The nature of these gangs allowed for a large degree of flexibility, giving women the option of working on a part-time basis for just a couple of hours a day or up to three days a week. A number of women were doing other wartime jobs at the time of registering; Miss Annie Williams from Llyswen was also employed as a postwoman whilst Mrs Annie Lewis, a married woman from the same village, was a school teacher and could therefore only work during the holidays.[56] Lewis and other married women like her also had family and domestic responsibilities. This was also the case during the organisation of gangs in Chepstow, where only 16 volunteers out of fifty-four who had initially registered could work with the gang on a regular basis. The wages provided were not truly an extra incentive either, with three pence per hour being the best women could expect to receive.[57]

During the harvest period of 1916, the need for this kind of casual labour grew in many small villages and districts throughout Wales, usually under the direction of a trained forewoman. In January 1916, the Women's Farm and Garden Union and the Board of Agriculture established the Women's National Land Service Corps (WNLSC). A recruit would either be trained as a forewoman leading a village agricultural gang or would be employed as a labourer engaged in an array of jobs on a farm. Forewomen arranged work for their group with local farmers, issued wages and updated time and pay sheets.[58] With most of the initial recruits being middle class and daughters of professional men from urban areas, recruiters hoped they would serve as a positive image for womanhood and female respectability.[59] But in many cases there were not enough suitably trained and experienced women available to organise and lead the groups. Silyn Roberts noted that

> [in many districts] it has been impossible so far to secure a sufficiently skilled and educated leader to make gangs of this type a success. It is not that there are no skilled workers in the district, but that all the skilled workers are themselves employed on their farms and are therefore quite unable to spare time from their own work to organise gangs.[60]

This meant that the availability of training for women in agricultural work had to be expanded.

The Women's Land Army

A certain degree of incredulity continued throughout the war surrounding the employment of women, however farmers increasingly requested trained and experienced workers for help during the harvest period. By 1917, the Women's Branch had realised that their recruitment criteria was far too restrictive with more workers needing to be instructed.[61] In correspondence with Miss Violet Markham of the National Service Department during 1917, Margaret Haig Mackworth noted that farmers in Wales wanted women with practical experience and training. She suggested that 'they [the farmers] are again getting very short of girls for the land, especially the more educated ones, whom they [the farmers] are particularly anxious to secure'.[62] The term 'educated' now referred to women with sufficient training and experience in agricultural work, rather than based solely on class. Even so, the terms 'educated' and 'trained' were often used interchangeably by wartime commentators.

The cultivation of agricultural land was intensified during the war, with food production along with its distribution being a primary concern. The Food Production Department, established in 1917, wanted farmers to plough open grasslands and sow cereals or potatoes.[63] With the vast majority of farms in Wales being pastoral and involved in the production of dairy, this change to a predominantly arable method of farming resulted in a great deal of reorganisation especially amongst smallholders. Large areas of previously uncultivated land were to be harvested for crops with help from different groups of substitute labour.[64] These included prisoners of war, discharged soldiers and members of the Women's Land Army (WLA).

Training in a wider variety of agricultural work continued after the formal establishment of the WLA in January 1917.[65] This centralised group comprised three sections: agriculture, forage, and timber cutting.

Alongside specialist instruction in market gardening and horticulture provided by Agricultural Colleges, demand for female labour increasingly came from larger farms and estates owned by landowners in Wales where training was often being organised. At a training camp established at Glanusk Park, Crickhowel, situated on the land of Lord Glanusk, sixty-eight women received board and lodgings at the camp and were then sent to adjoining farms for training.[66] Very often the location of such facilities provided an idyllic smokescreen to the physical demands of agricultural work for the vast majority of those employed on the land in Wales. After the initial period of training in relatively large groups, girls were often separated and employed individually at different farms. Pamela Horn has suggested that this caused a great deal of misery amongst some land army girls, especially if there was any degree of opposition from local people to their employment.[67] Local and national campaigns suggested that women who came to work in the countryside would feel revitalised for leaving the 'city life' behind them.[68] However, according to Doris Stapledon, this was far from reality for a group of women from the urban districts of south Wales working in the predominantly rural and mountainous counties of Breconshire and Radnorshire. She noted how:

> it began to dawn on me that there could be little demand for land girls on these small farms, and that the living conditions were not fit for them, nor could these girls, who mainly came from the towns

and mining villages of south Wales, stand the loneliness of the life on remote farms.[69]

WLA recruits were expected to move to any district, with large numbers moving to the countryside. There was not just movement towards industrial centres. One hundred and fifty women working in Cardiganshire had come from Glamorganshire, Denbighshire and as far afield as County Durham in England.[70] However, it gradually became apparent that although there were increasing numbers of women being trained across Wales, only a small number were actually being incorporated into the labour force. Aside from the difficulties and challenges presented by changing from a primarily pastoral system to one based on crop production, women also had to cope with the increasing physical nature of the work.[71] In June 1918, during a parliamentary debate concerning the potential consequences for rural areas of losing male workers as a result of the latest quota of men required for National Service, the position of women's labour in Wales was raised. The Parliamentary Secretary to the Ministry of National Service, Mr Beck, suggested that

> As regards Wales, I dare say the conditions are difficult in regard to small farms, but Wales has made extraordinarily small use so far of the trained women. Wales herself trained a number of agricultural women and could not absorb them, and those women who were trained in Wales for Welsh agriculture have actually had to be sent into England in order that their services may be utilised.[72]

Mr Walter Roch, the Member of Parliament for Pembrokeshire, argued that this was due to a lack of suitable accommodation for women in Wales.[73] After the harvest had been collected in the summer of 1918, the War Agricultural Committees in Wales were declared exempt from having to release more male agricultural workers for national service.[74] The shortage of labour during 1917 and 1918, combined with government changes in the method of land utilisation, was seemingly taking its toll on production in Wales.

Conclusion

Women were an integral part of the wartime agricultural labour force in Wales, providing valuable assistance in a variety of jobs. With strong local ties entrenched within rural areas, family members were an important source of labour for farmers. Attempts to recruit and organise female labour in particular areas demonstrated that gendered conceptions of women's work were an essential characteristic of local employment patterns. Factors including age, social background and the increasing availability of alternative employment options show how women themselves perceived certain kinds of work. Movement between rural and urban areas, alongside those working in their own locality was both a continuation of pre-war trends in patterns of employment and a demonstration of the alternative forms of work available to women.

Many factors influenced the extent of employment for women in different areas of Wales. Demand tended to be localised, with farmers and employers questioning women's physicality but also the practicality of employing them on certain farms. A shortage of accommodation severely curtailed the placement of trained female workers and demonstrated the economic deprivation clearly apparent in many rural areas of Wales at this time. There were simply not enough skilled women to begin with in order to organise and train gangs of village workers in some areas. Aside from farm work, women undertook training in market gardening, tended to allotments and carried out timber felling.

Although the provision of training in traditional areas of gendered work for different women in agriculture was expanded during the war, many were also expected to do jobs previously undertaken by men. Hence, if we take into account the various roles females took on in agricultural production, the meaning behind the term 'land girl' is far more complex than the preconceived image of the female farm worker reflected in government propaganda.

Notes

1. S. R. Grayzel (1999) 'Nostalgia', p 156.
2. D. A. Pretty (1989) *The Rural Revolt*, p 67; see also D. W. Howell (1992), 'Labour Organization Among Agricultural Workers', pp 63–92.
3. D. Jones (1989) 'Serfdom and Slavery', pp 86–100.
4. B. J. White (2011) 'Sowing the Seeds of Patriotism?', pp 13–27.
5. Government reports and private correspondence often used terms including 'women workers' or 'land girls', when referring to their employment on the land. This chapter refers to different groups of workers including those categorised as 'village women' and who were enrolled in wartime organisations.
6. A. Howkins (2003) *The Death of Rural England*, p 18.
7. See W. A. Armstrong (1991) 'Kentish Rural Society', pp 109–131; B. J. White (2011) 'Sowing the Seeds', pp 13–27.
8. M. S. Roberts (October 1918) 'The Women of Wales', p 817.
9. D. A. Pretty (1989) *The Rural Revolt*, p 64.
10. Census of England and Wales 1911, Volume X: Occupations and Industries Part II: Occupations (Condensed List) of Males and Females at Ages ir

Administrative Counties and County Boroughs, VII Agriculture (London: HMSO, 1913).

11. E. Whetham (1978) *The Agrarian History*, p 64.
12. M. S. Roberts (1918) 'The Women of Wales', p 822.
13. C. Twinch (1990) *Women on the Land*, p 27.
14. D. Jenkins (1971) *Agricultural Community*, p 75.
15. Glamorgan Records Office (hereafter GRO), GC/AG/7/1, Reports of Agricultural Lecturer, Agricultural Inspectors and Agricultural Analyst, February 1915–1920, R. Hedger Wallace, Agricultural Lecturers Report to the Chairman and Members of the Agricultural Committee, November 1915, p 3.
16. D. Beddoe (2001) *Out of the Shadows: A History of Women in Twentieth Century Wales*, (Cardiff: University of Wales Press) p 35.
17. *Daily Chronicle*, 1 June 1915, p 3.
18. P. E. Dewey (1991) 'Production Problems', pp 241–242.
19. Bangor University Special Archives and Collections, Bangor University [hereafter BU], Reference No. 14877, Women's Land Army: Reports, Letters, Newspaper Cuttings, etc., M. Silyn Roberts, Agricultural War Service for Women, July 1916, ff 5–6.
20. D. A. Pretty (1989) *The Rural Revolt*, p 64.
21. The National Library of Wales, Aberystwyth (hereafter NLW), The Welsh Army Corps, File No. C114/15, C: Administration, Report on Agricultural Work in the Counties of Glamorgan, Monmouthshire, Brecon and Radnorshire, 13 May 1916, p 2.
22. P. Horn (1985) *Rural Life in England* (Basingstoke: Palgrave Macmillan), p 120.
23. P. Horn (1985) *Rural Life*, p 120.
24. BU, 14877, War Agricultural Service for Women, ff 7–13.
25. BU, 14877, War Agricultural Service for Women, ff 7–13.
26. *The Carmarthen Journal*, 17 March 1916, p 4.
27. *The Denbighshire Free Press*, 24 June 1916, p 5.
28. *The Merioneth News and Herald and Barmouth Record*, 26 April 1918, p 3.
29. The National Archives, London (hereafter TNA), MF 59/1 (2), Women's County Committees: Organisation of Women's Labour, File I: Reports on Women's Employment, 4 October 1916, 'Summary of the Work of the Women's War Agricultural Committees, For the Year Ending August 1916', Sub-section: Wales Division, pp 31–33.
30. TNA, MF 59/1 (2), 'Summary of the Work of the Women's War Agricultural Committees, Sub-section: Wales Division, pp 31–33.
31. D. Jones (1989) 'Serfdom and Slavery', p 92.
32. *The Carmarthen Journal*, 31 March 1916, p 3.
33. K. J. Cooper (2011) *Exodus from Cardiganshire*, p 105.
34. *The Carmarthen Journal*, 31 March 1916, p 3.
35. London School of Economics (LSE), Beveridge Papers, Reconstruction, Box 6: Reconstruction Committee: Women's Employment Sub-Committee Documents, 6/124–154, No. 129, Report on the state of employment in all occupations in the United Kingdom in April 1918, pp 1–47, Table XV: Employment Exchange Areas, the State of Employment among Workpeople permanently employed in Agriculture, pp. 33–34.
36. NLW, The Welsh Army Corps, File No. C114/15, C: Administration, Report on Agricultural Work p 5.

37. I. Nicholson and L. Williams (1919) *Wales*, p 217.
38. D. A. Pretty (1989) *The Rural Revolt*, p 64.
39. R. J. Moore-Colyer (2009) 'Homes Fit For Heroes', p 86.
40. NLW Papers of Edgar Leyshon Chappell, 1896–1945, Class D: Agricultural Wages Board Enquiry and Research, 1918–1940, D2/1–11 Notebooks, Item: D2/1 Investigators Diary I, IV Cottage Accommodation, p 3–5.
41. NLW, Minor Deposits 375–403B, Records relating to the Y.W.C.A (Welsh Division) 1909–1942, 395B Aberystwyth Branch Minute Book, 1913–1924, Correspondence between Institute Secretary, Miss Kitts and Hon. General Secretary Miss Grace Williams, 12 April 1918.
42. *Western Mail*, 16 September 1918, p 2.
43. NLW, The Welsh Army Corps, File No. C114/15, C: Administration, Report on Agricultural Work p 2.
44. S. R. Grayzel (1999) 'Nostalgia', p 159.
45. *North Wales Chronicle*, 17 January 1919, p 2.
46. *Western Mail*, 23 October 1916, p 3.
47. D. A. Pretty (1989) *The Rural Revolt*, p 69.
48. D. Stapledon (August 1916) 'Women in the Root Fields', p 463.
49. I. Nicholson and L. Williams (1919) *Wales*, p 225.
50. C. Twinch (1990) *Women on the Land*, p 20.
51. B. J. White (2011) 'Sowing the Seeds', p 15.
52. S. R. Grayzel (1999) 'Nostalgia', p 158.
53. B. J. White (2011) 'Sowing the Seeds', p 17.
54. BU, 14877, War Agricultural Service for Women, Mrs Silyn Roberts' Report, April 1916, ff 14–27; Observations on Work Done in Cardiganshire, f 20.
55. BU, 14877, Women's Farm Labour Committee, Hay and Talgarth District, ff 53–56.
56. BU, Hay and Talgarth District, ff 54.
57. TNA, MF 59/1 (2), Sub-section: 'Special Schemes', V. Thorne, Work of Gangs in Villages, Chepstow, 23 June 1916, p 42.
58. G. Clarke (2008) *The Women's Land Army: A Portrait* (Bristol: Samson and Company) p 16.
59. G. Clarke (2008) *The Women's Land Army*, p 17.
60. BU, 14877, M. Silyn Roberts, Agricultural War Service for Women, July 1916, ff 5–6.
61. B. J. White (2011) 'Sowing the Seeds', p 19.
62. TNA, Ministry of National Service, Nats 1/1279, Correspondence between Lady Mackworth and Miss V. Markham, 25 June 1917.
63. P. E. Dewey (1991) 'Production Problems', pp 241–242.
64. *The North Wales Guardian*, 11 May 1917 p 3.
65. Imperial War Museum, Reference No. IWM PST 5996, 'National Service Women's Land Army', 1917.
66. *The Landswoman*, (October 1918) 1, 10, p. 227.
67. P. Horn (1985) *Rural Life*, p 128.
68. S. R. Grayzel (1999) 'Nostalgia', p 168.
69. Doris Stapledon (August 1916) 'Women in the Root Fields', p 464.
70. NLW, Minor Deposits 375–403B, Records relating to the Y.W.C.A (Welsh Division) 1909–1942, 395B Aberystwyth Branch Minute Book, 1913–1924, Correspondence between Institute Secretary Miss Kitts and Hon. General Secretary Miss Grace Williams, 12 April 1918.

71. B. J. White (2011) 'Sowing the Seeds', p 20.
72. *Hansard*, 1803–2005, House of Commons Debate, 'Agricultural Labour Pembrokeshire', 13 June 1918, vol. 106, cc 2494.
73. *Hansard*, 'Agricultural Labour Pembrokeshire', vol. 106.
74. TNA, MAF 42/8, Food Production Department Correspondence and Papers, 62265/D, Report of the Food Production Department for the year 1918, p 5.

References

Armstrong. W A (1991) 'Kentish Rural Society During the First World War', in B A Holderness. and M Turner. (eds), *Land, Labour and Agriculture, 1700–1920: Essays for Gordon Mingay* (London: The Hambledon Press) pp 109–131.

Cooper. K J (2011) *Exodus from Cardiganshire: Rural Urban Migration in Victorian Britain* (Cardiff: University of Wales Press).

Dewey. P E (1991) 'Production Problems in British Agriculture During the First World War', in B A Holderness. and M Turner. (eds), *Land, Labour and Agriculture*, pp 241–242.

Grayzel. S R (1999) 'Nostalgia, Gender and the Countryside: Placing the "Land Girl" in First World War Britain', *Rural History*, X, pp 155–170, p 156.

Howell. D W (1992) 'Labour Organization Among Agricultural Workers 1872–1921', *Welsh History Review*, XVI, 1, pp 63–92.

Howkins. A (2003) *The Death of Rural England: A Social History of the Countryside Since 1900* (London: Routledge).

Jenkins. D (1971) *Agricultural Community in South West Wales at the Turn of the Twentieth Century* (Cardiff: University of Wales Press).

Jones. D (1989) 'Serfdom and Slavery: Women's Work in Wales, 1890–1930', in D Hopkin. and G S Kealey. (eds), *Class, Community and the Labour Movement: Wales and Canada 1850–1930* (St John's Newfoundland: Committee on Canadian Labour History) pp 86–100.

Moore-Colyer. R J (2009) 'Homes Fit for Heroes and After: Housing in Rural Wales in the Early Twentieth Century', *Welsh History Review*, XXIV, 3, pp 82–103.

Nicholson. I and Williams. L (1919) *Wales: Its Part in the War* (London: Hodder & Stoughton).

Pretty. D A (1989) *The Rural Revolt that Failed: Farm Workers' Trade Unions in Wales 1889–1950* (Cardiff: University of Wales).

Roberts. M S (October 1918) 'The Women of Wales and Agriculture', *The Journal of the Board of Agriculture*, XXV, 7, p 817.

Stapledon. D (August 1916) 'Women in the Root Fields in Cardiganshire', *Journal of the Board of Agriculture*, XXIII, 5, p 463.

Twinch. C (1990) *Women on the Land: Their Story During Two World Wars* (Cambridge: Lutterworth Press).

Whetham. E (1978) *The Agrarian History of England and Wales, Volume 8, 1914–1939* (Cambridge: Cambridge University Press).

White. B J (2011) 'Sowing the seeds of patriotism? The Women's Land Army in Devon, 1916–1918' *The Local Historian* XLI, pp 13–27.

7
Ellen Wilkinson and Home Security 1940–1945

Paula Bartley

Introduction

The image of women usually portrayed on the Second World War Home Front is a positive one. They are seen to have been essential to the war effort, taking an active role in industry, agriculture, civil defence and community welfare. Many served with the Women's Royal Naval Service, the Women's Auxiliary Air Force, the Women's Auxiliary Fire Service, the Land Army and other uniformed services; large numbers worked in factories and others worked as mechanics, engineers, ambulance drivers, electricians and plumbers. Some became secret agents and underground operators working in occupied Europe. Even so, there is a myth that women tended to play a non-political supportive role, leaving the running of the war to male MPs. High politics, war and diplomacy continue to be seen as masculine fields with women largely relegated to the domestic, or Home Front. It is safe to say that the more public roles played by politicians like Ellen Wilkinson (1891–1947) remains forgotten. This chapter will examine Wilkinson's responsibilities during the war and assess the extent to which her role challenges another widely held belief that a new national wartime consensus emerged as British people buried their political, class and gender differences to fight a common enemy.

In May 1940, Winston Churchill replaced Neville Chamberlain as Prime Minister, formed an all-party Coalition and invited the Labour Party to join him. Ellen Wilkinson, Labour MP for Jarrow, one of only 12 female MPs, was appointed firstly to a minor Ministerial post in charge of hardship tribunals and later as Parliamentary Private Secretary to the new Home Secretary, Herbert Morrison.[1] From 1942 to 1945 she was Morrison's right-hand woman, carrying through Government policies with an unquestioning loyalty and focussed determination. Many were astonished at her appointment. At the time, 'Red Ellen' as she was known, was a strong trade unionist,[2] fierce left-wing feminist and a fiery orator who championed the poor and the vulnerable. Throughout the 1930s, she had bombarded the Conservative-dominated Coalition Government with impassioned attacks on its handling of the economic crisis, saying that she was 'blind and sick with rage' at the smug Neville Chamberlain and his Government's inhumane implementation of the Means Test. In October 1936 she led 200 unemployed men from Jarrow to London in the iconic Jarrow Crusade to protest against the Government's attitude to those who could not find work.

Ellen Wilkinson and Winston Churchill may have disagreed over domestic policy but they held two views in common: both had loathed the advance of Fascism and both had despised Chamberlain's politics of appeasement. Indeed, Wilkinson had fought against the growing Fascist menace throughout the 1930s, helping to acquit most of those accused of burning down the Reichstag and coordinating aid to the legitimate Government in the Spanish Civil War. She had launched one of Parliament's most vitriolic attacks on Chamberlain when he signed the Munich Agreement that allowed Nazi Germany to annex Czechoslovakia's Sudetenland. When Hitler marched into the rest of the country, she called it the 'Rape of Czechoslovakia'. On 3 September 1939, Chamberlain reluctantly declared war on Germany and shortly after Ellen insisted that he 'was not the man to lead the country'.[3] She considered Chamberlain's halting excuses about the initial failures of the war too painful to sit through, thought Chamberlain should resign, and in true conspiratorial fashion plotted to replace him with Churchill. Churchill was undoubtedly grateful to Ellen Wilkinson for her help in securing Chamberlain's resignation and, appreciative of her pre-war anti-fascist activities, was very keen to appoint her to a Government post.

It may seem remarkable that this former suffragist revolutionary supported Churchill's ambitions to be Prime Minister and was willing to work for a Tory well-known for his repressive role in crushing suffragette demonstrations, Irish rebels and industrial strikes in the United Kingdom. When interviewed about her appointment, she claimed that she 'felt that I had been in the presence of a very great man and a very great leader'. [4] She believed that 'the demands of Labour for a planned, all-out national effort were at last satisfied ... the Labour leaders entered a Coalition pledged to place the needs of the nation above sectional interests.'[5] In answer to her critics, she replied 'We are fighting for our very lives.'[6] Churchill, she believed, was the man for the hour: 'the ranks of labour have no cause to love him (but) he has been consistently anti-Nazi.' Certainly, the fact that two leading politicians like the normally combative Wilkinson and Churchill submerged their political differences to fight a common enemy suggests that a desire for national harmony occurred at every level.

The war proved to be a turning point for Ellen Wilkinson. She was now in a position to get things done rather than point out what others ought to be doing. Ellen had lived all her political life on the other side of the barricades, always opposing, constantly protesting but now as a junior member of Government she had to learn the art of being responsible. At first, her status as a compassionate radical politician was confirmed, but as the war dragged on and she abandoned many of the principles she had once held dear, her reputation as a fiery socialist diminished. Naturally, as a junior member of Government, Ellen had to compromise her political beliefs and accept the wartime restrictions imposed by the Home Office. She and Morrison faced colossal challenges as the British civilian population came under attack. The London Blitz began on Saturday 7 September 1940 and the series of heavy bombings continued until May 1941, leaving 20,000 dead and approximately 70,000 wounded. In other places, too, the bombardment was horrific: fifteen other cities from Plymouth to Glasgow suffered major raids. Of course, the bombings had a dreadful impact on public morale as those fortunate to survive frequently lost their family, their homes, their possessions and their courage. There was often no gas, no electricity, no water and no transport. Deprivation and bitter suffering were experienced by large numbers of people who allegedly soldiered on, buttressed by the belief that they were fighting against a tyrannical regime.

'Safety, Sanitation and Sleep'

Herbert Morrison, well aware of her popularity among the working class, placed Ellen Wilkinson in charge of shelter provision. Immediately she vowed to do as much as she could do to keep the population safe and public morale positive but it was a tough undertaking. Part of her new job was 'to put to bed each night, outside their own homes, 1 million Londoners.'[7] On the first evening of her new appointment she visited the East End, talked to people about their experiences, and listened. On a typically frightful night in London when buildings were burning and roads were blocked with rubble Ellen would be found driving around in the black-out, without any headlights 'cheering the people in the shelters, moving about all over the place from the church crypts to the pubs.' According to Ellen, five-sixths of her time was spent visiting shelters – in the first few months of her job she spent nearly every night inspecting a shelter, speaking to people and taking notes on how to improve the enforced communal life. A journalist from the *Daily Express* commented that 'going round with Ellen Wilkinson there were two things I liked about her, things that give me confidence in her approach to the problem – her energy and her natural touch with these people. She talked to the wardens and would always stop to talk to some man or woman and find their points of view.'[8] Certainly, Ellen's visible presence and comforting words, along with her rapid improvement of shelter provision and the subsequent favourable press reports, helped create the legend of a country united against the fearful aggression of their enemy.

Shelter provision was woefully inadequate when Ellen took over. Many upper-class families fled to their country houses, others took refuge in the safe basements of their expensive clubs and partied the night away. The Government requisitioned an unused tube station at Down Street and equipped it with bathrooms and other conveniences for its own use. Ellen, making a point of her solidarity with the poor and the politically insignificant, declined to use it. For the majority of people, there were simple corrugated steel Anderson shelters which could be erected in gardens or civic shelters but neither was sufficient; indeed many of the urban poor did not have the gardens in which to erect these shelters which anyway often badly built and were very damp. It certainly appeared as if no one in authority was concerned about the lives of the many thousands who were poor and without influence.

Soon after her appointment, Ellen Wilkinson and her boss put forward a scheme to improve shelter provision. She organised the distribution of new ones, soon called Morrison shelters, built to better withstand bombs. These were flat-topped table-like shelters with a steel frame and wire mesh sides. They could be erected within houses and did not collapse or shatter if a house was bombed. They had room for two adults and two children, were easy to erect and simple to produce and issued free to those who earned less than £350 a year. Ellen claimed that the 'ordinary reasonably well-built house afforded much more protection than was expected,'[9] and a booklet 'Shelter at Home' was distributed to show how people could turn their homes into 'an air-raid shelter giving a high degree of protection.'[10] At the beginning of the bombing, Ellen encouraged people to stay in these home shelters or use the newly erected street brick shelters. Small shelters, she said, were safer: the smaller the group, the fewer the casualties.[11] However once heavy bombing began, people wanted a greater degree of safety and somewhere quieter to sleep at night. There were a few deep shelters but those that existed soon became too crowded, too unsanitary or too unsafe to use.[12] Buckets were used as lavatories, no water was available; prostitutes and drunks mingled with families with young children. Even so, large numbers of people queued all day to enter 'Nightmare Arches', the shelter off the Commercial Road in the East End. More than 15,000 people slept there each night and the floor was soon covered with urine and faeces. Ellen had begun her new job by making a tour. 'There is new hope', said the *News Chronicle* on Ellen's new appointment, 'for the thousands of shelterers.'[13]

Londoners, fed up with the inadequacy of official provision, and oblivious to the legality of their actions, took the initiative and made their own arrangements. Many piled into the Underground stations, looking for protection from the incessant bombing. By the end of September 1940 nearly 200,000 people were sleeping in 'the tube'. Initially Ellen and the Government discouraged people from sheltering in the Underground because they feared that such a troglodyte existence would lead to a 'peculiar mentality of resignation' and thus compromise the war effort. The Government instructed London Transport to ban people from using the Underground as accommodation but was forced to reverse its decision when large numbers of people ignored these rules and made it their nightly home. Ellen was concerned that people 'were inviting tragedy' by grouping together in such large numbers.[14] In one incident on the London Metropolitan line, 61 died and 220 were injured when a bomb fell directly on the station. Some challenged Government provision in other ways. In September 1940, a group of people from Stepney, led by a local Communist, burst into the Savoy Hotel and occupied the basement shelter supplied for the wealthy guests. Ellen, reacting to public initiatives, requisitioned 569 private basements for Londoners to use.

In the early days of the war Ellen committed herself to improve the conditions of shelters and to make the London Underground stations safe havens. As usual, she threw herself into the challenge, battling with other departments for scarce materials and workers. She promised people, 'Safety, Sanitation and Sleep', a typical Ellen sound-bite highlighting people's understandable human urge for all three. She chivvied and bullied, encouraged and threatened, ordered and charmed. On one visit to Manchester, after Ellen had condemned the Manchester Corporation for its damp, unhygienic and uncomfortable shelters they quickly built new ones, renovated the old ones and provided bunk beds canteens and sanitation for their inhabitants. By the spring of 1941 thanks partly to the efforts of Ellen Wilkinson, Londoners were sheltering underground in some relative comfort. Ticket systems of entry were established, over 200,000 bunks were installed and allocated to regular users of the shelters, canteen facilities were set up, chemical lavatories, ventilation, lighting and running water became available. And in some shelters, people could attend night classes or watch films.

Despite these shelter improvements, people still got hurt and many were killed. Ellen, who always took her responsibility seriously, drove herself around to inspect air raid shelters immediately after they had been bombed. Soon she was dubbed the 'Shelter Queen'. One newspaper commented that 'Miss Ellen Wilkinson's personal visits to the East End...have done more to put heart and courage into East End families than anything that has gone before...they needed badly what Miss Wilkinson is giving them – womanly sympathy carried further than mere words.'[15] People knew that Ellen's sympathy was real: her own home was bombed in November 1940 and when she was given alternative accommodation that too was bombed.[16]

On 14 November 1940, 515 German bombers attacked Coventry. The city centre was laid waste: the magnificent cathedral destroyed, the medieval streets ruined, one third of factories irretrievably damaged and 4,000 homes flattened. Five hundred and sixty three people were killed and 863 seriously injured. Herbert Morrison and King George went to visit. Ellen was not considered important enough. Nearly a year later, however, Ellen was asked to visit Coventry to inspect its shelter provision. On her visit, she found that Anderson shelters had not been erected because of a lack of materials, surface shelters were falling down because they had been shoddily built, and large areas of the city were without shelter. At night, there were only 2,352 bunks for 150,000 people. Ellen blamed the Coventry National Emergency Committee, hinting that the 'municipality has been talking too much and acting too little'.[17] She accused the Committee of not using the money allocated by the Government for shelter provision, for not asking for a sufficient number of Anderson shelters and for being altogether 'slow off the mark'. 'Coventry has received many compliments for the heroism of its people, every one of them deserved', Ellen said, 'but the fact must not be used to cover up its own Council's slackness in providing shelters and the bad quality of much of what it did provide.'[18]

Regardless of the blackout and the dangers involved in any kind of travel, Ellen visited most regional cities to calm and encourage the population. In Plymouth after the dreadful bombing that destroyed much of the city she stayed overnight with Nancy Astor and went with her to inspect the damage.[19] She often visited Liverpool, one of the most heavily bombed cities outside London. For example, between 1 May and 7 May 1941, 680 bombers dropped 870 tonnes of bombs and over 112,000 fire-bombs over the city. On one of her visits, Ellen advised women and children to get out of the vulnerable areas as public shelters were not an appropriate place for them to be. 'The more I see', she insisted, 'of shelters in bombed areas the more convinced I am that the policy of dispersal is the right one ... Many underground shelters only give an illusory security. They will stand up to a 50lb bomb but not to one of 250lb.' Such experiences confirmed Ellen's belief that she was fighting a just war. She stated that 'I never realised what a vindictive person I was until I went through these cities.'

In January 1943, Ellen's soothing words were essential when she visited Catford Central School, Sandhurst Road, South East London. Here 32 children and four teachers had been killed in a lunchtime air raid. Ellen met as many bereaved parents as she could and tried to console them.[20] Where did she find the words to comfort Mr and Mrs Scholl whose 11-year-old daughter had been killed? Or to the parents of five-year-old twins, Ann and Judith Biddle who were eating their school lunch when the school was bombed? Ellen was well known for her compassion but she must have found this to be an especially difficult situation.

As Parliamentary Private Secretary, Ellen was required to defend Government policy, keep quiet on matters of national security and suppress her natural tendency for frankness. She often represented Herbert Morrison in the House of Commons and took questions from other MPs. In 1942 alone Ellen responded authoritatively and unemotionally to a range of queries about shelter provision, fire prevention, and the national fire service. She was severely tested over the Bethnal Green disaster. On 3 March 1943 at Bethnal Green Tube, crowds 'got out of hand and frantic with nervousness, confusion and worry' about the heavy gunfire and bombing outside, rushed into the station and someone slipped.[21] In a few seconds people were crushed to death as more and more attempted to gain entrance. One hundred and seventy three people died including 84 women and 62 small children. A full enquiry, held in secret, exonerated the local authorities and concluded that the disaster was caused by people losing their 'self-control' and causing the deaths and injuries. When asked in the House of Commons whether the enquiry into the disaster would be circulated to MPs, Ellen had to prevaricate. The enquiry was never published. Instead Morrison made a short statement in the House of Commons, and because of the risk to national security, made no reference to the panic of those involved. This generated resentment and the Government was blamed for hushing up a disaster caused by its own failures and shortcomings. Ellen remained silent. Her ex-colleague, Wright Robinson, noticed a marked change in her behaviour. On a previous meeting, he wrote in his diary, she had 'criticised rather drastically and hastily our Air Raid Shelters. She had had less experience of responsibility. Now she has had more and finds that rip and run raids of freelances do not apply to ministers in office... I admire her for facing up to responsibility and taking the raps that come to people who do.'[22]

In June 1944 a new threat emerged: the V1s known as flying bombs or doodlebugs. For three months over 5,000 of these bombs hit Britain. Towards the end of July 1944 one flying bomb wrecked a store and a bus full of passengers had its top blown off.[23] It was difficult to find an appropriate warning system without bringing the country to a halt so Herbert Morrison and Ellen Wilkinson were instructed to reduce the amount of notice given to the population. Nonetheless, in September 1944 as a result of better civil defence, Herbert Morrison was confident enough to announce that the battle of the flying bombs was over. The next day a V2, a more deadly version of the V1, dropped in Chiswick, killing a 63-year-old woman, a 3-year-old girl and a soldier home on leave. This time there could be no sirens or warnings: the bombs travelled at the speed of sound so were both silent and invisible until they crashed. Ellen was put in charge of providing help to those injured.

Fire-fighting and fire-watching

Later during the war Ellen was put in general charge of Civil Defence, working with Civil Defence teams, the National Fire Service, the Fire Guard and the W.V.S. Here, both Ellen Wilkinson's pre-war reputation as a left-wing feminist and the myth of a 'national war time consensus, based on a convergence of political beliefs, unity of goals and a heightened sense of national social solidarity'[24] were seriously challenged. On New Year's Eve 1941, Herbert Morrison, who wished to prevent vulnerable property being left unguarded at night, established compulsory unpaid fire-watching and put Ellen Wilkinson in charge of it. Trade unions objected, and accused the Government of violating the wartime consultation process and insisted that fire-watchers be paid for their time. Ellen, who in the past might have led the protest, endorsed the Government's position. 'The fires', she told the 1941 Trade Union Conference of Engineers, 'have got to be prevented or put out. Nagging and chivvying each other about an admittedly awkward job week after week just won't help the nation.'[25] She defended the Government's decision not to pay fire-watchers by arguing that 'while the demand that all fire-watching should be paid for at night and overtime rates might seem reasonable, where would it lead?...Nearly four million people would have to be paid, all at their different rates for their ordinary occupations. The result would be chaos and friction.'[26] In her opinion, the needs of the country overrode the rights of the working class.

Ellen drew even stronger criticism when she helped to re-organise the fire services. At the beginning of the war, Britain's fire services were made up of professionals and volunteers, largely under the control of local authorities. The service was not efficient enough to respond swiftly to wartime emergencies so Morrison merged them and put them under the control of a new Fire Service Council. At the end of May 1941, 1,400 local fire brigades amalgamated and were reduced to 32 brigades, allegedly one of the quickest administrative revolutions that ever took place. Ellen was on the Council and her job was to convince firemen to accept the changes. She was thought by the *Tamworth Herald* to be 'the most tactless woman who ever held minor office, whilst she staggered eight million fire guards when she remarked petulantly that the new regulations are not meant to be understood by them – all they had to do is just do what they are told.'[27]

A serious shortage of fire-watchers remained in spite of Government pleas and exhortations, so in August 1942 fire-watching was made compulsory for women. Their duties were roughly the same as men's: they were provided with a bucket of sand, a bucket of water and a stirrup pump to put out small fires. Later, they were given special training at the five Regional schools and 32 fire force schools set up especially for women. Women between the ages of 20 and 45 were liable unless they were pregnant, had children under 14 or worked more than 55 hours. They were only responsible for residential areas and, if they were married, to areas near their home.[28] Ellen was keen on women doing their share of war work, commenting that the only substitute for manpower was woman power.[29] 'We cannot let Britain burn down', she urged and it will be 'largely from the women that we shall get help.'[30] 'History', she told the *Daily Mirror*, 'shows that the firmness of a people's resistance depends on women.'[31]

The public reaction to women's compulsory fire-watching was overwhelmingly negative. Very many women claimed exemption; in Coventry 25,000 out of the 37,500 women registered excused themselves from fire-watching.[32] And very many women failed to register at all. Ellen, who had recently fractured her skull in a car accident, was in charge of converting the public to these new measures. In spite of the considerable pain of her fracture and severe bruising, she carried on until her doctor insisted that she stay in bed for a week. Nancy Astor remarked 'if you think women cannot stand the strain of war, let one of you try to do what Miss Wilkinson is doing.'[33] It was a demanding task even for a healthy person, particularly when she drew criticism from the people who had once been her strongest advocates. At one Liverpool meeting in October 1942, Ellen faced an angry audience of nearly two thousand people who opposed the new Government measures. Once or twice it nearly got out of hand as people screamed at her. According to the press, Ellen 'managed it with great humour and characteristic adroitness'[34] and succeeded in getting her points across. One month later, she had another 'somewhat stormy passage' when she spoke to a boisterous audience of 1,500 at the Coventry Hippodrome. The meeting was frequently in a 'state of uproar, interruptions, cheers, and questions' and she was scorned when she claimed that the Government had done a lot for Coventry.[35] Ellen insisted that she was not 'asking women to do what she did not do herself. I was out in the blitzes, every one of the nights. I have been a voluntary Fire Guard ever since there were voluntary Fire Guards and the place I watch is in the centre of London.'[36] And when women complained about their domestic and shopping difficulties if they were on duty as fire-fighters, she advised them to get their husbands to help more instead of going to the pub.[37] Ellen pretended to be unperturbed by the disturbances, commenting that 'I love a meeting of this sort; it is so democratic.'[38]

By 1943, despite grumblings from the civilian population, Ellen Wilkinson had recruited approximately 5 million fire guards. She was confident enough to inform Parliament that 'the country is really proud of its National Fire Service', now well trained, disciplined and effective.[39] She had helped set up a National Fire College which had trained nearly 6,000 students, 1,300 of which were women. Women, Ellen told the House of Commons, were playing an ever-increasing and more important part in the Service. 'I think with some amusement and pleasure of the good old type of fire guard officer who thought that the woman's job was to make a cup of tea when the men were coming off fire-guard.'[40] Women now did much highly-skilled work – dealing with calls for equipment, getting the right number and correct equipment and making decisions on which fires should take priority. Both sides of the House of Commons praised the 'Honourable Member for Jarrow' for her efficient handling of it all.[41]

Censorship and suppression

Ellen was fully committed to the Government and castigated those who criticised it. 'Back our men in Government', she pleaded with the left-wing journal, *Tribune*.[42] In January 1941, the viscerally anti-communist, Herbert Morrison banned the Communist Party's newspaper, the *Daily Worker*, after a number of inflammatory articles in the paper had called for 'revolutionary defeatism'.[43].This was one of the most notorious acts of press censorship during the war, and an example of the inability of Government to win over oppositional voices. In the past Ellen had protested against the curbing of free speech but now, as a loyal Parliamentary Secretary, she retracted her views, justified the ban and accused the *Daily Worker* of undermining the war effort.

Meanwhile, more compromise and more criticism followed. The Emergency Powers Act 1939 gave the Government the right to direct and control labour. Strikes and lock-outs were banned. Oppressive measures such as these would once have been anathema to Ellen but now, as a member of Government, she supported them. In the First World War, which she regarded as an unjust war, she had engineered a number of strikes and had been critical of a Government which curtailed trade union rights. During the first few months of the war there were over 900 strikes, thus dashing Ellen's hope that unions would choose to place national solidarity against a common enemy over their own needs. Although strikes were illegal, strikers were not prosecuted because the Government preferred to negotiate rather than take legal action. In August 1941, a dispute involving 2,000 skilled men in the North East was settled when Ellen persuaded the men to resume work.[44] 'If you want a fight' she told them 'fight Hitler.'[45]

Tensions between Ellen and trade unionists intensified. In October 1942, Ellen condemned workers at a shipyard in Newcastle on Tyne who had gone on an unofficial strike. She hoped, she said, that they would lose.[46] The Government, keen to squash industrial action, also prosecuted 1,000 of 4,000 striking miners at a Kent colliery and imprisoned its main leaders. Eventually the case was dropped but such incidents led to further criticisms of Ellen Wilkinson. At her 1943 Union Conference, one delegate accused 'their' MP of colluding in the repression of the working class, remarking that 'you cannot convert a prison van into a Rolls Royce merely by putting Ellen Wilkinson at the wheel'. In1944 alone, despite Government clampdowns, there were over 2,000 strikes and this led to a new law making incitement to strike illegal.

To the astonishment of her socialist friends and colleagues Ellen supported the release of Oswald Mosley. In May 1940, Mosley had been imprisoned without trial for his fascist sympathies and activities; in November 1943 Herbert Morrison freed the increasingly frail Mosley from prison and instead placed him under house arrest. Both Ellen Wilkinson and Herbert Morrison despised Mosley's politics but because they no longer considered him a threat to the nation they could not justify his continued incarceration. This may have been a triumph for the right of free speech but it was an ill-timed and ill-judged decision. When Mosley's release was announced the trade union movement, the Labour Party National Executive Committee (NEC), the National Council of Labour, half the Parliamentary Labour Party, the press and popular opinion were enraged. Morrison faced deputations, a back-bench revolt and a threat of resignation from Ernest Bevin. Hugh Dalton wrote that 'Little Ellen who is apt to be much too publicly emotional about her 'Chief' makes an impassioned defence, with sobs in her throat, but it really isn't very convincing.'[47] In 1943, at her Union conference, some delegates tried to get Ellen dismissed: 'I believe that Miss Wilkinson's action in agreeing to the release of Mosley was one of the greatest crimes that any individual could possible perpetrate against the working class ... We must condemn Miss Wilkinson's action in the most forceful terms.'[48] Ellen did not attend the Conference to hear the resolution because she was in a nursing home recovering from a heavy bout of bronchitis. She had spent much of her life fighting Fascism long before it was recognised a menace and must have been upset, angry and very hurt by these comments.

Ellen, faced with the demands of office, had undoubtedly mellowed but she claimed that she had not changed her fundamental views. When an old comrade asked her 'Are you still uncompromisingly a Socialist?' she gave him a straight look and said with remarkable intensity 'Much more so than ever!'. As a member of the Government she had to exercise restraint but at times her public comments remained as radical as ever. She told audiences she feared fortunes would be made by the 'worst kinds of speculators' if the Tory party gained power after the war. The post-war election, she maintained, would be fought over whether the national needs would be met 'by the ethics of the poker table or by trained and intentional planning'[49] and accused the Tory Party of wanting to give employers all power in industry and the bankers all power in finance.

Conclusion

Ellen's role in the Second World War encourages historians not just to re-appraise her life but to re-evaluate the Home Front more generally. It is thought that Ellen's tough and unpopular commitment to civilian conscription, strike breaking, censorship and Mosley, as well as her willingness to work under the right-wing Churchill, undermines her pre-war reputation as a left-wing feminist. Yet, in Ellen's opinion, the end justified the means. Faced with the menace of Hitler, she temporarily abandoned her socialist convictions in favour of an unqualified resistance to Fascism and its advancement. It is assumed that many shared Ellen's convictions and the war is often thought to have engendered an unprecedented community spirit with a population unanimously united against a common enemy. However, not everyone shared Ellen's sense of collective danger; indeed the diverse response of the civilian population to wartime requirements challenges the somewhat sentimentalised idea of a self-sacrificing nation bound together by an irresistible national consensus.

On 30 April 1945, Hitler committed suicide; a few days later Germany surrendered and the war officially ended in Europe. By now Ellen Wilkinson was the most important woman in the Labour Party, helping to set out the socialist principles of the Labour Party and co-authoring the manifesto, Let Us Face the Future in preparation for the post-war election. I believe that 'Let us Face the Future', a passionate, expressive, radical manifesto, had Ellen's hand, and principles, written all over it. The manifesto declared that the 'Labour Party stands for freedom – for freedom of worship, freedom of speech, freedom of the Press... But there are certain so-called freedoms that Labour will not tolerate: freedom to exploit other people; freedom to pay poor wages and to push up prices for selfish profit; freedom to deprive the people of the means of living.' And in an even more radical paragraph – with direct reference to Clause IV in the Labour Party's constitution – and in hardly the words of Herbert Morrison – the Manifesto stated 'The Labour Party is a Socialist Party, and proud of it. Its ultimate purpose at home is the establishment of the Socialist Commonwealth – free, democratic, efficient, progressive, public-spirited, its material resources organised in the service of the British People.' The transformation of society that Ellen had worked for all her life now seemed possible.

On 5 July new parliamentary elections took place with the Labour Party winning a sweeping victory. The new Prime Minister, Clement Attlee, had a high regard for Ellen Wilkinson and appointed her Minister of Education, the first woman to take this post, the second woman to become a Cabinet Minister and the only woman in a Labour Cabinet of twenty. In her short time as Minister she raised the school-leaving age, organised a huge school building programme, set up a fast-track system of teacher-training, instituted state-funded university scholarships and provided free school milk to all British primary school children. Sadly Ellen died in February 1947 before she could be fully effective as a socialist and feminist member of Government and was largely forgotten until feminist historians began unearthing the traces of her life.

Notes

1. Florence Horsburgh, Conservative MP, was appointed Parliamentary Secretary to the Minister of Health, largely responsible for the evacuation of children from the cities.
2. Ellen was sponsored by the National Union of Distributive and Allied Workers (NUDAW). See P. Bartley (2014) *Ellen Wilkinson*.
3. *Daily Herald*, 5 September 1938.
4. *Herald*, 27 May 1940.
5. Ellen Wilkinson, *Plan for Peace*, 1944.
6. *Tribune*, 24 May 1940.
7. *Yorkshire Post*, 28 October 1940.
8. *Daily Express*, 11 October 1940.
9. *The Guardian*, 12 June 1941.
10. *The Guardian*, 12 June 1941.
11. *Hansard*, 27 February 1941.
12. D. Bernard and G. W. Jones (2001) *Herbert Morrison, Portrait of a Politician* (Sheffield: Phoenix Press).
13. *News Chronicle*, 11 October 1940.
14. *The Guardian*, 28 February 1941.
15. *Nottingham Evening Post*, 15 October 1940.
16. *The Guardian*, 18 November 1940.
17. *Midlands Daily Telegraph*, 20 September 1941.
18. *Midlands Daily Telegraph*, 10 October 1941.
19. *Western Morning News*, 9 August 1943.
20. *The Times*, 22 January 1943.
21. Tube Shelter Enquiry, April, 1943.
22. Wright Robinson diary, 13 April 1942.
23. *Nottingham Evening Post*, 28 July 1944.
24. J. Harris (1992) 'War and Social History', pp 17–35.
25. *The Guardian*, 21 June 1941.
26. *The Guardian*, 21 June 1941.
27. *Tamworth Herald*, 30 October 1943.
28. *The New Dawn*, 10 October 1942.
29. *News Chronicle*, 30 October 1941.
30. *The Guardian*, 15 May 1941.
31. *Daily Mirror*, 2 July 1940.
32. *Coventry Evening Telegraph*, 23 October 1942.
33. *Western Daily News*, 7 March 1941.
34. *Manchester Guardian*, 5 October 1942.
35. *Coventry Evening Telegraph*, 5 October 1942.
36. *Coventry Standard*, 10 October 1942.
37. *Birmingham Gazette*, 5 November 1942.

38. *Coventry Evening Telegraph*, 5 October 1942.
39. *Hansard*, 30 June 1943.
40. *Hansard*, 30 June 1943.
41. *Hansard*, 30 June 1943.
42. *Tribune*, 3 January 1941.
43. In Lenin's view it was better for an imperialist power to be defeated rather than the working class of one country fight against the working class of another.
44. *The Guardian*, 25 August 1941.
45. *Daily Herald*, 18 August 1941.
46. *Daily Express*, 12 October 1942.
47. Hugh Dalton, 24 November 1943.
48. Annual Delegate Conference, 1944.
49. *Reynolds News*, 4 March 1945.

References

Bartley. P (2014) *Ellen Wilkinson: From Red Suffragist to Government Minister* (Cambridge: Pluto Press).

Harris. J (1992) 'War and Social History: Britain and the Home Front during the Second World War', *Contemporary European History*, 1, pp 17–35.

Smith. H L (1984) 'Womanpower Problem in Britain during the Second World War', *The Historical Journal*, 27, 4, December, pp 925–945.

Summerfield. P (1998) *Reconstructing Women's Wartime Lives* (Manchester: Manchester University Press).

Figure 1.1 William (Will) Brown, a young soldier from Worcester who wrote regularly to his mother. By kind permission of Sean Brown, Worcestershire.

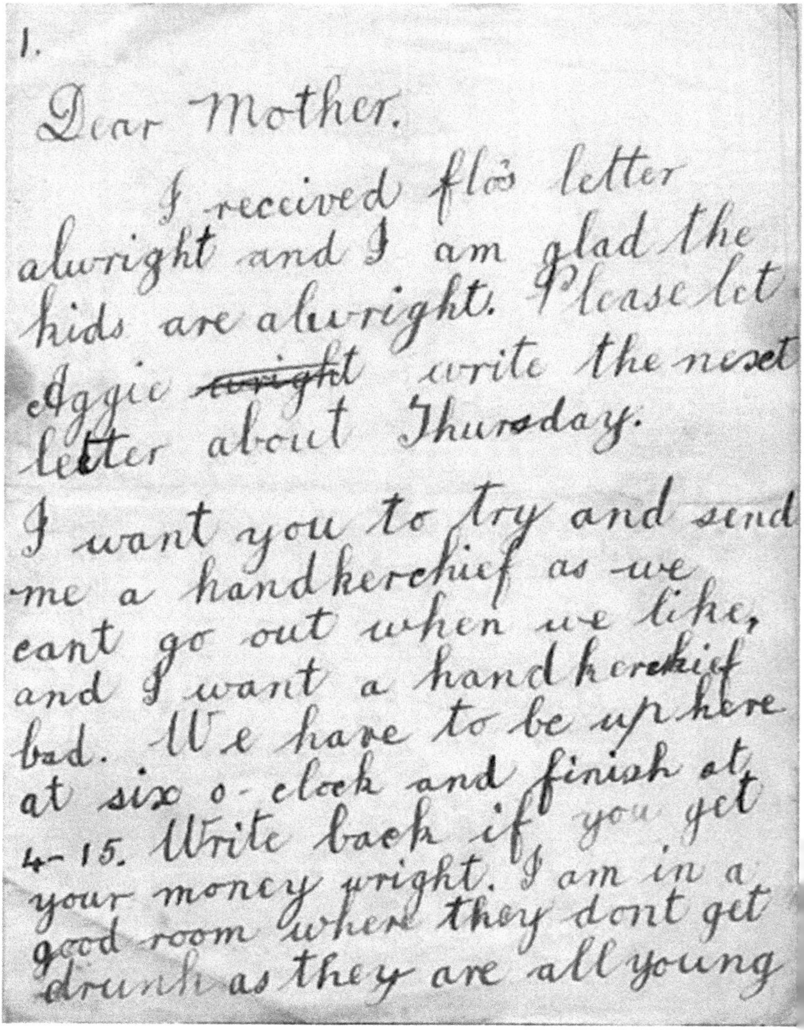

1.

Dear Mother.

I received flo's letter
alwright and I am glad the
kids are alwright. Please let
Aggie ~~wright~~ write the next
letter about Thursday.

I want you to try and send
me a handkerchief as we
cant go out when we like,
and I want a handkerchief
bad. We have to be up here
at six o-clock and finish at
4-15. Write back if you get
your money wright. I am in a
good room where they dont get
drunk as they are all young

Figure 1.2 Letter from Will Brown to his mother. By kind permission of Sean Brown, Worcestershire.

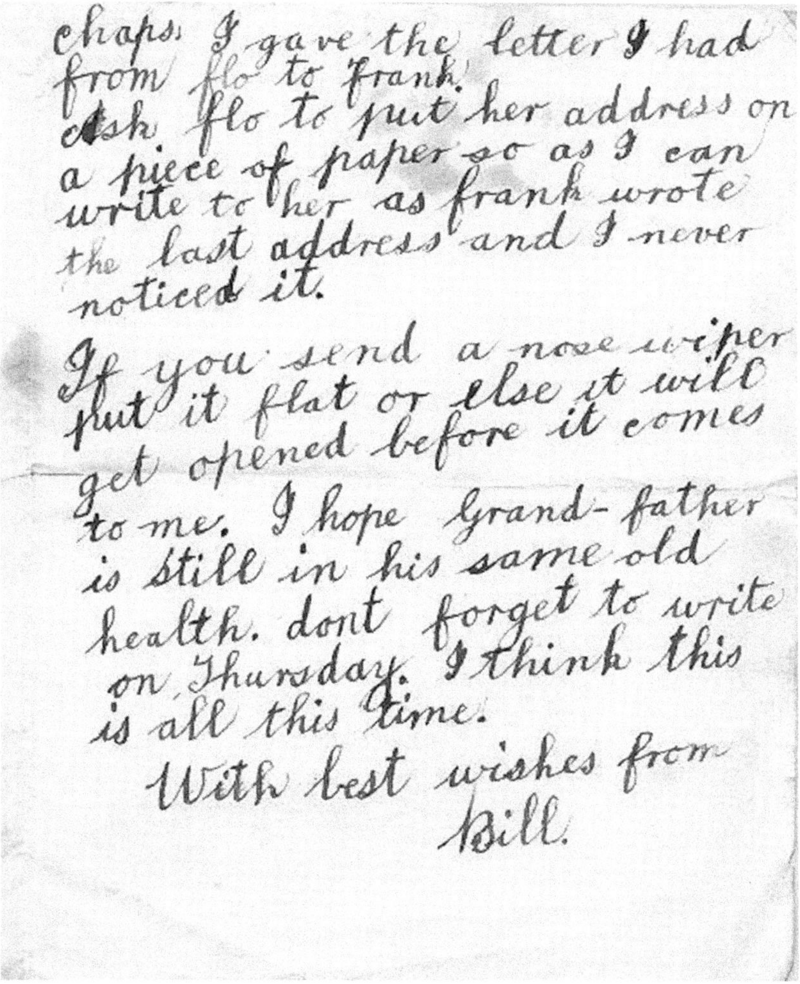

chaps. I gave the letter I had
from flo to frank.
ask flo to put her address on
a piece of paper so as I can
write to her as frank wrote
the last address and I never
noticed it.

If you send a nose wiper
put it flat or else it will
get opened before it comes
to me. I hope Grand-father
is still in his same old
health. dont forget to write
on Thursday. I think this
is all this time.

With best wishes from
Bill.

Figure 1.3 Letter from Will Brown to his mother. By kind permission of Sean Brown, Worcestershire.

L. J. Allchin. (3357)
Signal Section
"A" Squad,
Norfolk S.Y.Y.

Dear Lois,

In your last letter, (a long, long, time ago,) I think I remember you expressing a desire to hear from me again soon.

I'm afraid you will think by this time that I have quite forgotten you all over in Stone, but that is really not the case at all. Billy will tell you I often enquire about you, and I hope he does not fail to remember me to you whenever he writes home.

Letter-writing, I am sorry to say, is not one of my accomplishments, dear Lois, but this time I felt I must write and thank you somehow for those delicious little macaroons you sent in Billy's parcel, specially for me. They were just extra while they lasted, in fact I never remember tasting nicer, and that's without the teeniest bit of flattery. I wish you would come and give our cooking staff one or two lessons, (not on macaroons, but on how to cook meat and potatoes,) they need it dreadfully.

Well, Dear Lois, any news I might have had to send you, even after such a long time, would most probably only be second-hand, as I expect Billy keeps you pretty well informed, so I'm not going to risk it. We are still living and waiting for the one great thing to happen which will bring us all back home again, but which seems such a horrible long while coming. At any rate I think it will have taught us to appreciate things which we never used to before, (decent cooking, for instance; and Macaroons for example, eh! Dear Lois?)

I expect Billy has told you that I have been transferred into "A" Squadron now, so we don't see quite so much of each other, but of course we are still the best of friends, except for little arguments sometimes on which Squadron has the best football or cricket team, etc. He always beats me at this of course, because I shall always remain a "B" at heart.

Well I think this is quite all this time Dear Lois. Please remember me to Mater and Pater and all at home, and altho it is perhaps hardly right to expect it, after keeping you waiting so long, a reply soon, would make me Your most happy and sincere friend
Len.

Figure 1.4   Letter to Lois Turner in Stone, Staffordshire. Reproduced by kind permission of Staffordshire and Stoke on Trent Archive Service (SRO 5778/1/21).

Figure 2.1 Jack and Gert Adam. Courtesy of the Board of Trustees of the Armouries.

Figure 2.2   Jack Jnr., Peggie and Madge. Courtesy of the Board of Trustees of the Armouries.

Figure 2.3   Jack with his unit. Jack is centre fourth row from the left. Courtesy of the Board of Trustees of the Armouries.

BRITAIN.
SWANSEA WOMEN WHOSE HUSBANDS AND SONS ARE ON ACTIVE SERVICE WAITING TO REGISTER FOR ARMY PAY.

Figure 3.1 Swansea Women whose husbands and sons were on active service waiting to register for army pay, note many are wearing their husbands hats. Originally published in local and national newspapers.

POTATO DAY. Kingston May 4ᵀᴴ 1917.

Figure 5.1 Potato Day at Bentalls of Kingston – 4 May 1917. When it became known that Bentalls would be stocking potatoes during the war years (there were shortages although no direct rationing of potatoes), people queued round the block to purchase their spuds, sold as a special promotion at the store. Reproduced with permission of the Mary Evans Picture Library.

Figure 6.1   Women's Land Army recruitment poster, showing four young women carrying tools and a basket of produce, and leading a team of horses, 1918. Reproduced by permission of Mary Evans Picture Library.

Figure 7.1   Ellen Wilkinson on the hustings. Reproduced by kind permission of the People's History Museum, Manchester.

Figure 8.1 Guernsey Mothers prepare to evacuate. By kind permission of the Priaux Library, Candie Gardens Guernsey.

Figure 8.2   Eva and Bert le Page and baby Anthony, August 1940. By kind permission of Anthony Le Page, Petit Creux, Guernsey.

Figure 8.3 Mrs Kath Ozanne with Tony and Mike Cheshire, 1942. By kind permission of Mr Anthony Ozanne.

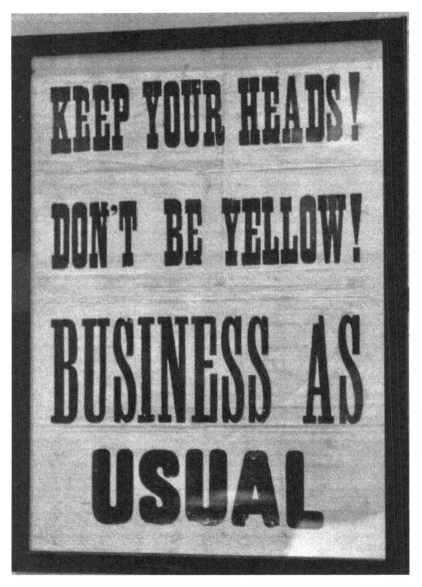

Figure 8.4 By kind permission of the German Occupation Museum Forest Guernsey.

Figure 9.1 Firefighters with their dog mascot during the Second World War. Reproduced with the permission of Mary Evans Picture Library.

Figure 11.1   Hat crocheted out of garden string. Hat from the collection of the Fashion History Museum, Cambridge, Canada. Photography by Jonathan Walford, reproduced with his kind permission.

Figure 12.1   Kit Gayford and women trainees walking along a dock. Reproduced with the kind permission of the Canal and River Trust.

Figure 13.1   War Industry 'Wings for Victory Week' 1943. At a factory two women war workers fill bombs which have been covered in savings stamps following 'Wings for Victory' week in London. A third worker looks on. Behind them can be seen posters listing their target figures for the saving scheme. Ministry of Information, Second World War Official Collection at the Imperial War Museum.

8

Guernsey Mothers and Children: Forgotten Evacuees

Gillian Mawson

Introduction

In September 1939, on the outset of war, millions of evacuees in mainland Britain, school children and mothers with children, were sent from industrial areas and ports to the relative safety of the countryside. In June 1940, 17,000 child and women evacuees from the island of Guernsey, a British territory, were sent to the industrial areas that had been vacated by English evacuees just nine months earlier. Yet the experiences of these Guernsey evacuees have been marginalised from both academic and popular accounts of the Second World War Home Front; they rarely appear in the images, myths and memories of evacuation. This chapter draws upon twenty interviews conducted with evacuated Guernsey mothers between June 2008 and February 2012, which are supplemented by the letters and diaries of mothers who have passed away, and interviews with their children to reveal the private world of these women's wartime experiences. In doing so it builds upon the methodology of Penny Summerfield and Corinna Peniston-Bird's work which uses oral testimony to explore the nature of women's wartime lives[1] and acknowledges the increasing interest that historians such as Summerfield, Sonya O. Rose, Peniston-Bird, and Julie Summers have brought to the study of gender history of Britain during the Second World War.[2]

These personal histories of Guernsey mothers disrupt myths of the typical British wartime family as comprising a wife who remained at home when her husband left to join the forces, for their experience of the Home Front was very different to that of their English neighbours. The German occupation of the Channel Islands in 1940 resulted in many Guernsey women and children leaving their homes and having to negotiate the social and cultural challenges of new communities on mainland Britain where they sometimes struggled to maintain a sense of their Guernsey identity. In Lancashire, Cheshire and Yorkshire they encountered a mixed reception from local people, and elements of gender bias meted out by English officials. Some women also experienced re-displacement upon returning to post-war Guernsey; however their recently rediscovered stories have not only restored their place in Guernsey's history, but also challenged myths and memories of British wartime evacuation.

The evacuation of Guernsey

In June 1940, German forces swept through occupied France towards Cherbourg, just 30 miles from Guernsey. The British Government concluded that Guernsey, one of the Channel Islands, and British territory, should be demilitarised. On 19 June 1940, Guernsey parents were advised to register their children for immediate evacuation to England.[3] Mothers with infants were also offered passage and Mrs Trotter recalled the panic in Guernsey 'banks still had their long queues, and one heard on every side the question – "are you going?" Some shop girls panicked and went off onto the boats with just their handbags and very little money'.[4] Many teachers registered for evacuation with their pupils whilst mothers with infants decided to accompany the teachers as 'helpers'. Ruth Alexandre wrote, 'Chaos and confusion reigned, didn't know what to do, but was advised to go.'[5] Reta Batiste left as a helper with the Forest school, and described leaving her husband, 'Wilf took our suitcases down for us, his last words were "I cannot bear to see you off". It was a dreadful feeling the whole party in the bus, waving crying goodbye. The children were singing away not realising what it all meant.'[6] Eva Le Page left with an infant under each arm and a bag which contained only nappies and feeding bottles.[7] Merle Roberts recalled, 'The harbour was thronged with agitated people trying to decide what to do. The noise was terrific, with broadcasts telling people not to be yellow and not leave the island. Some decided to go back home and take the consequences, others to stick to their decision to go.'[8]

Between 20 and 28 June, around 17,000 evacuees, near about half the population, left Guernsey.[9] They left for Weymouth in mail boats, cattle boats and cargo boats, and the Captain of the *SS Whitstable* noted, 'Alarm at Guernsey appeared rather acute. The officers quarters were reserved for the aged and infirm, invalids and nursing mothers.'[10] During the crossings the mothers cared for distressed children and Mary Champion wrote, 'The journey in a cattle boat was rough and cold, toilet facilitie were basic. The crossing was awful and I looked after eight children. I remember helping one child to vomit, and then both of us slid around in it on the floor.'[11] At Weymouth, the mothers disembarked with few possessions, little or no money and no idea where they would live.[12] Meanwhile, in Guernsey, on 28 June, as evacuees were boarding the mail boat, *Isle of Sark*, the harbour was bombed by the Luftwaffe, and Mrs Trotter wrote 'We were startled by two terrific explosions, followed by machine gun fire; then a terrible bombardment started. The boat shook and trembled but did not get a direct hit. When we came up, we saw the tomato lorries along the quayside blazing. It was a dreadful piece of brutality on an unprotected island.'[13] On 30 June Guernsey was occupied by German forces and one English MP remarked, 'For the first time in our history, British territory has been invaded without any resistance whatsoever.'[14] Charles Cruickshank believes that the fate of the Channel Islanders became symbolically important to Britain, and that 'it was a blow to British morale that British territory was occupied at all.'[15]

At Weymouth, Ministry of Health officials directed the majority of evacuees, by train, to three designated 'neutral areas', factory towns in Lancashire, Yorkshire and Cheshire, where accommodation had previously been earmarked for refugees expected from Belgium.[16] Given no clue as to their final destination, these women cared for thousands of children who were crammed into railway carriages without toilet facilities. Norah Flint recalled, 'The journey was a nightmare, one child was sick, then another developed a high fever. We waited for a doctor but he didn't meet the train.'[17] When these rural women eventually reached evacuee reception centres in the industrial towns of northern England, they were traumatised, not only by the long and difficult journey, but also by the industrial landscape of Manchester, Stockport, Bradford and Oldham. Molly Cowley was amazed to see 'trains, trams, and wide roads with two or three lanes.'[18]

Although welcomed by the local community, the women encountered ignorance regarding Guernsey's relationship with Britain. They assured locals that Guernsey was British and that they were not foreigners. Some recalled comments such as, 'so you're from the Channel Islands then? We've read about you in the papers. Is it hot there?'[19] Mrs Tippett was told, 'we thought you would be wearing grass skirts.'[20] Salvation Army and Women's Voluntary Service (WVS) volunteers appeared to know that Guernsey was near France, but assumed that the evacuees spoke only French, which offended and disorientated some of the mothers.[21] Olive Quinn described her arrival at a parish hall in Burnley, 'The WVS made 'signs' for us to start eating. We thought this rather odd and would have laughed if we hadn't been so tired from all the travelling. Suddenly the penny dropped! They thought we were all French, and as they couldn't speak French, they had performed this sign language.'[22] However, it was the evacuees themselves who needed the services of a translator, as they attempted to decipher local accents and dialects and Kathleen Cowling wrote, 'We later came to understand the Lancashire accent and the different words that people used. Sweets were 'toffees', streams were 'brooks' and dishes were 'pots'.[23]

Due to the hasty way in which the evacuation had been organised, mothers who sailed with their infants had great difficulty finding their children who had evacuated with their schools. No coordination appears to have been carried out by the authorities to ensure that family members could be reunited in England. Bridget Macey believes that 'no efforts were made to link the evacuation of school children with their mothers and younger siblings'[24] which determined a long separation between evacuated mothers and their children. Richard Titmuss noted that, in 1939, only four female Ministry of Health inspectors had attended conferences on evacuation, contributing to 'the failure to foresee the conditions in which mothers and children would arrive, and the kind of services they would require.'[25] Local authorities did what little they could to reunite mothers and children, and the few surviving evacuee registration lists are marked with notes which indicate that families had been reunited.[26] However, the women's initial joy in finding their children was often cut short because of a lack of suitable accommodation. In *Churchill's Children*, John Welshman describes the instance when an evacuated teacher was separated from her own baby upon arrival in a reception area.[27] In 1940, Guernsey mothers in Stockport endured a similar experience and a teacher wrote at the time:

> Officials had not been informed that there were mothers with children in our party, so they were not prepared to billet them together. They were split up – one child here, one child there, and the mother elsewhere. The scene defies description, we shall never forget it, these mothers had lost their homes, their husbands and everything they possessed, and just clung to their children as their last joy.[28]

Facing new challenges

Wartime newspaper reports show that, in 1939, many English and Scottish evacuated mothers returned home after a few weeks, despite the dangers they might face.[29] Guernsey mothers did not have this choice and had to cope with receiving the dreadful news that Guernsey had been occupied by Germany on 30 June 1940 and that they would therefore possibly require long-term accommodation in England for themselves and their children. The gender bias was suggested by billeting officers who questioned the Guernsey women's abilities to care for their children without their husbands; some even recommended that the mothers hand their children over to local families for the duration of the war. Jean Le Prevost's daughters were cared for by local families until Jean found suitable accommodation, 'Housewives would try to take one of my girls to live with them, and I would say that we all had to stay together until we could find our own home! Some women actually said to me "Sorry love, but I don't have room for you and two kiddies."'[30]

Some mothers were offered homes by families who primarily wanted them to assist with housework and childcare, and Dorothy Johnson recalled, 'A well-spoken lady came towards me, looked me up and down and said "Can you cook?" "Yes I can", I replied. The woman said "Right, you look strong enough, you will do." I became their housekeeper, I worked very hard indeed and never received a smile from either of them. After six months of this, my husband, Henry, left the Forces as he had failed a medical. Eventually we managed to get our own home.'[31]

Olive Quinn and her baby daughter, Carol, were billeted with a Burnley woman who insisted that Olive work in the family shop to earn her keep, despite the fact that a billeting allowance was being provided, 'It was a poky little shop in a dirty dismal street, I worked all day for her and wondered if I would ever be able to adapt to my surroundings. I cried myself to sleep that night and the following morning the woman wanted nothing to do with me. She said that my crying had put her off taking in refugees and she sent for the WVS lady to take me away.'[32] English women evacuated in 1939 had suffered a similar fate, as Titmuss explained, 'More often than not she is accepted but not welcomed into the billeting household...these conditions create a very bad psychological disturbance both for the mothers and children.[33]

Guernsey mothers also discovered that, unless their husbands were in the forces, they were not eligible to rent properties. To combat this, they formed alliances so that those whose husbands were in the forces shared accommodation with those whose husbands were trapped in Guernsey. Sharing childcare and household duties, many also undertook part-time shift work as John Tippet recalled, 'Mum and Aunt Cissy shared an unfurnished corner shop, as my Dad was in the Forces and Cissy's was in Guernsey. They took turns to work and to look after each other's children, and they worked in the same cinema but on different shifts.

It was a new thing for them, being housewives and breadwinners.'[34] However, despite their shared status as Guernsey evacuees, there were tensions within these overcrowded households. The mothers suffered multiple problems in managing budgets and negotiating a new way of life, whilst dealing with the added trauma of sudden evacuation. Rose Duquemin recalled,

> Each of the four mothers and her children had a bedroom in the house, with my Mum as the leader. There was also a woman 'overseer' who was from the WVS. This constant interference from the overseer didn't work very well as you can imagine, and there were arguments sometimes between the mothers, mainly over cooking and childcare.[35]

Over time the Guernsey mothers integrated into their new communities and played their part in the defence of the British Home Front. They faced the terror of air raids, contributed towards fund-raising schemes and stood alongside local people undertaking vital war work. Agnes Scott recalled her first week at a Manchester factory,

> I had to work a week in hand before getting paid, and had no money so walked to and from work. The foreman, John Dewhurst, noticed that I never went to the canteen and wanted to know the reason. He gave me a loan of ten shillings! I was delighted, it was so unexpected. I never forgot him.[36]

Guernsey women shared their Britishness with their neighbours and Sonya O. Rose argues that 'this recognition of common jeopardy contributed to making national identity particularly meaningful for individuals.'[37] One Guernsey mother wrote a letter to the *Sunday Express*, stating 'I have lost in this war many things that were dear to me. A cosy little home in Guernsey, now occupied by jackbooted ruffians and the companionship of a young husband who dreams his dreams behind barbed wire in Germany. We are behind you to a woman.'[38] This letter reveals the writer's attempt to show, not just her loyalty to the British war effort, but how the German invasion of Guernsey had ripped her family relationships apart. For her English neighbours, the Home Front meant a life in England, surrounded by the support of family and friends, with male relatives serving in the forces. Certainly, some Guernsey women had husbands and sons in the forces, but for the majority 'the Home Front' consisted of an unfamiliar life in England, cut off from husbands, family and friends who were trapped in occupied British territory.

The evacuees had arrived with nothing, but their visibility in local press reports resulted in countless donations from members of a wartime population that had little themselves. These reports presented the British nation as the rescuer of vulnerable mothers and children from the steam-rolling invasion of the Nazis, although group photographs of evacuees tended to depict the children rather than the mothers. One newspaper advised readers 'These evacuees have only beds, a few chairs and an occasional teapot. Readers of the Express probably possess furniture and household utensils for which they have no further need but which would be a God send to evacuees who have been unfortunate enough to lose all their goods and chattels.'[39]

One Guernsey family moved into an empty house in Rochdale, which, within three hours, was filled with furniture donated by neighbours.[40] The mothers received not only gifts, but friendship from locals who understood what the evacuees had left behind. Joan Le Page wrote, 'These northern women, are very sympathetic. They say things like "We are all on the same side love, what bits do you need for your house? We will see what we can give you. It's terrible, you, a woman here on your own with those three kids, and your poor husband stuck at home with them bloody Nazis."'[41] The evacuees also took steps to maintain some sense of their own identity and community, never losing sight of the fact that, one day, they would return home. They would then need to reintegrate into their parish communities and pick up the pieces of their pre-war lives. Guernsey adults formed approximately 100 Channel Island societies which provided emotional support and social interaction for adults and children. They also provided a safe space in which to share cultural aspects such as traditional songs, stories and recipes and to discuss their hopes and fears for Guernsey's future. Cruickshank argues that, without such efforts, the evacuees' re-assimilation into their islands at the end of the war would have been much more difficult.[42] Mrs Lowe noted the importance of regularly meeting other Guernsey mothers, 'There are a lot of us crammed in this house, and my father in law is quite badly behaved and unreasonable most of the time. I am so glad to get out to the meetings on Saturdays for some respite.'[43] The evacuees also shared the contents of their occasional Red Cross messages.[44] Unlike mainland evacuees, Guernsey women were unable to write letters or telephone their families because all communications between Guernsey and England had been cut. Anne Le Noury explained the importance of these 25 word messages, 'The few censored words meant that Dad and the family in Guernsey were still alive.'[45]

The long-term consequences of evacuation

On 9 May 1945, Guernsey was liberated by British forces, and Mrs Hamel heard the German surrender on the radio, 'To us, this was the greatest broadcast ever! The lapping of the water could be clearly heard as the launch carrying the German commander drew alongside. The BBC did a grand job. We sat there, not knowing whether to laugh or cry.'[46] The postal service and telephone lines were reinstated, but these long awaited communications often brought tragic news from Guernsey. Mrs Ingrouille discovered that her mother had died during the occupation.[47] The return to Guernsey did not mirror the speed of the evacuation, and those selected for early return were those for whom there was immediate employment.[48] However, some mothers foresaw problems associated with reconstruction in Guernsey, whilst many had come to appreciate the modern amenities that England could offer. Eight Guernsey families decided to remain in the Lancashire council estate where they had been placed in June 1940.[49] Many Guernsey children, now in their late teens, had found promising employment or become engaged to locals, and Yvonne Bristol recalled 'Mum and dad decided to stay in England as they thought it gave us all a better chance.'[50] Hazel Knowles' father was granted compassionate leave from the army, to visit his mother in Guernsey, and Hazel recalled,

> Whilst there he inspected our house which we had all left so hurriedly in 1940, and on his return, he and my mother decided, after a great deal of thought, to stay in Stockport until I had completed my schooling. In the event, father found a job with Manchester Corporation then started his own business in landscape gardening.[51]

Of the women interviewed, 75 per cent returned to an island that had been torn apart physically, socially and economically. Their hope was to assimilate quickly into their family and parish community, but they encountered a multitude of dilemmas that had a high emotional cost. Studies of couples separated during wartime have shown how estrangement occurs, and Julie Summers has pointed to situations where the dislocation caused by years of separation can have extreme consequences for a family.[52] Certainly, soldiers faced difficulties returning to their families after a long absence, but in the case of Guernsey, thousands of mothers found themselves preparing to return home to their husbands after five years apart. Some feared that they would be unable to reconnect emotionally with their husbands and during their journey home, their thoughts were complex. Mrs Quinn recalled arriving at St Peter Port, 'My heart was beating 60 to the dozen! Then I saw my husband and we experienced the lovely feeling of holding each other after five long, weary years.'[53] Freda Langlois also recorded her feelings, 'How lovely to set foot on our native soil once again and to be met by those loved ones.'[54]

Older women can find it difficult to share aspects of their private lives, especially when their accounts will be made public. Off the record some women revealed insights into their sexual lives. One returned home to discover that her husband had formed another relationship. He met his wife and child at the harbour, bluntly advised her of his affair, and stated that he did not want either of them in his home.[55] A child from another family recalled, 'when my Mum and I got back to Guernsey and met my dad, I noticed that they didn't hold each other's hands as we walked away from the harbour.'[56] Households encountered difficulties with reunion and settlement and many mothers found it difficult to adjust to their pre-war lives. In England their role had become enhanced as they had gained power and independence as breadwinners and sole decision makers. In post-war Guernsey they were defrocked of these responsibilities, expected to relinquish their skills and independence and return to the traditional role of housekeeper and child minder. Kath Ozanne's son, Tony, recalled, 'In England Mum had enjoyed her new found career, giving her a different outlook on life than that of a grower's wife. After the war, women like my mother had to rebuild their homes and re-establish their marriages with husbands they had not seen for years.'[57] Cecilia Le Poidevin also found it difficult to adjust, and her daughter recalled, 'In Guernsey we had Dad, an Uncle and Grandfather in the house. There was lots of tension at first.'[58]

Julie Summers argues that the varied personal experiences of life in wartime played a powerful part in shaping the character of children and their parents[59]. Guernsey mothers had to negotiate the emotional relationships of their families and encourage children to reconnect with fathers and siblings. By 1945, John La Mare had been separated from his father for so long that 'we were like strangers. We never formed a proper relationship'[60]. Mothers also had to manage the disappointment of children who were forced to abandon their career aspirations to help on the farm, assist with child care, or undertake relatively menial work. Irene Moss recalled: 'there was no decent work for young women in

Guernsey. All that English education and I ended up scrubbing floors'.[61] One particularly distressing factor which emerged during interviews was that, upon their return to Guernsey, the women discovered a two tier system at work. There appeared to be a stigma attached to those who had evacuated; a perception that, by leaving the island, they had been cowardly and disloyal to Guernsey. In effect, the occupied were made heroic and could not see beyond the terror of their own experiences. There was no acknowledgement whatsoever that the evacuated had suffered in any way.[62] During the 1940 evacuation itself, anti-evacuation posters warning islanders not to leave had been pasted around the harbour. The most inflammatory poster had stated, 'Keep Your Heads! Don't Be Yellow!! Business as Usual'.[63] By 1945 the experience of occupation and notions of loyalty to Guernsey had created a context suitable for anti-evacuation sentiment to flourish on the island, and one returning mother stated: 'Each time I started to talk about my time in England, someone would say 'well, here, during the occupation it was much worse' so I was frozen out of the conversation. After a time I shut up and never brought the subject up again'.[64]

When Mrs Le Poidevin and her husband, a Headmaster, returned to Guernsey with their pupils, the parents expressed grateful thanks in public. However, behind closed doors, the couple faced accusations of having run away, rather than being viewed as protectors of the island's next generation. Their son Nick recalled that for many years at family gatherings, 'we were constantly reminded that we had run away from the Germans'.[65] In many families, the experience of being on the mainland became a taboo subject, and when Edna Cave returned with her children, her family never asked her about the evacuation, 'They just weren't interested in what I had gone through'.[66] Most women maintained this pattern of silence and failed to discuss their evacuation experiences, even with their own children. In this way the women's experiences were forgotten, relegated to the margins in any national discourse of the island's history. My interviews with these women, conducted more than sixty years after the island's liberation, provided a safe space in which their stories could be aired for the first time. Yet even in this space, breaking the pattern of silence was no easy feat as wartime traumas were relived and emotions aired.

Conclusion

The gathering of these overlooked histories of the Guernsey evacuation to Britain during the Second World War has brought the subject of evacuated mothers into the open, challenging myths of the experience of women on the Home Front in both Guernsey and the UK. Prior to 2010, Guernsey had no official commemoration of the evacuation, and the interviewed mothers carried a legacy of enduring hurt because their wartime experiences had been ignored at a national and local level. Now their oral histories are being retrieved and recognised, breaking the long established pattern of silence. As a direct result, a commemorative evacuation plaque was unveiled in Guernsey in May 2010 by The Bailiff, Sir Geoffrey Rowland, whose own parents were evacuated to Stockport.[67] Sir Geoffrey Rowland stated: 'In June 1940, many Islanders arrived at railway stations in a tired, distressed and confused state and feeling embittered by the impact of the War on their lives, and for some, their livelihoods. This was particularly so in the case of adults.'[68] Today, the surviving evacuated mothers appreciate that their voices, silent for so long, are now being heard, and they can collectively project their stories within the national imagination.[69] The recovery of their testimony will add to the histories of wartime displacement, and gender – challenging the myths, images and memories of evacuation on the British Home Front.

Notes

1. P. Summerfield and C. Peniston-Bird (2007) *Contesting Home Defence*.
2. See for example, S. Rose (2003) *Which People's War?*; or J. Summers (2009) *Stranger in the House*.
3. *Guernsey Star*, 19 June 1940, p 1.
4. Imperial War Museum, ref. P338, Personal Account of Mrs M. Trotter, p 7.
5. Misselke family papers, Diary of Ruth Alexandre, June 1940, p 2.
6. Batiste family papers: Diary of Mrs Batiste June–July 1940, p 5.
7. Interview with Eva Le Page, 6 February 2011, p 1. Eva passed away in 2012.
8. Weston Family Archive, Memoirs of Merle Roberts, p 2.
9. For a more detailed account of the evacuation to England, refer to G. Mawson (2012) *Guernsey Evacuees*.
10. B. A. Reade (1995) *No Cause for Panic*, p 30.
11. Imperial War Museum, Ref. P338, Personal Account of Mrs M Trotter p 2.
12. B. A. Reade (1995) *No Cause for Panic*, p 8.
13. Imperial War Museum, Ref. P338, Personal Account of Mrs M. Trotter, p 10.
14. *The Times*, 31 July 1940.
15. C. Cruickshank (1975) *The German Occupation*, p 54.
16. Bury Archives Service, Channel Island files, MOH memo to Bury Town Council, June 1940.
17. Flint family papers, letter written by Norah Flint, 27 June 1940, p 1.
18. Interview with Molly Cowley, February 2010, p 1.
19. E. J. Hamel (1975) *X Isles*, p 19.
20. Interview with John Tippett, August 2009, p 4.

21. Although some evacuees who were interviewed spoke a Guernsey French 'patois', the majority spoke clear English in 1940.
22. *Guernsey Press Supplement*, 20 June 2000, Evacuation Memories of Olive Quinn, p 13.
23. Rochdale Archives, Guernsey Evacuee file, Memories of Kathleen Cowling, p 3.
24. B. Macey (1991) 'Social Dynamics', p 4.
25. R. Titmuss (1950) *Problems of Social Policy*, p 111.
26. Stockport Heritage Library ref. B/T/5/32 Stockport Sunday School's Channel Island evacuee lists, June 1940.
27. J. Welshman (2010) *Churchill's Children*, p 80.
28. Martel family private papers, School Diary of Percy Martel, 1 July 1940, pp 936–937.
29. *Campbelltown Courier* 'Many evacuees have gone home', 30 September 1939.
30. Le Prevost family papers, Diary of Jean Le Prevost p 21.
31. Interviews with Herbert Quick and Linda Thompson, the children of Dorothy Johnson, June 2008.
32. *Guernsey Press Supplement*, June 2000, p 13.
33. R. Titmuss (1950) *Problems of Social Policy*, p 168.
34. Interview with John Tippett, October 2008, p 4.
35. Interview with Rose Short, February 2010, p 2.
36. Interview with Agnes Scott, May 2010, p 2.
37. S. O. Rose (2003) p 11.
38. *Sunday Express*, Letters Page, 9 July 1944.
39. *Stockport Express*, 1 August 1940, p 7.
40. Brian Reade Archive Refugees folder, Section R, unidentified Rochdale newspaper, July 1940.
41. Le Page private papers, Diary of Joan Le Page, August 1940, p 14.
42. C. Cruickshank (1975) *The German Occupation*, p 47.
43. Diary of Mrs Lowe, March 1942 – this is a pseudonym, as the interviewee wishes to remain anonymous.
44. Red Cross messages were sent from England to Paris then through several European countries, reaching Guernsey up to six months later, after German censorship. The Stockport Channel Island Society published a newsletter, *Channel Islands Monthly Review*, between May 1941 and August 1945, which printed some of the Red Cross letters received from Guernsey. The newsletters also give a detailed insight into the activities of the Channel Island societies in England.
45. Interview with Anne Le Noury, February 2012, p 5.
46. E. J. Hamel (1975) *X Isles*, p 35.
47. *Stockport Advertiser*, 18 May 1945, p 9.
48. *Manchester Guardian*, 11 June 1945, p 6.
49. Bury Archives Service Channel Island files ref. AB U/T/792, Billeting Office memo, 31 March 1947.
50. Interview with Yvonne Bristol, October 2009, p 3.
51. Testimony of Hazel Knowles, August 2009, p 11, (Hazel's uncle Cyril had remained in Guernsey during the war and joined the GUNS organisation (Guernsey Underground News Service). GUNS had circulated a daily newssheet compiled from the BBC news bulletins, which they were illicitly listening to on a hidden radio.
52. J. Summers (2008).

53. O. Quinn (1985) *The Long Goodbye*, p 90.
54. Langlois family papers, Testimony of Freda Langlois, Spring 1946, p 12.
55. For personal reasons this interviewee wished to remain anonymous. She lives in Guernsey and has remarried.
56. For personal reasons, this interviewee wished to remain anonymous.
57. *Guernsey Press*, 8 May 2010, p 15. During a subsequent interview Tony was keen to stress the difficulty his mother faced in post-war Guernsey.
58. Interview with Margaret Parkyn and Kath Munro (née Le Poidevin) 2009.
59. J. Summers (2011) *When the Children Came Home*, pp 302–303.
60. Interview with John La Mare, October 2009, p 3.
61. Interview with Irene Moss, February 2011, p 2.
62. For a detailed account of the stigma faced by Guernsey evacuees, see G. Mawson (2012) *Guernsey Evacuees*, pp 180–184.
63. Ozanne family papers, interview with escaped evacuee, Fred Hockey, *Daily Herald*, undated, but prior to November 1940.
64. This evacuee wished to remain anonymous.
65. N. Le Poidevin (2010) *Torteval School in Exile* (Jersey: Ex Libris Self Publishing) p 66.
66. Interview with Edna Cave, February 2011, p 5.
67. Interview with Sir Geoffrey Rowland, May 2010, p 1.
68. Speech delivered by Sir Geoffrey Rowland at The Royal Court Guernsey, 8 May 2010, p 2.
69. I have used my interviews with evacuee mothers to create a Guernsey Mother's 1940 Diary: http://guernseyevacuees.wordpress.com/diary-of-an-evacuee-jun-1940/

References

Cruickshank. C (1975) *The German Occupation of the Channel Islands* (London: Oxford University Press).

Hamel. E J (1975) *X Isles* (Guernsey: Paramount Lithoprint).

Macey. B (1991) 'Social Dynamics of Oral History Making: Women's Experiences of Wartime', *Oral History*, 19, 2, pp 42–48.

Mawson. G (2012) *Guernsey Evacuees: The Forgotten Evacuees of the Second World War* (Stroud: The History Press).

Quinn. O (1985) *The Long Goodbye* (Guernsey: Guernsey Press) p 90.

Reade. B A (1995) *No Cause for Panic: Channel Island Refugees 1940–45* (Jersey: Seaflower Books).

Rose. S (2003) *Which People's War: National Identity and Citizenship in Wartime Britain 1939–45* (Oxford: Oxford University Press).

Summers. J (2008) *Stranger in the House* (London: Pocket Books).

Summerfield. P and Peniston-Bird. C (2007) *Contesting Home Defence: Men, Women and The Home Guard in the Second World War* (Manchester: Manchester University Press).

Summers. J (2011) *When the Children Came Home: Stories of Wartime Evacuees* (London: Simon and Schuster).

Titmuss. R (1950) *Problems of Social Policy*, (London: HMSO).

Welshman. J (2010) *Churchill's Children: The Evacuation Experience in Wartime Britain* (Oxford: Oxford University Press).

9

The Home Front as a 'Moment' for Animals and Humans: Exploring the Animal–Human Relationship in Contemporary Diaries and Letters

Hilda Kean

Introduction

The 1939–1945 war – often called the 'People's war' – is imbued with mythic qualities that show the British on the Home Front in a favourable light.[1] It is a war which people today still want to remember, as evidenced by the range of new memorials to former war workers including 'Women of World War Two' in Whitehall; Bomber Command in Piccadilly; 'Blitz, the National Firefighters' Memorial' near St Paul's Cathedral; the wide range of memorials at the National Memorial Arboretum; or the new memorial in Bethnal Green 'Stairway to Heaven'.[2] Richard Overy's magisterial *The Bombing War* has persuasively elaborated the implications of seeing the Second World War as a total war that promoted the idea that 'all citizens had a part to play and encouraged the view that warrior identity was linked to new ideals of the civil warrior.'[3] Although the Home Front is key to 'total war' nevertheless little research has been undertaken on the all-encompassing nature of that totality through the inclusion, in different ways, of non-human animals. Domestic animals played a large part in the events on the Home Front not least in creating emotional support for a population under aerial bombardment or acting as signifiers of 'home' for evacuees.[4] In an important wartime study of the experience of evacuated children, many stated that what they missed were their pets, eliding the animals with their sense of home. The survey of children evacuated from Islington and Tottenham to Cambridge noted that the third most mentioned 'miss' for girls was pets, and for boys the eighth.[5] Certainly the traumatised children observed and interviewed in a different study by Dorothy Burlingham and Anna Freud also cite animals in their narratives. As one small child said, 'My mummy and I were under the table and my poor little sister was in bed all by herself covered with stones, and my pussycat was thrown away.'[6]

In addition to their inclusion in contemporary press reports and records such as Mass Observation Reports or Home Office or Ministry of Agriculture and Fisheries files, animals, particularly domestic cats and dogs, feature prominently in published and unpublished diaries and letters. These are not simply 'personal' stories but are often situated in more widely known war stories and, of course, add a wider picture of the war. Thus, movingly, the teenage diary of Colin Perry refers to the death on the Arrandora Star[7] of the Italian owner of the local pet shop, 'It was only a few short weeks ago that my brother, Alan, took our canary to him to have its nails cut; and only a few short weeks ago that we bought weed for the goldfish bowl from him.' Azario had lived in Tooting for 42 years but, in 1940 with growing anxiety and the expectation that Britain would soon also be at war with Italy, he was 'immediately taken off in a police car for internment ... it seems incredible that an old man who kept a pet store in Upper Tooting Road has suddenly been snatched away to forfeit his life in the Atlantic. I can see him now attending to his pets ...'[8] Equally poignant was the letter sent to Beryl Myatt, evacuated to Canada from Hillingdon by her parents, intended to reach her on arrival. At the top it says, 'Chummy sends his love' accompanied by his pawprint. But the little girl never received her parents' letter, having been lost at sea on the torpedoed ship, Benares.[9] These are just two of many examples of the domestic animal presence in established war narratives. Nevertheless when popular editions of published war diaries do discuss the human author's relationship to animals, this tends to be ignored in both the indexes and subsequent analysis.[10] Thus although the Mass Observation diary of Nella Last has received much critical attention since its publication in 1981 and has even been adapted as a television film, Nella's relationship with Mr Murphy her cat and Sol her dog have been resolutely ignored,[11] even though she discussed both extensively and commented on the treatment of animals by neighbours and relatives. She even pleaded – successfully – to save the life of Tiger Tim, the 'entire' tom cat at the Women's Voluntary Service (WVS) canteen, who other women wanted to kill because he smelt. As she noted 'Will one more smell make any difference to the general odour of mice, mouldy bread, a room with practically no ventilation, gas stoves, dirty sinks and lavatory?'[12]

This chapter focusses upon aspects of the way in which animal–human relationships were documented in the personal diaries and letters of four people, three of whom lived in London and one, Nella Last, in Barrow in Furness in the north-west of England. Nella Last's whose published account is drawn from the Mass Observation archive.[13] The second unpublished diary is a handwritten contemporaneous daily account of Gladwys (sic) Cox a 57-year-old housewife living with her husband Ralph and Bob, a tabby kitten, in a mansion block in West Hampstead.[14] The third, also unpublished, diaries I discuss are those of advertising businessman Laurance Holman living in Bedford Square, near the British Museum, from where he also ran his business. He described his daily rides on his horse Mariana and then Trump around Hyde or Regent's Park, including peregrinations to view the previous night's bombing.[15] While horses may not be conventionally seen as 'pets' in that they live outside the perimeters of a human's geographic home, certainly the horses featuring in Holman's life fulfilled the function of 'creating stability for a human'.[16] Mariana and Trump possessed names and by being named were, as Nik Taylor puts it, '[brought] into our human worlds'.[17] Finally the collected early wartime letters to friends in America of criminologist and writer Fryniwyd Tennyson Jesse will be considered. She is perhaps best known now for her 1934 novel *Pin to see the Peepshow*, re-issued by Virago Press in its distinctive dark green covers in 1979.[18]

The focus on London is both because letters and diaries exist for the capital but also because the city witnessed an unprecedented mass killing of cats and dogs at the start of the war. The slaughter of around 400,000 cats and dogs at their owner's behest in London alone in the first week of the war is forgotten though recorded widely in the national press at the time and in Humphrey Jennings documentary *The First Days 1939*.[19] The figure was later corroborated both by the Royal Society for the Prevention of Cruelty to Animals (RSPCA) and Brigadier Clabby, the author of the official history of the Royal Army Veterinary Corps.[20] So extensive was the voluntary killing of pets that animal campaigners, such as the National Canine Defence League, referred to it as 'the September holocaust'. The same description was employed by diarist Gwladys Cox on 15 September 1939 when criticising her neighbour who 'smilingly' had told Gwladys she had had their cat and two kittens destroyed, 'There has been a perfect holacaust [sic] of cats in London, and as a result, some districts ... are threatened with a plague of vermin so now the authorities are begging people to keep their pets, if possible.'[21] This opening act of the war was therefore obviously a significant moment for animals in London. Although generalised killing of pets would happen later in the war, particularly in south-eastern coastal towns when they were due to be evacuated in the event of invasion,[22] it was however only in London that slaughter took place in the first days of the war, something that was recorded by London diarists – and extensively in the press.[23] In the course of the war the animals who survived (who were the majority)[24] and their human companions often became physically, and emotionally, closer. Responses to a recent Mass Observation directive on animal–human relationships endorse the view that during the 1930s a rather different relationship between domestic animals and humans had existed than that which is generally found today.[25] The comments of an 87-year-old respondent are typical of perceptions of the norm,

> I am not so sure that domestic animals were even thought of as pets then. The fact that they weren't there to be pampered or for orna-mental reasons, or indeed to live lives any better than their owners' made it so that they had to justify their existence. Cats were there to deal with mice and dogs to take care of the rats.[26]

The nature of the diary form: physical closeness

The material circumstances of war ensured that people became more aware of their animals' physical presence. Cats and dogs moved into air raid shelters together with their keepers, often ensuring that the humans went to their shelter more speedily alerted by the acute hearing of the animals. As one Londoner described it, 'the dog's ears used to go up and it used to run and was in the dug-out before us.'[27] Cats tended to be more house-oriented especially at night time and initially some cats were disoriented by the blackout. They were used to seeing the reflec-tion of lighted rooms on the garden, as a sign that the family was in and without this stayed out. One cat's keeper explained, 'Since then he has stayed at home more than usual, and has shown every symptom of puzzlement and disquiet.'[28] The Cats Protection League gave specific advice such as 'Feed it [sic] regularly. Provide it with an elastic collar and some form of identification, above all *keep it in at night.*'[29] Dogs, who would often walk themselves during the 1930s, were in wartime less likely to be allowed to roam freely during the day; as in the event of bombing, surviving humans needed to be able to direct emergency serv-ices to retrieving family 'pets'. This physical closeness of animals and humans is a factor in the accounts that exist of the daily life of humans and animals together during the war as the writers recorded their quotidian routine, of which animals were an integral part. Furthermore, specific canine and feline skills were increasingly valued – as hunters of mice and rats, as 'advance warners' of aerial bombardment, and as beings responsive to humans' moods. By April 1944 *Cats and Kittens. The*

Magazine for Every Cat-lover could confidently declare that 'Never has the cat been so popular in this country as at the present time' helping to provide 'relief from the strain of war.'[30]

The form of a diary focussing on daily activities within a set, regular, timespan is a good genre to demonstrate small features of everyday life and of a life shared with other living beings. However, as various recent research has shown, there is no one set framework for the rationale of diary-keeping. Whilst the famous may see diary writing as a way of 'having the last word',[31] others may see the process as a way of working through ways to live their lives, to control and organise time, or simply because of ensuring they remember a particular moment.[32] Gwladys Cox, for example, seemed only to keep a diary during the war, recognising this as both personally and publicly important for posterity. Holman and Cox created their own rationales but Last's initially anonymised account was written to the framework of Mass Observation.[33] Holman and Cox had no externally imposed framework but frequently recorded tiny details of prices or the difficulties of buying food, setting this against broader accounts of the war. Some recently published war diaries, such as that of air raid warden Richard Brown, were specifically written to capture the moment of war. Brown's last entry on Victory Day, 8 June 1946 concluded:

> Yes we are celebrating today so I suppose it's a suitable day on which to close this diary. I've enjoyed it; it's run to nearly 3,000 pages, readable possibly only to myself, but I hope it will provide a little relaxation, if not interesting reading in its recorded experiences and impressions, some future period, years hence.[34]

In Brown's diary much attention was paid to coverage of the progress of the war abroad and a commentary, such as, 'News in general is very disturbing'.[35] The diaries I discuss here tended to have a different approach. Thus Laurance Holman juxtaposed different aspects of his life in one small daily entry, eliding features of the war 'abroad' with routine business activities and riding his horse. With his omission of some explanatory names – he was clearly writing the diary for himself – external events such as defeat or progress in Europe were elided into the personal narrative. Thus on 31 May 1940 he wrote: 'News a shade better British Expeditionary Force (BEF) being saved more than we dared hope Vet gave the OK today for walking only. I rode her [Mariana] in Regent's Park.' His later lines on 2 April 1945 are also typical: 'CEASEFIRE – a noon to-day in Italy; TG!* Easy day, no meeting with Mr King until to-morrow: ride from 2 to 5: home to a spot of modelling, cold pork salad & tea.' [*Thank God]

Gwladys Cox emphasised the impact of war upon animals in general in London, not just her own cat, describing, for example:

> ... the zoo, which has been terribly hard hit by the war though lack of gate money, now has a system of 'adoption'. People all over the country have adopted animals there by promising funds for their keep. A dormouse costs 1/- board per week.[36]

Unlike the diaries of Cox and Holman, Tennyson Jesse's letters were authored by a published writer and were meant to be read widely, both by her American friends who were the first recipients of her writing and the unknown audience when they were published just months after being written. Although at first it seems that her bull terrier and two cats were incorporated into the narrative simply as part of the household activities, a letter of March 1940 reveals other, broader, motivations:

> I watch [our cats] with a sense of relaxation and pleasure because they know nothing about war. I think everybody sat a time like this should keep animals, just as royalties and dictators should always keep animals. For animals know nothing of politics, nothing of royalty, nothing of war unless, poor creatures, they also, knowing not why, are wounded and killed.[37]

By situating animals as apart from politics, albeit included in the suffering of war, she articulates a position commonly held at the time. 'This quality of something untouched by the social, snobbish and more serious matters that torture us, is what animals give us, and as a contribution to civilisation, believe me it is of inestimable value: it has become our only rest-cure.'[38] The diaries of Nella Last were similarly intended to be read by a wider audience. In seeking to obtain details and observations of all aspects of daily life Mass Observation was providing a useful service for subsequent readers but, of course, also circumscribing the content of diarist's entries in the attempt to create 'an anthropology of ourselves'.[39] In writing about her observation of the animal–human relationship, Last was also – consciously or not – asserting the validity of this particular experience.

Traces of animals changing behaviour during the war or human projections?

Within the broader field of Animal Studies some have suggested that historical discussion of animals can only ever be representational since archival materials about the lives of animals are only ever produced by humans.[40] Erica Fudge, for example, has argued that as access to animals in the past is through humans 'then we never look at the animals, only ever at the representation of the animals by humans. The difficulty then can be', she continues, 'that animals themselves disappear, abandoned in favour of the "purely textual"'[41]. Certainly this is what happened in some wartime propaganda in which pets simply became symbolic of home. I have previously suggested that this approach can be too sweeping.[42]

In the Home Front diaries discussed here Cox, Tennyson Jesse and Holman, in their own ways, did not just present accounts of the impact of animals' lives on humans, though this was there in the very practice of being included in the writing process, but they also portrayed aspects of the daily activities of animals in their narratives. Animals may have relative autonomy from the framework of the human writer if they have acted or behaved in different ways to the norm or in circumstances (such as war) in which their presence is more noted. Of course, the incidents recorded rested upon the decision of the human.[43] For example, Gwladys Cox specifically discussed how Bob, a tabby cat with honey-coloured eyes who was only seven months old at the start of the war,[44] reacted to many of the changes in lifestyle imposed by war, but these were as she witnessed them. Gwladys imagined Bob's feelings when placed in a basket in the middle of the night and moved to a nearby basement cellar in response to air raid alerts 'he must think us mad, such goings-on in the middle of the night'.[45] This is obviously a human projection. Nevertheless we do learn that Bob, like Gwladys, had adopted different night-time routines because of the war. We also learn about Bob's changing diet. He ate different types of fish such as whiting or cod or herrings, although he refused to eat one of the favourite fish of Londoners 'rock eel' (otherwise known as dogfish); but enjoyed rabbit that was purchased weekly.[46] We also learn about the concurrently changing human diet – including the sharing of this with Bob. The cat's toileting habits were also sometimes affected because of war. For example, at the beginning of October 1940 the top floor of Gwladys's mansion block had been destroyed by incendiary bombs so humans and Bob had relocated to a friend, Mrs Shepp in Alvanley Gardens. She took Bob outside,

> hoping he would make use of the garden. Not he! Never before had he seen a garden, much less walked in soil, and was nervous of the unfamiliar surroundings so back to the dining room, where he squatted on the fine pile carpet. Fortunately Mary loves cats, and Mrs Snepp being blind, we mopped up and no one was any the wiser.[47]

Tennyson Jesse recorded a similar story to this fine pile carpet encounter. As a precaution against possible fire the humans had placed buckets of sand on every landing, 'after a few weeks we discovered the kitten misunderstood the purposes of these, so we emptied them again. Now they are re-filled and have a piece of cardboard laid over the top so that the kitten can't make the same mistake. Besides, anyway now it prefers ruining my best plants.'[48] Because of the war, the humans had acted differently by placing the buckets in the house – so too did the cat!

Through such detailed observations the reader becomes aware of the behaviour of particular animals during the war and how this changed. We are not only presented with a human analysis of an emotional relationship. The animals in the diarists' pages do not simply exist as the recipients of human projections but are beings in their own right. Not only were the lives of 'pets' in the home changed; the lives of horses kept for recreational purposes were also disrupted not only through dietary restriction but changes in the form of rides or being sold for war work.[49] Mariana, the horse Holman rode regularly was stabled near Regent's Park and later near Hyde Park. Holman noted, for example, on Monday 30 Sept 1940, 'Said a little prayer of thanks for another night of safety: midday ride with raid shelter in L.G. Barracks* on the way back. Mariana went home so walked her from the Victoria Gate.' *[Life Guard] Here the horse's usual routine and riding route (as well as that of Holman) was changed because of aerial bombardment. I am not suggesting that any of the aspects of individual animals' lives referred to above are intrinsically significant (any more than the lives of the humans writing the accounts.) However, they are indications of the way in which their lives, like those of their human keepers, were also disrupted or changed because of the war, irrespective of any anthropomorphic projections. Total war is also a concept that can be applied to the context of their circumstances, which we can access to some extent – if we choose to acknowledge interest in an animal existence – through diaries and letters.

Broader concerns and observations about the human–animal relationship on the Home Front

In addition to the 'owned' animals included in the diary narratives, the writers were also conscious of animals and their wider treatment beyond their own household. That is, animals were not discussed simply because of a personal relationship with the human writer. Instead they were seen to be an integral part of broader social and political circumstances witnessed by the diarist. The three women, in different ways, commented on the killing of companion animals.[50] Like many others at the start of war, Nella Last had contemplated killing her own companion animals, 'Wonder if I should give my faithful old dog, and my funny comedian cat "the gift of sleep".'[51] However she did not do this and became critical of others who later killed their animals for no good reason, as she forcefully explained:

> Aunt Eliza decided to have her old spaniel put to sleep. I protested for, although 13, he is clean in his habits and has no 'old dog' smell. The only thing is, he is going deaf and short-sighted. Poor old auntie, she was broken-hearted. I could see that daughter and son in law had worked on her till she decided it was for the best. They don't like dogs and they have such a marvellous home – no, house – all chrome and glitter.[52]

For Tennyson Jesse the acquisition of a new cat at the start of the war was circumscribed by the wider circumstances of the mass pet killing. Her flat was over-run with mice so she decided to:

> ... give an abandoned cat a good home and rang the RSPCA.
>
> I said: 'I want to talk about a cat.'
>
> And a very weary voice answered: 'Oh yes, you wish to have a cat destroyed.'
>
> 'Not at all,' I cried, 'I want to get a cat.'
>
> The voice said: 'What! You want to adopt a cat? Hold on, don't ring off whatever you do.[53]

Unfortunately, the cat escaped during his first days in his new home but providentially was discovered by the daily help some two weeks later, in the course of which he had had an accident that badly affected his hind legs. He was unable to catch mice: 'Muff thereupon became a luxury cat – a pleasure cat – and we still had to look around for some way of dealing with the mice.' A kitten was duly adopted.[54] Tennyson Jesse used the plight of lost and distraught Muff to comment on her own attitude towards war, indicating the emotional transference between animal and human, 'The terror and hunger of one cat seems very little in times like these, but nevertheless gave me an ache at the heart and filled me with pity that there should even be this tiny pin-point of needless suffering.'[55]

Cox was the diarist to comment most extensively on the killing and abandonment of pet animals and the work of the National Air Raid

Precautions Animals Committee and animal charities in rescuing, treating and identifying lost animals. Bob, for example, was the 97,354 animal to be registered and to then sport an identity disc.[56] Cox particularly noted the presence (or absence) of particular animals she observed in the street and was empathetic towards the comfort such animals gave to human companions, not just to herself. Thus, on Sunday 15 November 1942 she observed, 'It is a dark, cold foggy day. I look out on a rather dreary street and watch a neighbour taking the dog out. He walks slowly, with bowed head – his only son was killed at the Front last week.' On another occasion in the street, it was the dog first rather than the human who she noticed, 'I seemed to recognise a Cairn terrier – Robbie!' Behind him came a thin, tired-looking woman, whom I next recognized as Ward! [The dog lived with elderly Mrs Snepp, she of the carpet upon which Bob had urinated, who had died and the dog was now being cared for by her former servant].[57] The comfort that dogs brought to humans was not just valued by Cox. It frequently featured in contemporary Mass Observation reports. As one young working-class man, whose mongrel had died some months before, suggested in 1941, 'Probably dogs do more to uphold morale among their owners than anything else.'[58] Or as a woman explained earlier that summer, 'I've been all alone in the house since my husband went and the children were evacuated – and that dog's been wonderful company.'[59]

Although her diary was a personal response to living through war, many of Cox's sentiments were shared with others as this example illustrates. Near the start of the war the Cats Protection League had believed that cats would be neglected by officialdom if they were in bombed buildings. They based this view on the low status in which cats were held at that time. 'Wherever you are and whatever happens to you, you will be rescued before long, but rescue parties will not trouble over animals.'[60] Cox told the story of the mother of her cat Bob who had lived in a grocer's that had been bombed. The grocer, customers and demolition workers were all concerned about finding the cat. The workers searched through the rubble for some days 'Bob's mother alive! Demolition workers found her, as they dug away debris in the shop and carried her in a sack to the Finchley Road Cullens. When I saw her this morning days without food, she is very thin, but seems none the worst.'[61] Gwladys Cox's recording of other people's reactions was not simply a noticing of an isolated event. Humans observing the animals around them and rescuing them was more prevalent than has been previously acknowledged. Cox's own response of empathy is drawn out by the form of writing she is employing, rather than because of any rarity of the incident per se.[62]

Both Last and Cox also discussed the way in which their animals provided companionship and emotional support for them. Cox defined Bob as her 'constant companion' and 'consolation' in all her wartime trials.[63] For Nella Last, the dog's value was in providing both emotional and empathetic support,

> To me he is more than an animal: he has kindness, understanding and intelligence and not only knows all that is said but often reads my mind to an uncanny degree. He knows when I am sad and dim and lies with his head on my foot, or follows me closely as if to say, 'I cannot help you, but please understand I love you and will stand by.'[64]

Unlike her human partner who seemed unable to understand his wife, the dog could apparently do this. Instead of dismissing this as simply a product of an imaginative human mind we might consider the position of animal ethologist, Marc Bekoff. He has argued that if animals did not show their feelings then it would be unlikely people would bond with them, 'We form close relationships with our pets not only because of our own emotional needs but also because of our recognition of theirs.'[65] Similarly anthrozoologist, John Bradshaw has suggested that both cats and dogs have a relationship with a human keeper that is 'fundamentally affectionate'.[66] Animals and humans alike benefitted from such a relationship. Thus one man interviewed by Mass Observation elaborated his relationship with his dog thus: 'I've had this old fellow six years, I wouldn't think of life without him...I don't like shelters because of my asthma so I never go to one, so he's not alone ever.'[67]

Holman's diaries are rather different in that the main animal with whom he interacted was a horse who lived in stables away from his house. His daily routines, for example on a Saturday when he brought home shopping from near the stables or his observation of the first spring flowers in Hyde Park were influenced by where he (and Mariana) rode. Thus he noted the location of dropping of bombs in relation to his own house and the stables where Mariana lived: 'bomb dropped Russell S[quare] and one of the big houses in Portland Place was wrecked within 100 yards of "Mariana": mid-day ride.'[68] On various occasions, he chose to witness bomb damage from astride Mariana. 'An easy night for us, last night, but Whitehall got it: 2 in Birdcage Walk, 1 behind F[oreign]O[ffice], 1...in St James' Park: 3 in Whitehall: 2 in Trafalgar Sq[uare]...Mariana passed all these spots in my ride.'[69]

Holman saw riding – and developing expertise in the recreation that he had come to in middle age – as a key part of his own existence even though doctors often warned him against such strenuous exercise. Perhaps, because of this relatively new acquaintance it was important for him to record both his own daily riding – and aspects of the horse's behaviour. As a popular horse-riding guide of the time explained, 'balance … is the sine qua non of riding.'[70] The aim was to move as one harmonious whole: horse and human together. With both Mariana and Trump he tried to obtain an understanding, or 'feel': 'Went to the bottom of the Row with Trump and received a glorious "bucking" on the way back: He's a grand ride, now, and we well understand one another.'[71] The tone of the diary generally is that of a no-nonsense type of man concerned with figures, sales, personal expenditure and having a fairly prosaic and resilient approach to life. Yet in his attitude towards the old age and deteriorating physical condition and subsequent deaths of Mariana and Trump he expressed himself with compassion. The language changed: 'No ride today: poor old Mariana so lame that I brought her back from Harley St. I fear very much she is "for it" this time' and shortly before her euthanasia she became 'the old dear'.[72] He described her last ride thus: 'Mariana takes her last ride to HP [Hyde Park]: to Lancaster Gate (Victoria G[ate]) and back: poor dear, she's done.'[73] Mariana was killed the following Saturday by his friend. Describing the event dramatically in his diary 'Mariana's zero hour: 9 am.' He commented on the preceding week thus: 'Mariana was part of my life, how much I didn't fully know until this week.'[74] He also recorded his grief towards the death of his subsequent horse, Trump: 'Trump was taken at 9 am: he went quietly into the Horse Box. By now he will be where the good horses go. R.I.P. I've shed more tears over "Trump" than I've done over many humans.'[75]

Laurance Holman is probably the only writer discussed here who is solely writing for himself. Thus there can be initials or abbreviations to refer to individuals since he did not need to differentiate between 'external' and 'personal', events were intertwined as being equally important to him. He used the diaries to reflect back on earlier years and to constantly sift for personally significant events to record.

Conclusion

In these four examples, the diarists and letter writer were including events extrinsically (as well as intrinsically) important. As Walter Benjamin put it, 'A chronicler who recites events without distinguishing between major and minor ones acts in accordance with the following truth: nothing that had ever happened should be regarded as lost for history.'[76] The lives of Bob, Muff, Mariana, Trump, Sol and Mr Murphy were directly affected by the war on the Home Front: so too were the lives of Gwladys, Fryn, Nella and Laurance. Their relationships were a product of that particular moment. As Gwladys Cox noted of Bob, her tabby cat, 'He was our constant companion and consolation in all our war-time trials'.[77] Speaking of contradictory views, a young man interviewed in August 1941 said, 'Well, I know dogs are unpopular nowadays. I know when I had mine some people were downright rude to me. And it's grown worse lately. It's foolish really. Probably dogs do more to uphold morale among their owners than anything else.'[78]

James Serpell has argued that humans use animals as alternative sources of social support, and benefit emotionally and physically from this.[79] These examples from the past seem to confirm this. Some scholars working within Animal Studies seek to go further by rejecting human-centred worldviews, 'an aim [is] to move away from humanist theoretical conceptions of the world'.[80] These accounts of the war on the Home Front are not just 'about' humans but are animal-centred too. For historians, 'It is the choices historians make that define the parameters of their studies and this gives them a great responsibility. They are, in relation to their own society, guardians of sound knowledge of the past, and in relation to past societies, instrumental in making sure that justice is done.'[81] If we choose to start thinking in different ways about the Home Front during the Second World War then contemporary diaries and letters may be a useful starting point for acknowledging the, as yet largely unspoken, role of non-human animals at that time. The experience of war changed all living beings – and also the relationships between them.

Notes

1. A. Calder (1992) *The People's War* and *The Myth of the Blitz*. For discussion of turning 'the home front into a fighting front' see R. Overy (2013) *The Bombing War*, p 127–130.
2. See P. Ward-Jackson (2003) *Public Sculpture of the City of London*, pp 392–394; P. Ward-Jackson (2011) *Public Sculpture of Historic Westminster*, pp 428–432; Andrews. M. with Bagot-Jewitt. C. and Hunt. N. (2011) *Lest we Forget*, http://www.stairwaytoheavenmemorial.org/ (accessed 27 October 2013).
3. Overy (2013) *The Bombing War*, p 128.
4. See 'These are temporary parents', *Daily Express*, 2 September 1939, p 16; and *Daily Mirror* 4 September 1939, p 6.
5. S. Isaacs (ed.) (1941) *The Cambridge Evacuation Survey*, pp 68–70.
6. D. Burlingham and A. Freud (1942) *Young Children in War-time*, p 6.
7. For discussion of the responses to the sinking of the Arrandora Star, see for example, W. Ugolini (2011) *Experiencing War*.

8. C. Perry (1974) *Boy in the Blitz*, p 13.
9. Photocopy of letter dated 21 September 1940 to Miss Beryl Myatt, Imperial War Museum archives, 05/56/1.
10. P. Ziegler's (1995) popular *London at War 1939–45* (London: Mandarin Paperbacks) features many animals in the text but no references in the index. Similarly F. Partridge (1999) *A Pacifist's War Diaries 1939–1945*, Volume 1 (London: Phoenix, reissued 2009); R. Scott (ed.) (2011) *The Real Dad's Army*; S. Garfield (2005) *We are at War. The remarkable diaries of five ordinary people and extra-ordinary times* (London: Ebury Press).
11. R. Broad and S. Fleming (eds) (1981) *Nella Last's War*
12. R. Broad and S. Fleming (1981) *Nella Last's War*, p.251.
13. R. Broad and S. Fleming (1981) *Nella Last's War*.
14. It was subsequently neatly re-written, though apparently not edited, and donated to the Imperial War Museum.
15. The Laurance Holman diaries from 1937–1950 (with the omission of part of 1939) were donated to the Camden Archives.
16. E. Fudge (2008) *Pets*, p 20; see too, S. Swart (2010) *Riding High. Horses, Humans and History in South Africa* (Johannesburg: Wits University Press).
17. N. Taylor (2013) *Humans, Animals, and Society*, p 18.
18. F. Tennyson Jesse and H. M. Harwood (1940) *London Front*, (Harwood was her husband). F. Tennyson Jesse (1974) *A Pin to see the Peepshow* (London: Virago) (first published 1934).
19. A short film made in collaboration with Harry Watt and Pat Jackson. See K. Jackson, *Humphrey Jennings*, pp 211, 220–223.
20. E. Kirby and A. Moss (1947) *Animals Were There*, pp 18–19; J. Clabby (1963) *A History of the Royal Army Veterinary Corps*, p 41.
21. G. Cox, 'Unpublished wartime diary', (15 September 1939) Imperial War Museum 86/46/1.
22. State initiated killing of animals did take place in areas subject to forced evacuation orders. See for example Rodney Foster in Sussex. Scott, (2011) *The Real Dad's Army*, p 36.
23. The diaries of Laurance Holman are missing the second part of 1939. Cox and Tennyson Jesse refer to the killing – as do others.
24. The figure of 400,000 accounts for about 26 per cent of cats and dogs in London. The *Veterinary Record* estimated in Greater London alone there were 73,000 horses, cattle, sheep and pigs and 2,000,000 dogs and cats. See 'Animals and ARPs', *Veterinary Record* (19 August 1939) p 1011.
25. See H. Kean 'The changing human–feline relationship in Britain c.1900–1950', Paper given to ISAZ University of Cambridge, July 2012. http://www.youtube.com/watch?v=YFHFg41dS-Y
26. R1418 male 87, widower, Summer directive 2009, Animals and Humans, Mass Observation Archive, University of Sussex.
27. Mrs Croucher, in E. Hostettler (ed.) (1990) *The Island at War: Memories of War-time Life on the Isle of Dogs, East London* (London: Island History Trust) p 31.
28. M.W. 'Cats at Home', *The Cat*, Cats' Protection League, September 1939, p 67.
29. A. A. Steward, 'The Secretary's Comments', *The Cat*, September 1940, p 131.
30. G. Cox-Ife, Editorial, *Cats and Kittens: The Magazine for Every Cat-lover*, April 1944, p 1.

31. See critique of diary-keeping by Australian historian, Manning Clark, by Mark McKenna. M. McKenna (2011) *An Eye for Eternity: The Life of Manning Clark*, (Melbourne: Melbourne University Press).

32. See C. Feely (2010) 'From Dialetics to Dancing', pp 91–110; T. Brennan (2000) 'History, Family, History', pp 37–50; M. Tebbutt (2012) *Being Boys*.

33. See J. Hinton (2013) *The Mass Observers*.

34. H. D. Millgate (ed.) (1998) *Mr Brown's War*, p 271.

35. *Mr Brown*, 8 August 1942, p 148.

36. G. Cox, Diary, 9 December 1939.

37. Tennyson Jesse and Harwood, *London Front*, p 287.

38. Tennyson Jesse and Harwood, *London Front*, p 287.

39. Mass Observation Archive. http://www.massobs.org.uk/original_massobservation_project.htm accessed 1 September 2013.

40. D. Brantz (ed.) (2010) *Beastly Natures*, p 10.

41. E. Fudge (2002) 'A Left-handed Blow', p 6.

42. H. Kean (2012) 'Challenges for Historians', pp s57–s72.

43. H. Kean (2012) 'Challenges for Historians'.

44. G. Cox, foreword to diary.

45. G. Cox, 5 September 1939.

46. G. Cox, entries for 22 January 1942, 20 February 1943, 2 February 1942, 24 December 1942.

47. Cox, 2 October 1940.

48. Tennyson Jesse, *London Front*, letter 12 June 1940, pp. 426–427.

49. Because of petrol rationing, traffic regulations preventing horse-drawn vehicles from central London were rescinded and the number of working horses increased. J. N. P. Watson (1990) *Horse and Carriage*, p 65; J. Bellamy (1975) *Hyde Park*, pp 99–103.

50. Holman used pre-war diaries starting mid-year and then changed in 1940 to a January–December version. Holman regularly fed the cats in the stables and seemed to be aware of animals' presence.

51. Entry for 31 August 1939: cited in File Report 621, p 11.

52. Broad and Fleming (1981) *Nella Last's War*, entry for 4 May 1940, p 43. She also noticed birds and bird song, for example 4 May 1941, p 131.

53. Tennyson Jesse (1940) *London Front*, letter 4 October 1939, p 67.

54. Tennyson Jesse (1940) *London Front*, letter 16 October 1939, p 106.

55. Tennyson Jesse (1940) *London Front*, letter 4 October 1939, p 70.

56. G. Cox, 14 December 1940. Cox described the work of local animal activist Miss Clara Lowenthal in 'hunting London' for specific stray animals: 'in fair weather and in foul, we have met her on her way to help some animal in distress – now to trace a lost dog with glass splinters in its paws, now to report to the coal merchant that some brute had flogged his horse unmercifully ... ', Cox, 26 January 1943, 7 September 1943.

57. G. Cox, 21 November 1941.

58. M 20 C Hendon JS 27 /8/41 TC 79 /1E, Mass Observation Archives.

59. Mill Hill F 40 C 11/7/41 TC 79 /1E, Mass Observation Archives.

60. *The Cat*, November 1939, p 16.

61. G. Cox, 25 February, 1 March, 3 March 1944. This retrieval was not unique. Such animal rescues even merited inclusion in quasi-official accounts. F. R. Lewey (1944) *Cockney Campaign*, p 93; See also C. Demarne (1980) *The London Blitz*, p 65.

62. This is also reflected in the rather sentimental account by a novelist A. G. Rosman (1941) *Nine Lives*, pp 165–166.
63. Foreword to G. Cox diaries, written retrospectively.
64. N. Last, 10 November 1942, pp 216–217.
65. M. Bekoff (2007) *The Emotional Lives*, p 19.
66. J. Bradshaw (2013) *Cat Sense*, p 191.
67. Male Euston 45 D, Dogs in Wartime, TC1/B, Mass Observation Archives.
68. L. Holman, Unpublished diaries, Wednesday 16 October 1940.
69. L. Holman, Friday 18 October 1940.
70. Pegasus (1948) *Horse Talks*, pp 25–30.
71. L. Holman, 2 December 1942. See Kate Dashper 'The Elusiveness of "Feel" in the Horse–Human Relationship: Communication, Harmony and Understanding', Paper presented at Cosmopolitan Animals conference, Institute of English Studies, University of London, 26 October 2012.
72. L. Holman, Wed 10 June 1942; 26 September 1942. Mariana had become lame but Holman persevered with veterinary treatment and he resumed riding with her in March 1942 although her lame condition returned.
73. L. Holman, 25 October 1942.
74. L. Holman, 31 October 1942 and comment for preceding week.
75. L. Holman, 9 May 1947.
76. W. Benjamin (1970) 'Theses on the Philosophy of History', pp 247–249.
77. Foreword to G. Cox, Diary.
78. M20 C 27 /8/41 Dogs in War Time TC 79/1/E, Mass Observation Archives.
79. J. Serpell (2005) 'People in Disguise', p 132.
80. N. Taylor (2013) *Humans, Animals, and Society*, p 159.
81. J. Kalela (2011) *Making History*, p 24. See also, H. Kean and P. Martin (2013) *The Public History Reader*.

References

Andrews. M with Bagot-Jewitt. C. and Hunt. N. (eds) (2011) *Lest we Forget. Remembrance and Commemoration* (Stroud: History Press).
Bekoff. M (2007) *The Emotional Lives of Animals* (Novato, California: New World Library).
Bellamy. J (1975) *Hyde Park for Horsemanship* (London: J A Allen).
Benjamin. W (1970) 'Theses on the Philosophy of History', in H Arendt. (ed.), *Illuminations* (London: Cape).
Bradshaw. J (2013) *Cat Sense: The Feline Enigma Revealed* (London: Allen Lane).
Brantz. D (ed.) (2010) *Beastly Natures. Animals, Humans, and the Study of History* (Charlottesville VA: University of Virginia Press).
Brennan. T (2000) 'History, family, history', in H Kean, P Martin. and S Morgan. (eds), *Seeing History. Public History in Britain Now* (London: Francis Boutle) pp 37–50.
Broad. R and Fleming. S (eds) (1981) *Nella Last's War* (Bristol: Falling Wall Press).
Burlingham. D and Freud. A (1942) *Young Children in War-time: A Year's Work in a Residential War Nursery* (London: Allen and Unwin).
Calder. A (1992a) *The People's War, Britain 1939–45*, New Edition (London: Pimlico).
Calder. A (1992b) *The Myth of the Blitz*, New Edition (London: Pimlico).

Clabby. J (1963) *A History of the Royal Army Veterinary Corps 1919–61* (London: J. A. Allen).

Demarne. C (1980) *The London Blitz: A Fireman's Tale* (London: Parents' Centre Publications).

Feely. C (2010) 'From Dialetics to Dancing: Reading, Writing and the Experience of Everyday Life in the Diaries of Frank P Forster', *History Workshop Journal*, 69, pp 91–110.

Fudge. E (2002) 'A Left-handed blow: Writing the History of Animals', in N Rothfels. (ed.), *Representing Animals* (Bloomington, IN: Indiana University Press) pp 3–18.

Fudge. E (2008) *Pets* (Stocksfield: Acumen).

Hinton. J (2013) *The Mass Observers. A History 1937–1949* (Oxford: Oxford University Press).

Hostettler. E (1990) (ed.) *The Island at War: Memories of War-time Life on the Isle of Dogs, East London* (London: Island History Trust).

Isaacs. S (ed.) 1941 *The Cambridge Evacuation Survey* (London: Methuen & Co).

Jackson. K (2004) *Humphrey Jennings* (London: Picador).

Kalela. J (2011) *Making History: The Historian and Uses of the Past* (Basingstoke: Palgrave Macmillan).

Kean. H (2012) 'Challenges for Historians Writing Animal–Human History. What is really enough?', *Anthrozoos 25th Anniversary Supplement Issues in Anthrozoology*, pp 57–72.

Kean. H and Martin. P (2013) *The Public History Reader* (Abingdon: Routledge).

Kirby. E and Moss. A (1947) *Animals Were There. A Record of the Work of the RSPCA During the War of 1939–1945* (London: Hutchinson).

Lewey. F R (1944) *Cockney Campaign* (London: Stanley Paul and Co).

McKenna. M (2011) *An Eye for Eternity: The Life of Manning Clark* (Melbourne: Melbourne University Press).

Millgate. H D (ed.) (1998) *Mr Brown's War: A Diary of the Second World War* (Stroud: Sutton Publishing).

Overy. R (2013) *The Bombing War. Europe 1939–1945* (London: Allen Lane).

Pegasus. (1948) *Horse Talks: A Vade-Mecum for Young Riders* (London: Collins).

Perry. C (1974) *Boy in the Blitz. The 1940 Diary of Colin Perry* (London: Corgi).

Rosman. A G (1941) *Nine Lives. A Cat of London in Peace and War* (New York: G.P. Putnam's Sons).

Scott. R (ed.) (2011) *The Real Dad's Army. The War Diaries of Col. Rodney Foster* (London: Pension).

Serpell. J (2005) 'People in Disguise. Anthropology and the Human–Pet Relationship', in L Daston. and G Mitman. (eds), *Thinking with Animals. New Perspectives on Anthropomorphism* (New York: Columbia University Press).

Taylor. N (2013) *Humans, Animals, and Society: An Introduction to Human–Animal Studies* (New York: Lantern Books).

Tebbutt. M (2012) *Being Boys* (Manchester: Manchester University Press).

Tennyson. Jesse F and Harwood. H M (1940) *London Front. Letters Written to America, August 1939–July 1940* (London: Constable).

Ugolini. W (2011) *Experiencing War as the 'Enemy Other': Italian Scottish Experience in World War II* (Manchester: Manchester University Press).

Ward-Jackson. P (2003) *Public Sculpture of the City of London* (Liverpool: Liverpool University Press).

Ward-Jackson. P (2011) *Public Sculpture of Historic Westminster*, Volume 1 (Liverpool: Liverpool University Press).

Watson. J N P (1990) *Horse and Carriage: The Pageant of Hyde Park* (London: Sportsman's Press).

10
The Weak and the Wicked: Non-conscripted Masculinities in 1940s British Cinema

Paul Elliott

Introduction

The BBC series *Dad's Army* (1968–1977) was a classic of the British sitcom. Often cited as an exemplar of comic form and characterisation it also, as Jeffrey Richards details, existed as a quasi-mythical vision of a Golden age of Englishness, where 'a nation of eccentric individualists could be blended together to defend the country in wartime'.[1] In this chapter, however, I want to suggest that, underneath the jokes, the men of *Dad's Army* shed light on what was a very real problem for filmmakers in the war itself: how to depict non-enlisted, non-conscripted males and, at the same time, aid in the war effort. Privates Jones, Pike and Walker especially (as the pensioner, the mummy's boy and the spiv) represented, as Summerfield and Peniston-Bird convincingly detail, reoccurring and preformed versions of non-conscripted masculinity that also appeared time and time again in British wartime narrative cinema.[2] They directly mirrored character types that provided a noticeable counterpoint to the more dominant hegemonic versions of mythic maleness proliferated by mainstream and government-sanctioned culture. Here I want to concentrate mainly on popular narrative cinema (drama and comedy) rather than either documentary or newsreels, as throughout the war the latter forms were noticeably more varied in their depictions of masculinity, although the line between what was fictional and what was fact was continually blurred.

In 1942, at the height of the war, there were around 15,000,000 males between the ages of 14 and 64 registered as British subjects. Of these 3,784,000 were in the armed and auxiliary services leaving 11,216,000 (almost three times as many) male civilians working and fighting on the Home Front.[3] Most of these men worked in the engineering and building trades but transportation, shipping and the railways provided a constant source of employment throughout the conflict. The figures here, provided by the Government after the war, do not include the influx of men from the various parts of Europe – from France, from Poland, from Germany – and neither, of course, does it include servicemen and military personnel who were stationed in Britain itself.

Escalations in male conscription during 1941 drastically affected the country's workforce and heightened the sense of a nation being slowly drained of its able-bodied men. Angus Calder cites one labour manager as saying 'Men over sixty and even over seventy. Men taken from non-essential work. Women and girls from all sorts of jobs and from no job at all. Cripples, weak hearts, discharged servicemen, halfwits, criminals, all sorts of people so long as they can stand or even sit and turn a handle. These are our material.'[4] However, most of the labour shortages were in areas outside of direct war work (especially those that provided civilian goods and services) and even by Calder's conservative estimates, two-thirds of the male population were still in Britain, still on the Home Front, challenging the myth that it was a feminine space peopled by women and the 'left-overs' of masculinity.[5]

The early (and much maligned) propaganda film *The Lion Has Wings* (1939) is one of the few British wartime films to specifically depict masculinity on the Home Front. Aside from the fairly recognisable characterisations of upper-class airmen, aircrew and female war workers, audiences were also presented with images of the millions of men it took to keep the British war machine fighting. Here, in the opening sections of the film are scores of fit, intelligent-looking aircraft workers, miners, engineers, steel workers, railway men, mathematicians, draftsmen, builders and foundry men, none of whom conform to the dominant image of the non-enlisted wartime male as someone who failed the call-up or who languished in reserved occupations. Aside from documentary representation, such willingness to depict the full variety of non-conscripted maleness becomes noticeably weaker as the war progresses. I want to suggest here that this elision of a vast portion of the masculine wartime public was not only supported by the majority of British fiction films but formed part of the mythical construction of the People's War and consequently the Home Front. It was in the country's interest to proliferate an image of non-hegemonic masculinity that reached an apogee in *Dad's Army* and that still has never quite been challenged.

Hegemonic masculinity

War galvanises masculinity. What it means to be a man, or rather what it means to be manly, is culturally distilled before being mobilised through official and unofficial channels and blended with concepts of what it means to be a good citizen. Conflict also affects the range of masculine possibilities, so that what was permissible in peacetime is often seen as both unmanly and, by extension, unpatriotic in war. As Leo Braudy states in relation to First World War: 'In the diffuseness of peacetime, different masculinities might be indulged, but in war military masculinity [is] the core of national cohesiveness, and, not coincidentally, the essence of defining us against *them*.'[6] Naturally, hegemonic images of masculinity in wartime become irreducibly connected to the armed forces and to the various historical and cultural narratives that support them; evocations of mythical manliness seek to create continuity between successful conflicts of the past and the present, and the feminine is often seen as a luxury that, *perhaps*, can one day be returned to. In times of mass communication the media has a vital role to play in this process and can be used both to shape and ultimately to trace the shifts in gender construction.

World War Two was no exception. As Sonya O. Rose has argued, it was a time when British hegemonic masculinity was constructed using two, seemingly contradictory, images of manliness: 'the temperate hero' who provided a more humane alternative to the perceived hyper-masculinity of the German male, and a 'soldier hero' who represented a form of ordinary valour in the face of overwhelming physical danger.[7] These two versions of masculinity were, as Rose details, intimately connected to the larger strategy of opposing the perceived characteristics of the Nazi party with a British sensibility that was *both* chivalrous and homely. If the soldier hero presented an image of the stoic British bulldog, then the temperate hero presented one of the warm family man who could play with his children and miss his wife as well as fight on the front line. Some of this sense was explored by J.B. Priestley in his famous radio broadcast of Sunday 9 June 1940:

> The Nazis understand – and it is their great secret – all the contempt-
> ible qualities of men. They have a lightening eye for an opponent's
> weakness. But what they don't understand, because there's nothing
> in their nature or experience to tell them, is that men also have their
> hour of greatness, when weakness suddenly towers into strength,
> when easy-going tolerant men rise in their anger and strike down evil
> like the angels of the wrath of God.[8]

This image appears time and time again in the cinema of the era. In films like *Went the Day Well?* (1942), *Millions Like Us* (1943) and *The Bells Go Down* (1943) it is possible to detect the mixture of the warrior spirit and the homely father that Rose describes as being 'cobbled together ... from aspects of both anti-heroic and heroic forms of masculinity.'[9] Andrew Spicer also details how the war mobilised a specific form of cinematic hero that was characterised by his 'unexceptional ordinariness'. Such heroic images can be seen to have been concretised in the performances of a range of different actors from John Mills to Tommy Trinder.[10]

The images that form the basic store of manliness in any given period are always surrounded by a series of dialectically positioned traits and characteristics. The Home Front, especially as it was depicted in wartime cinema, was a place where masculinity was both questioned and upheld and representations of non-conscripted males (i.e. those not in the services) were a perennial problem for British filmmakers eager to aid in the war effort but also to offer narratives that were set at home. It is worth pausing for a moment here to revisit the concept of hegemony especially as it relates to gender and sexuality. For Antonio Gramsci, hegemony was the process by which subaltern populations and groups are suppressed and ruled by dominant ones. Hegemony then does not merely refer to the dominant mode *per se* but to the mechanism through which it assumes its dominance on what Gramsci terms 'the domain of contradictions'.[11] The hegemonic power or image not only accepts oppositions and contradictions but thrives upon them, as long as they never usurp it. The dominant group is also in constant development and revolution; it has superseded previous regimes and will, itself, be superseded eventually. Taking an idea from Marx's 'Preface to a *Critique of the Political Economy*' of 1859, Gramsci also makes the prescient point that these competing modes and ideologies are formed long before they materialise in a given culture. Hegemonic dominance does not happen overnight, it draws upon familiar ideas and cultural images that are already in existence, sometimes reinventing them, sometimes reviving them.

This last point is particularly important for our topic here because both the dominant and the subaltern images of British wartime masculinity were in existence long before the war began. They were not invented by a propaganda machine but were instead part of a continually moving field that stretched back to the 1920s and before. Raymond Williams' notions of 'residual' and 'emergent' cultures describe neatly the tectonic shifting of masculine modes in this period, as residues of older masculine images were redeployed to aid in the war effort.[12] Films like 1941's *Love on the Dole* and Humphrey Jennings' *The Silent Village* (1943) are as much concerned with pre- and post-war Britain as with the period 1939 to 1945 and the same can be said of its depiction of masculinity.

Here I would like to examine three 'versions' of non-enlisted masculinity that repeatedly occur in fictional British wartime cinema – the pensioner, the mummy's boy and the spiv – and make specific reference to three films of the period: *The Life and Death of Colonel Blimp* (1943), *Band Waggon* (1940) and *Waterloo Road* (1945). As stated earlier, there are direct lines to be drawn between these films and representations in later cultural texts like *Dad's Army*, suggesting, I hope, that these three character-types were not contingent or accidental, but formed an integral part of what many writers have conceived of as the myth of the People's War.[13]

Jones – or, the Pensioner

The image of the Home Guard as a collection of old men and outsiders did not begin in 1968 with *Dad's Army*, as Angus Calder writes:

> The Old Sweat of the First World War was known to refuse to drill, to refuse to accept responsibility, or to get hoity-toity when he found he had to share a rifle with two (or perhaps ten) other Volunteers. One swore irreverently that its zone commander had been tended personally by Florence Nightingale in the Crimean War; but the press concluded that the oldest L.D.V. [Local Defense Volunteer] was probably a former regimental sergeant major from Crieff, in Perthshire, who had first seen action in the Egyptian Campaign of 1884–85.[14]

This image not only suggests a distillation of the character of Private Jones but also what his character-type represented for surrounding notions of masculinity. Like Jones, the 'Old Sweat' of the Home Guard was a residual mode of maleness that stretched back to colonial and therefore simpler forms of warfare. It was not simply a case that these particular old men differed in degree from modern hegemonic masculinity, they differed in type: their frames of reference, particularly of course in relation to the fighting, were not only outmoded (as with, for instance, Powell and Pressberger's *The Life and Death of Colonel Blimp*), they dangerously underestimated the current situation.

J.B. Priestley's Postscript of Sunday 16 June 1940 is instructive here. Priestley likens the L.D.V to the shepherds and woodsmen of 'Thomas Hardy's fiction in which his rustics meet in the gathering darkness on some Wessex hillside.' He then goes on to draw parallels between the

Napoleonic wars of Hardy's boyhood and the present day conflict, concluding that 'all this raiding and threat of invasion, though menacing and dangerous enough, was not some horror big enough to split the world – but merely our particular testing time; what *we* must face, as our forefathers faced such things...'[15] By the middle of the war, this position was becoming untenable and the sense that the rules of war had changed drastically, and that Britain had also to change, was gaining prominence.

The Home Guard however formed only one of the residual narratives that surrounded depictions of ageing men in wartime films. The music hall provided a stable of comic male characters that would be deployed throughout the period; uppermost in this was the image of the 'old codger', enshrined in performers like Frank Randle, Will Hay, Moore Marriott and Robb Wilton. British cinema had a long tradition of borrowing from music hall and variety theatre, and production companies such as Butchers and Mancunian regularly plundered the popular stage for their performers. The translation of stage act to screen was often a simple one and the films of character actors like Frank Randle and Arthur Lucan (Old Mother Riley) are often passed over by film criticism because of this. However, as Richards and Sheridan state, these cheaply made comedies and melodramas were hugely popular and their stars were big draws in their day.[16]

Will Hay's characters in films such as *The Goose Steps Out* (1942) and *The Black Sheep of Whitehall* (1942) provided a more nuanced depiction of non-hegemonic masculinity than any of those in *Dad's Army*. Hay's characters were satires on class and pretention as well as age and stretched far back into a career that began in 1914 after he joined Karno's Speechless Comedians.[17] Hay's career was built on the subtle and gentle satirising of the bourgeoisie – the pretentious but ultimately ignorant schoolteacher, the inept barrister or the unorganised fire chief. His characters had social power but they were out of control and it's easy to see what they would have meant for music hall audiences during the privations of the inter-war period. Throughout his life, Hay played characters that were far older than he was himself and they were as inept as they were middle aged. Hay's wartime films placed him firmly on the Home Front as he assumed roles in reserved occupations like policemen, firemen and schoolmaster (teacher and schoolmaster were covered in the Schedule of Reserved Occupations of 1938). Even without Moore Marriott to accentuate the problems of age, Hay's characters were always men out of their time: Captain Benjamin Viking of *Where's That Fire?* 1940) more closely reflected Priestley's Hardyesque collection of rural mechanicals than the technologically advanced fire service they found themselves up against; and William Potts in *The Goose Steps Out* recycled Hay's familiar character from the film *Boys Will Be Boys*, initially released in 1935.

Hay's masculinity is certainly outside of the wartime hegemonic norm and clearly represents a residual mode that stretches back to the 1920s and 30s. However this residue was redeployed by filmmakers and producers and gleefully consumed by a cinema-going public wary of the kind of red tape and small minded bureaucracy that threatened British action in the 'phoney war' years of 1939 and 1940. In the People's War it was upper middle-class males who were viewed with the most suspicion, most particularly intellectuals who fell outside of the twin images of the temperate hero and the warrior spirit. Mass Observation cites a surveyor who, in 1942, suggested that Sir Stafford Cripps might be 'too closely surrounded with "bright" intellectuals to provide popular appeal' for most people and, as Rose details, the links between intellectualism and dangerous pacifism were seen as almost inevitable.[18] Perhaps because of this, Hay's brand of humour, that pricked the fragile bubble of bourgeois pretence, proved hugely popular throughout the war.

The most noticeable ageing character however throughout the war was that of Colonel Blimp. Created by David Low in the 1930s in a series of cartoons for the London Evening Standard, Colonel Blimp was not strictly non-enlisted (he was after all a Colonel) however there are obvious parallels between Blimp and characters like Private Jones and Captain Mainwaring.

Powell and Pressberger's character of Clive Wynne-Candy both draws, and departs, from Low's cartoons. Wynne-Candy is satirical *and* sympathetic and, again, represents the combination of age and class in transition. The narrative of *The Life and Death of Colonel Blimp* compares the successive military campaigns of the Crimea, the First, and then the Second World War, finding in these conflicts a manifestation of an increasingly precarious position regarding the British sense of fair play and mannered civility. Both in the cartoon and in the film, Blimp is contrasted with the ideological needs of total war. The statesmen-like gentility of nineteenth century conflicts (and, to a lesser extent, the First World War) has no place in a war characterised by mass extermination doodlebugs and Nazism. Throughout the film, Wynne-Candy comes to realise that he is an anachronism, a fact that he (and the film) sees as regrettable but necessary.

The Life and Death of Colonel Blimp can be considered in terms of it positioning in the conflict, coming after the phoney war but before wha

Churchill euphemistically termed 'the rough and tumble of D Day'.[19] In February 1942, the House of Commons debated what Frederick Pethick Lawrence called 'Blimpery in all fields of life'.[20] It is obvious from this discussion that Blimp represented something fundamental in terms of masculinity to British society and moreover something that the authorities wanted to distance themselves from. Sir Stafford Cripps ends the debate with the resounding phrase that they should bury the 'the late and not lamented Colonel Blimp' forever. As Rattigan discusses, Powell and Pressberger's depiction of Blimp is less condemnatory than might be suggested from this exchange.[21] There *is* nostalgia in their characterisation, a nostalgia that is only heightened by the dreaminess of the technicolour cinematography; however there is also regret that contemporary politics has forced humanity to abandon the values it once had and that once meant so much. Clive Wynne-Candy is, like Private Jones, a relic of simpler wars that were characterised by colonial might and a comforting geographical distance. Throughout the film he comes to realise this but it is a truth that contemporary audiences on the Home Front would have been well aware of; in fact this image appears in other films of the period most noticeably the Chelsea pensioners in Carol Reed's *The Way Ahead* (1944) who offer advice and criticism in equal measure whilst sitting on the sidelines.

British wartime cinema's depiction of ageing masculinity skirts the line between propaganda and satire. Clive Wynne-Candy's foolishness is more than mere folly, it is a dangerous naiveté in the face of total war and the Nazis' industrial military complex. It is difficult in this dismissal of ageing maleness not to see a reflection of the public attitude towards Neville Chamberlain who, despite being only five years older than Churchill, was always associated in the public mind with age and privilege. Sonya O. Rose, for example quotes an article in the *Picture Post* that frames this in no uncertain terms:

> Above all the leaders [of Britain] must be men. For the last twenty years they have been a lot of old women. The Old Woman Democracy of Neville Chamberlain, John Simon and Samuel Hoare has got to give way to the Leader Democracy of such men as Churchill, Duff Cooper, Bevin, Morrison and Amery.[22]

What is interesting here is the cross-party nature of this list. What is being suggested as a panacea for the country in 1940 is not political (Churchill, Duff Cooper and Amery were Conservatives, Bevin and Morrison, Labour) neither was it based in class but linked inevitably to the hegemonic vision of masculinity.

Pike – or, the Stupid Boy

In his extensive study of masculinity in British cinema, Andrew Spicer isolates two 'alternative masculinities' in wartime film, the Fool and the Rogue. As Spicer details, these not only existed outside of the usual hegemonic boundaries but also had a relationship with each other; for every fool there was a rogue and for every rogue a well-meaning fool. Spicer's conception of the wartime Fool posits a continuum between characters played by the likes of George Formby, Will Hay and The Crazy Gang and the Shakespearian jester who possess licence to prick the pretensions of the King because '[a]s Fools or Rogues, they battle ... the pompous, the pretentious, the bullies and the kill joys.'[23]

This is a liberating image and it certainly has validity, the characters played by Frank Randle, Arthur Lucan or George Formby can all be read against the concept of the carnivalesque that Andy Medhurst asserts is endemic within the music hall tradition.[24] Their drunkenness, stupidity, ignorance and downright doltishness were, in their own right, a liberating force from the constraints of wartime austerity. At the end of George Formby's *Let George Do It!* (1940) for example, Formby is famously depicted punching Hitler after first hailing him mid-sentence with the line 'Oi windbag!' It was a sequence that Mass Observation detailed as being the most popular in the film and was one only a fool could carry off. [25]

The foolish however, although undesirable, are not necessarily unmanly and in wartime cinema the masculine hegemony is re-enforced by other, more subaltern images. Arthur Askey played a series of foolish characters throughout his career, beginning in the concert parties of the First World War and cutting his teeth in variety and music hall. Big Hearted Arthur was a huge success in the radio series *Band Waggon*, which ran from 1938 to 1940. *Band Waggon* displays elements of variety theatre rooted in the 1930s and heralds the emergence of a new form of zanier Marx Brothers-inspired comedy that would find its natural apotheosis in *Round the Horne* and *The Goon Show* in the 1950s and 1960s. Askey starred in eight wartime films and in all but two (*King Arthur was a Gentleman* (1942) and *Bees in Paradise* (1944)) he plays non-enlisted parts. Askey's size and cheerfulness alone placed him outside of traditional notions of manliness but, as Robert Murphy outlines, in his early films especially there is also an effeminacy that is gradually abandoned throughout the war:

> In *Band Waggon* 'Stinker' [Richard Murdoch] and 'Big' [Arthur Askey] are to all intents and purposes a gay couple. [In one scene] Askey

puts a bolster between them when they have to share a bed in the castle, but the clanking of the ghost (Moore Marriott) soon has them clutching each other in terror.[26]

Murphy goes on to describe how subsequent films re-negotiate the relationship between Askey and Murdoch, lessening the suggestion that both are un-conscripted through reasons other than occupation. In two of their next three films (*Charley's (Big-Hearted) Aunt* (1940) and *I Thank You* (1941)) the hint of homoerotism is neatly avoided through Askey's cross-dressing that nods towards pantomime and female impersonators such as Arthur Lucan and Robb Wilton. In *The Ghost Train* (1941), as Murphy states, Murdoch takes a much more traditional male lead and is clearly a counterpoint to Askey's effeminate childishness.

Askey's characters are, like Private Pike, Mummy's boys; their relationship to women is child-like with very little of the shy proto-sexuality of George Formby. If the latter acts like a teenager on a first date, the former acts like a toddler, blissfully unaware of the inappropriateness of his behaviour and his inability to acknowledge the charms of women. In *Back Room Boy* (1942) Askey begins the film in a relationship with a woman but this is soon lost and he travels to a lighthouse to escape women forever; in *Miss London Ltd* (1943) he traverses a whole agency full of beautiful women without a hint of the sexual interplay that would undoubtedly characterise a Formby or a Frank Randle film.

Crucially Askey's characters are mostly depicted living on the Home Front. However this is never overtly thematised as it is with many comedy films of the period where non-enlistment becomes a barrier to be overcome and, more often than not, also a way of getting the girl. It might be tempting to view Askey as a manifestation of a country's desire for the carnivalesque but it is just as possible to view this as yet another playing out of non-hegemonic masculinity. Even when Arthur is called up (in 1942 and 1944) his status is more platoon mascot than serious soldier or airman. The ideological subtext of this is clear: children and fools have no place in a man's army.

The seminal moment for the Askey character however comes in *Back-Room Boy* (1942), as Arthur Pilbeam makes his way to carry out the important war work which is described initially as 'terribly important' and having 'millions depend on him'. After a series of scenes designed to inflate the importance of his employment, it is revealed to be nothing more taxing than the pressing of a button that provides the pips for the World Service clock. Arthur is a pipsqueak himself and so it makes sense that his role in the war should be reduced to providing such insignificant noises. Although there is an attempt at a romantic storyline with Betty,

Arthur's closest relationship in the film is with Jane the young evacuee, played by Vera Frances, who acts as a surrogate sibling that only serves to accentuate his own childishness. In the final scenes, Arthur's emasculation becomes complete as Betty is given his job and, despite getting the girl for once, Arthur runs off holding Jane's hand rather than Betty's, a suggestion that he is more at home with the sexless children than the sexy adults.

Walker – or, the Spiv

Robert Murphy first identified the cycle of films that detailed the figure of the spiv.[27] The spiv skirted the borderline between legality and criminality and experienced a brief popularity in the films of post-war austerity Britain. As Peter Wollen points out, their initial characterisation was dark, drawing from Film Noir but given a distinctly British sheen.[28] By the late 1950s and 1960s however, depictions of the spiv had solidified into the comic and a long line of gaudy suited, trilby wearing wide boys from Max Miller, through Flash Harry to Private Walker denuded and declawed what were originally deeply ambiguous examples of maleness. Although linked to rationing and wartime shortages, the spiv only really makes his presence known in cinema after 1945. The 'spiv cycle' begins with Gainsborough's *Waterloo Road* (1945), although Wollen makes a convincing case that Clifford Odets' film *None but the Lonely Heart* (1944) predates it by a year. It is however only with films like *Appointment with Crime* (1946), *Dancing with Crime* (1947), *Brighton Rock* (1947) and *They Made Me a Fugitive* (1947) that the genre really begins to take shape.

The social and cultural position of the spiv in the post-war period has been covered neatly by writers like Murphy and Wollen, however as David Hughes suggests, there was another aspect to the spiv that is instructive for considerations of non-hegemonic masculinity: his sexuality. The familiar look of the spiv, his sartorial exuberance in the form of loud silk ties, flashy suits and wide brimmed hats was in direct contrast to the greyness of clothing rationing but also provided a flashy alternative to the acceptable image of the enlisted male, as Hughes states: '[The spiv] over-compensated for the drabness, becoming almost feminine in the process, decked out in the patterns and shades of cheap bulls-eyes, all their tough swagger just a device to conceal a soggy cowardice underneath.[29] The spiv was a rare peacock on the Home Front, his louche sexuality was depicted as both dangerous and fascinating. In *Waterloo Road*, Stewart Granger's character Ted Purvis exemplifies the early (pre-comic) conception of the spiv; he possesses a flashy masculinity that is held in direct contrast to the temperate hero of John Mills' Jim Coulter, a serviceman. Purvis' suits (cut in the American style) display a suspicious disregard for rationing and he is constantly linked to the gaudiness of the amusement arcade where he and his cronies spend most of their time.[30] The narrative sees him pursuing the affections of Tillie Coulter, Jim's wife, whilst he is away on active service, articulating the perceived fear that non-enlisted men were free to steal the women of the enlisted. The spiv, with his flamboyance and easy money was as much a figure of sexual licentiousness as criminality. He was also forever linked to the consumerist desire so interrupted by rationing. The spiv was both provider and consumer of black-market goods and as such was held with doubled suspicion by authorities.

As Adrian Horn details, the uniform of the spiv also reflected the increasing influence of American culture in British society.[31] The wide lapels and broad shoulders of the zoot suit were taken from US gangster movies and imported into England via US servicemen. The link between the spiv and the more dangerous elements of American culture was summed up in the 1949 Mass Observation study on Juvenile Delinquency when it described the scene at a local dancehall:

> Most of the people here are of the working class. Only one or two 'Dago' or 'Spiv' types are present. They are dressed in their own, or rather the American singular style – i.e. cut back collar with large knotted tie; 'Boston Slash Back' hair cut; and a 'house coat' style of jacket usually in light fawn with brown flannels to match.[32]

Ted Purvis is obviously the older brother of these young ne'er-do-wells and as such represents an emergent masculine mode that would solidify in the 1950s with youth subcultures like the Teddy Boys and the Mods.[33] In *Waterloo Road* however he represents a sexually excessive danger lurking within the bosom of British society, a criminal but also a flashy outsider who would steal your wife as well as your watch.

As Britain struggled through the age of austerity, the spiv became more and more prominent in crime cinema. As Richard Hornsey details, he became an image of excessive consumption, not only a route into the black market but the antithesis of the upstanding masculinity needed to build the New Jerusalem.[34] The introduction of bread and potato rationing in 1946 and 1947 meant that the need for black market goods became more pressing and widespread; however the reasons for such measures were no longer based in the fight against evil but in governmental mismanagement of national resources. However, the post-war spiv cycle was always more concerned with sin than crime as the petty thievery and racketeering associated with these gatekeepers of the black market were constantly twinned with transgressions of a more sexual kind. In this way the spiv represented a quilting point for numerous social anxieties and said as much about the sanctity of the family unit as the law. Primarily created after the war, the spiv would continue to feature in comedies like *Dad's Army* and the *St Trinians* films right up until the 1970s. However much of their louche sexuality would find its way into the youth and popular culture of the 1950s as the Teddy Boys would adopt much of their sartorial extravagance, if not their petty criminality.

The image of the temperate hero, as Rose details, was crucial to the war effort and appears in many British films of the period. It offered a palatable alternative to what Lynne Segal calls 'the martial men' of the Third Reich and formed an integral part of the folklore of the People's War.[35] However, in order for this image to be concretised, alternatives needed to be posited and discarded and depictions of what was not manly were as important as what was. The old, the weak and the wicked were beyond the bounds of the hegemonic mode and therefore provided alternative expressions of masculinity both for those who were fighting and (perhaps more importantly) for those on the Home Front.

Williams' notion of residual and emergent cultures (although based on large-scale epistemic shifts in his own work) offers a way of viewing the constantly moving state of masculine hegemony. It is not the case that alternative masculinities are *created* simply to shore up the dominant mode, instead residues of previous identities are seized upon and emerging trends are highlighted. This is perhaps why issues of gender can never be untangled from age, class and social history, they are always in constant negotiation, always processual. Privates Jones, Pike and Walker – as the pensioner, the fool and the spiv – represented this process occurring, as British society drew upon the music hall of the 1930s *and* the influx of American culture that would manifest itself fully in the 1950s, for its images of errant men.

Notes

1. J. Richards (1997) *Films and British National Identity: From Dickens to Dad's Army* (Manchester: Manchester University Press) p 362.
2. P. Summerfield and C. Peniston-Bird (2007) *Contesting Home Defence: Men, Women and the Home Guard in the Second World War* (Manchester: Manchester University Press) pp 170–190.
3. P. Howlett (1995) *Fighting with Figures*, p 38.

4. A. Calder (1992) *The People's War*, p 269.
5. A. Calder (1992) *The People's War*, p 321.
6. L. Braudy (2003) *From Chivalry to Terrorism*, p 378.
7. S. O. Rose (2003) *Which People's War? National Identity and Citizenship in Wartime Britain 1939–1945* (Oxford: Oxford University Press) p 195.
8. J. B. Priestley (1940) *Postscripts* (London: William Heinemann) p 8.
9. S. O. Rose (2003) *Which People's War?* p 181.
10. A. Spicer (2001) *Typical Men: The Representation of Masculinity in Popular British Cinema* (London: I B Tauris) p 7.
11. A. Gramsci (1988) *The Antonio Gramsci Reader*, p 204.
12. R. Williams (2005) *Culture and Materialism* (London: Verso) p 40.
13. See for example A. Calder (1998) *The Myth of the Blitz*.
14. A. Calder (1992) *The People's War*, p 124.
15. J. B. Priestley (1940) *Postscripts*, p 9.
16. J. Richards (1997) *Films and British National Identity: From Dickens to Dad's Army* (Manchester: Manchester University Press) p 14.
17. P. M. St. Pierre (2009) *Music Hall Mimesis in British Film, 1895–1960* (Madison: Farleigh Dickinson University Press) p 190.
18. Mass Observation (FR1375).
19. W. S. Churchill (1989) *The Second World War: Abridged Edition* (London: W&N) p 775.
20. *Hansard*, 24 February 1942.
21. N. Rattigan (2001) *This is England*, p 218.
22. Cited in Rose (2003) *Which People's War?* pp 168–169.
23. A. Spicer (2001) *Typical Men: The Representation of Masculinity in Popular British Cinema* (London: I B Tauris), p 19.
24. A. Medhurst (2007) *A National Joke*, p 69.
25. J. Richards and Sheridan (1987) p 334.
26. R. Murphy (2000) *British Cinema*, p 42.
27. R. Murphy (1992) *Realism and Tinsel* (London: Routledge).
28. P. Wollen (2002) 'Riff-Raff Realism', in *Paris Hollywood: Writings on Film* (London: Verso) p 184.
29. D. Hughes (1964) 'The Spivs', p 93.
30. See S. Chibnall (1985) 'Whistle and Zoot', pp 56–81.
31. A. Horn (2009) *Juke Box Britain*, p 119.
32. H. D. Willcock (1949) *Report on Juvenile Delinquency* (London: The Falcon Press) p 49.
33. A. Horn (2009) *Juke Box Britain*, p 123.
34. R. Hornsey (2010) *The Spiv and the Architect*, p 19.
35. L. Segal (1990) *Slow Motion: Changing Masculinities and Changing Men* (London: Virago) p 115.

References

Askey. A (1975) *Before Your Very Eyes: An Autobiography* (London: The Woburn Press).

Braudy. L (2003) *From Chivalry to Terrorism: War and the Changing Nature of Masculinity.* (New York: Vintage).

Calder. A (1992) *The People's War: Britain 1939–1945* (London: Pimlico).

Calder. A (1998) *The Myth of the Blitz* (London: Pimlico).

Chibnall. S (1985) 'Whistle and Zoot: The Changing Meaning of a Suit of Clothes', *History Workshop Journal*, 20, Autumn, pp 56–81.

Gramsci. A (1988) *The Antonio Gramsci Reader* (London: Lawrence and Wishart).

Horn. A (2009) *Juke Box Britain: Americanisation and Youth Culture 1946–1960* (Manchester: Manchester University Press).

Hornsey. R (2010) *The Spiv and the Architect: Unruly Life in Postwar London* (Minneapolis: University of Minnesota).

Howlett. P (1995) *Fighting with Figures: A Statistical Digest of the Second World War.* (London: Central Statistical Office).

Hughes. D (1964) 'The Spivs', in M Sissons. and P French. (eds), *The Age of Austerity: 1945–1951* (London: Penguin) pp 86–105.

Medhurst. A (2007) *A National Joke: Popular Comedy and English Cultural Identities* (London: Routledge).

Murphy. R (2000) *British Cinema and the Second World War* (London: Continuum).

Orwell. G (2002) 'The Art of Donald McGill', in *Essays* (London: Everyman), pp 373–383.

Priestley. J B (1940) *Postscripts* (London: William Heinemann).

Rattigan. N (2001) *This is England: British Film and the People's War 1939–1945* (Madison: Farleigh Dickinson University Press).

Richards. J and Sheridan. D (eds) (1987) *Mass Observation at the Movies* (London: Routledge).

11
Second World War Rationing: Creativity and Buying to Last

Elspeth King and Maggie Andrews

Introduction

Rationing and shortages, have come to pervade popular representations of the Home Front. The introduction in 1940 of food rationing, followed by clothing in June 1941 and the removal of the small petrol ration for private motoring in March 1942[1] significantly extended the war into the domestic sphere, the 'Home Front'. Rationing made the battle to materially provide for the family a battle against the enemy whilst aiming to ensure that all the civilian population in the Second World war had access to basic necessities at a reasonable price. Contemporary official rhetoric suggested rationing contributed to the 'People's War' whereby a cohesive nation united in common sacrifices for a single purpose: defeating the enemy. For many housewives for whom it became an almost moral obligation to maintain the home and, as the popular song suggested, 'keep the home fires burning', rationing, food shortages, fuel targets and official dictates against waste turned everyday life on the Home Front into hard work.

Furthermore shopping and consumption were not merely about meeting basic material needs in the 1940s. Rappaport has charted the nineteenth-century rise of department stores[2] which were followed in the early twentieth century by the introduction of chain stores such as Marks and Spencer (1894) and Woolworths (1909). These all served to democratise the pleasures of consumer culture and turn shopping into a leisure activity.[3] Bourdieu's observations on the significance of taste and consumption[4] were developed in relation to everyday life in 1960s France, however, whether it was cars or food, clothing or home furnishings, consumption and shopping were established as markers of social class – and as importantly, perhaps, strata within classes – in inter-war period in Britain. The growing interest in shopping was reinforced by media and popular culture including women's magazines, broadcasting and the Ideal Home exhibition[5] which, despite the inter-war economic recession, encouraged fantasies of purchasing and legitimated envy particularly for the lower middle class and the working class who as they worked in new industries or white collar jobs had rising real incomes. Janis Winship has demonstrated that Marks and Spencer allowed socially mobile young women in this period to shop for clothing which both expressed their individuality and fitted comfortably into working lives in teaching, clerical or retail work.[6] The now familiar pastime of looking at magazines, exhibitions or catalogues and imagining what life would be like with the products advertised was firmly established before the war and continued despite shortages.

The basic premise of rationing was simple: an individual allowance of basic foodstuffs, furniture and clothing was obtained in exchange for money and coupons. If a person's allowance had already been claimed, it was illegal for a shopkeeper to sell products to the customer.[7] Rationing however offered little satisfaction for housewives' consumerist dreams and as women bore the brunt of household responsibilities they felt the impact of the shortages most acutely when shopping. Queueing became a daily occurrence, with working women using their lunch hours or losing pay when they took time off to shop.[8] Everyday domestic activities which gave a sense of home and identity, a shared meal, the purchasing of clothes and presents, decorating a house or a drive in the country, all became problematic. This chapter draws upon Mass Observation diaries, autobiographies, oral histories and memories to suggest that in the face of these problems housewives utilised their creativity, resourcefulness and innovation to mitigate the constraints created by rationing and shortages of clothing and furniture. They continued to find ways to express their individuality in their clothes and to care for their families by providing them with more than basic necessities. Popular narratives of women, unable to get stockings, using gravy browning on their legs were, it will be suggested, only one of a multitude of practices which pre-occupied women's everyday life on the Home Front in the Second World War. Whatever the official rhetoric of a 'People's War' these practices were, however, shaped by social differences and most particularly by class.

Having to make do meant buying to last

The constraints of clothes and furniture rationing, whilst perhaps secondary to the rationing of food in a hungry nation, presented serious problems to a war weary people. An added pressure to those battling to clothe themselves and their families were the endless exhortations to keep up appearances as a boost to the morale of the country, particularly men in the forces; to fail in this task as *Vogue* stressed in August 1942: 'undermines present usefulness'.[9] As Pat Kirkham suggests, the beauty as duty ethos was part of a national call for a 'united front to maintain the illusion of normality in extraordinary times'.[10] For housewives trying to enhance or even maintain their home; shortages and rationing of furniture were also a concern, particularly for the middle classes. Frances Partridge noted that inflation and purchase tax meant prices were exorbitant; whilst Mr Brown, an engineer from Ipswich, suggested that a replacement carpet which would have cost £5 pre-war were in 1944 costing about £30;[11] and Vera Hodgson living in London and doing social work, noted that tallboys (tall thin chests of drawers) in Barkers department store, that previously cost 25/- were £5 in 1942.[12] For those with the time to spare, auctions were a possible source of furniture, but again prices had soared making them the preserve of the wealthier. Maggie Joy Blunt, a Mass Observation diarist who later worked for an architectural journal, remarked when friends tried to buy furniture at an auction, they found that an oak table which would have cost £4 pre-war in 1943 was priced at £27.[13]

Consequently shopping in an era of rationing and shortages required not just endless resourcefulness but also the adoption of a 'buying to last' mentality wherever feasible. This was less of a problem amongst wealthier groups, given such increases in prices. The government endorsement of 'buying to last' resulted in the introduction of clothes rationing in 1941 was quickly followed in 1942 by utility clothing. Although conforming to strict government guidelines to ensure economy of materials and durability and with a limited range, much utility clothing was designed by top fashion designers such as Hardy Amies.[14] It was intended to reduce the civilian consumption of raw materials and also to release workers from the clothing industry for the war effort. Payment for utility garments was by a combination of coupons and cash, with initially 66 coupons issued to each adult which were nominally enough to buy one complete outfit.[15] *Vogue* praised the utility scheme for its 'beautifully designed clothes', saying it was a 'revolutionary scheme...an outstanding example of applied democracy'[16] in October 1942, but the public were not entirely convinced by such rhetoric.

George Springett, a conscientious objector with communist sympathies living in Kent, whilst committed to a 'buy to last' approach, dismissed a 'lot of utility trousers [as] shoddy stuff' when shown them by a local outfitters. Instead, on asking 'haven't you got any pre-war trousers?', the response from the manager was negative but following a conversation which included a discussion of pacifism, things altered as 'he went to the back of the shop and produced a really fine pair of *pre-war* trousers.'[17] If George Springett's criticisms were of the durability of utility clothing, a more common complaint was that the clothes did not offer the pleasures of consumer culture and did not allow individuals selecting clothes 'to define and describe' themselves.[18] An attitude, Anne Seymour, editor of *Woman and Home* blamed the media for. She complained, in an interview with Mass Observation, that the media did not articulate the scope for expressing individualism within the scheme.[19] Subsequent articles in the magazine suggested there was no restriction on the design of utility clothes, other than conforming to the regulations. As Anne Scott James suggested 'Mrs Brown need not look like Mrs. Robinson's twin sister ... for there is yet no question of standard clothing.[20] The term 'utility' clothing was disliked by clothing manufacturers who felt it insulted their products, but clothing and fashion did not remain static with clothes remodelling agencies flourishing during the war.[21] Magazines were filled with suggestions of how to accessorise your clothes to give them a new look. Hats particularly, magazines suggested, could be 'primped' with artificial flowers and feathers which were 'off coupons',[22] not least because the government recognised the morale-raising power of 'jaunty ... headgear'. Hats became one of the few ways in which to express individuality within the confines of utility wear.[23]

By 1943 the utility scheme was extended to cover furniture and other essential household goods including pottery and cooking utensils. Initially called 'Standard Emergency Furniture', utility furniture could only be obtained on production of a permit, in itself only granted to those newly-weds who were setting up home for the first time or to people who had been bombed out. Each item had a unit value such as 1 unit for a dining room chair and a couple would receive a basic allowance of 60 units plus an additional 15 for each child.[24] By making simple, standard designs, what might be called 'minimalist' today, a lot of people got value for money and what is viewed retrospectively as a high quality item which would have a long and useful life.[25] Advocates of 'good design' appropriated the utility scheme to impose their principles[26] on a nation who favoured a 'Jacobethan' style of furniture, made popular because it was thought it would not date.[27] The simplicity and clean lines of utility design were often contrasted with, according to O. H. Frost, the 'frills and fancies' of the reproduction furniture which dominated the 'lower end' of the British furniture trade in the early twentieth century.[28]

One tactic employed by the lower-middle and better off working classes with limited incomes was to 'buy to last' by purchasing on the 'never-never'. Kays, a well established catalogue store, who made this a promotional feature claimed that they offered 'everything on credit...at the same price as it is obtainable in any London store for cash'[29] and supplied a multiplicity of products from household goods such as 'long life' quality sheets made 'for strength' to chicken coups.[30] They sold 'Gambroon' trousers produced in special cloth and designed to 'wear like iron' for 24/- and eight coupons under the strapline 'For Hard Wear' and Boots 'made to wear like iron' with a grain hide upper and 'specially selected for water resilience and toughness of fibre' for 26s 6d and nine coupons.[31] The catalogue which had once offered a relaxing read and fantasies of consumerism to customers now brought military terminology and phrases into the domestic sphere, suggesting that resistance, defiance, strength and resilience were all part of domestic war effort.[32] The Times Furnishing Company Ltd. similarly stressed the quality of its products, reminding its customers: 'even in the making of a standard article there are grades of quality' and that although some were better than others 'it is from these "better" makers that *your* Utility will come.' Again they provided options to pay in cash or 'on our easy terms', making the furniture accessible to all who had been issued with the necessary permits, regardless of their income.[33]

If the original quality of the materials was important to ensure that clothing and furniture lasted, so was avoiding damage and mending. Kays supplied large Horrockses' cloth overalls, which offered the 'utmost protection for housework' and were available in one size only[34] and were designed to go over and protect other clothes. They had the added advantage of saving precious time for the hard-pressed housewife who could wear their work clothes underneath and be ready to go to the office/factory. Clothing repairs were either done within the home or, if money allowed, by a seamstress. For the very wealthy there was always Harrods. Utilising a tactic only available to a few, Frances Partridge on one of her and her husband Ralph's frequent visits to London, took a windcheater of his to have a new zip fitted at Harrods where the assistant reassured them that 'nothing's impossible'.[35] Peter Jones and John Lewis also offered a renovation service that 'will undertake to do almost everything...make a dress out of a pair of flannel trousers...turn evening gowns into day dresses, men's suits and shirts into women's suits and blouses…mend handbags, repair hinges and reline.' Bourne and Hollingsworth, whose dressmaking department was famed for its clever re fashioning of clothes offered to perform 'similar miracles upon wilting hats'.[36] Women's organisations such as the Women's Institute both provided the skills and championed working-class women who employed similar make-do-and-mend tactics.[37]

Those who came from comfortable, well-connected backgrounds were able to see the war out relatively untroubled when it came to furniture and, to a significant degree, clothes also. Vera Brittain or Frances Partridge, both of whom were well off with large houses in un-bombed areas of the country, had a plentiful supply of good quality, often inherited, pre-war furniture to last the duration. The most obvious sign of the war was the wear and tear on carpets and soft furnishings as Mr. Brown, a designer at an engineering firm, living in East Anglia, commented 'our carpet is showing signs of wear, but it will just have to last'.[38] Whilst Frances Partridge, the pacifist and member of the 'Bloomsbury Set' who lived in Wiltshire where a stream of visitors sought refuge from London noted: 'I catch myself thinking what covers to put on the chairs. As they have needed the sacrifice of clothes coupons they are pretty shabby.'[39] Such issues were not a concern for many of the working class who would at times resort to selling their clothing coupons to make ends meet.

Self-sufficiency, creativity, resourcefulness and innovation

The added workload of voluntary or paid war work, consequent constraints on shopping time and the frustration of queues, which might have nothing left to buy when housewives reached the end, encouraged self-sufficiency. Many with suitably sized gardens or allotments turned their hands to vegetable growing and to poultry keeping, some with the benefit of the Chicken Kit, which could be ordered from the Kay's catalogue.[40] Out of necessity, this culture of self-sufficiency, established in woman's magazines in the inter-war years, evolved not just for food but also other household necessities.[41] Magazines in the inter-war period had revived feminine crafts such as crochet or embroidery, modernising and adapting them to contemporary expectations.[42] Fiona Hackney notes 'commercial magazines…recast home craft as a modern activity and the housewife as an agent of modernity'.[43] Thus 'making' with its allied feminine values was considered an appropriate means of modifying the 'masculine' tendencies of the modern interior in favour of social display. In the war years adaption was certainly required and a

Harrods advertisement was able to point out that 'A sewing machine can be almost as much a weapon as a spade'.[44]

Magazines were not the only medium to encourage self-sufficiency, the propaganda film *In Which We Live: Being the Story of a Suit Told by Itself* (1943) demonstrated how to get maximum wear from a man's suit. Narrated by the suit in a semi-autobiographical style, it moves from the man being fitted for the suit in the 1930s to the start of the war and the suit initially being put away 'for the duration' only to be brought out and cut up to make clothes for the children. All is accompanied by encouragement to look after the suit by protecting it from moth and careful ironing.[45] Women were not spared from the government message to recycle clothing. In the Pathé newsreel film *Evening and Day Frock Issue* (1943), Anne Edwards, fashion expert from *Woman* magazine, pointed out how to turn a dance frock into a practical daytime dress. She is shown cutting out patterns and stitching, before a woman models the recycled dress with a matching turban to her serviceman boyfriend. Thus creativity and resourcefulness enabled woman to fulfill her duty to be beautiful.[46] Other accounts of an innovative approach to clothing include an evacuee living in Shropshire who, on finding a shop selling cheesecloth and dusters, transformed the cheesecloth into nightwear and the dusters into parts of a dress. The use of nuns veiling for nightwear, was not however an unparalleled success as it was made of wool and rather prickly when first put on.[47]

Knitting was perhaps the most common area of self-sufficiency, with no wool garment ever thrown out, they were instead unravelled and the wool was rolled up around a piece of cardboard until required. Women knitted jumpers, scarves, balaclavas, socks and mittens for their families and for those in the armed forces. Thus knitting enabled women to care for their family, making items to give as gifts when purchases were limited. Fake sweater necks, which looked like a jumper under a suit or coat, were popular as they used little wool. Knitting is portrayed in popular images of the 'nuclear' family gathered in the living room: father in his Home Guard uniform, two children playing cards at the Morrison table shelter and the mother using her precious 'spare' time knitting, with the radio playing in the corner.[48] Perhaps the cult of knitting has been over romanticised as a communal activity done in front of a roaring fire by happy women[49] but as one woman recollected less than enthusiastically: 'we didn't do anything else except listen to the wireless and knitting, we were always knitting.'[50] Patching, knitting and darning were time consuming boring pastimes often done after a long day of war work or child care, forced on people by necessity, not choice.[51]

Make do and Mend, one of the foremost slogans associated with the Home Front, was not just confined to knitting and repairing. The war and accompanying shortages presented a challenge to those who had grown used to expressing their individuality and identity through their clothing in the inter-war years. Women instead altered, accessorised and the January 1943 edition of *Women's Wear Daily* suggested they 'reconfection' clothes and particularly hats[52] which were one item of clothing where self-sufficiency and the ingenious use of available materials led to imaginative designs including turbans like the one that London vicar's wife Molly Rich concocted when her hat 'died on my head during a thunderstorm'.[53] Women used everyday household goods creatively to express their individuality, even garden string was crocheted into a hat.[54] Hats were subject to a 33 per cent luxury goods tax levy and some thought they were an unpatriotic frivolity especially as so many women were wearing them as part of their service uniform. Mass Observation had commented in 1939 that 'increasing hatlessness has gone along with churchlessness', however wearing a hat outside remained for most women a sign of respectability and styles which won favour also included berets or miniature versions of male styles. Many unique fashion statements resulted from using precious material in original ways, if not always with a great deal of skill.[55]

As McDowell suggests, considerable ingenuity was employed to ensure that odd pieces of material could still create something presentable.[56] Thus a Mass Observation file report noted '66 coupons were quite generous for "those who use their hands" in wartime'.[57] Of course much of this was dependent on having access to the 'raw ingredients', whether existing good quality clothes or lengths of material. Indeed a Board of Trade leaflet implored 'No material must lie idle, so be a magician and turn old clothes into new',[58] so materials were used for items other than their original use. Olivia Cockett wrote in her diary entry for July 1941 that she had 'made a housecoat for winter evenings – to save office clothes. Curtain material no coupons 12s'.[59] Magazines ran their own 'coupon saving pattern service' including the *Girls Own Paper* which encouraged its readers to send for the pattern for a two material jacket to 'make this useful garment from two discarded coats or frocks!'[60] With furnishing fabrics included in the coupon scheme 'Make do and mend' extended into the home and there are accounts of kitchen tablecloths made from flour sacks and trimmed with bias binding, and milk bottle tops stitched together to make table mats. One interviewee's mother managed to get hold of some flour bags that she unpicked, washed, dyed green and turned into curtains.[61] Many evenings were used making rug by threading strips of old clothes through hessian. As one rug maker recalled 'there were doormats, kitchen sink mats and posh ones for the sitting room'.[62]

The war made its presence felt in all aspects of appearance and many items were appropriated and used in unconventional ways to maintain the 'whole' appearance. Artificial or costume jewellery, seen as an essential part of any formal outfit, which in peacetime might have cost three guineas was now valued at nineteen. More reasonably priced felt jewellery such as bracelets and earrings were also available at around 12s 6d.' prime examples of making do and substitution.[63] The lack of gold for wedding rings meant either an inherited one had to be used or a 'utility' version with a high copper content which turned the wedding finger green.[64] Little wonder many found the acquisition of a 9 carat wedding rings and engagement rings (18 carat), purchased by instalments from Kays catalogue, appealing.[65] Unlikely materials found their way into jewellery; perspex, aluminium and brass were fashioned into presents often made by factory workers or servicemen in a reflection of the trench art of First World War and sometimes decorated with military insignia.[66] Even bottle tops, clip hooks, film spools and corks were reinvented as jewellery[67] and country residents experimented (not necessarily successfully) with acorns and other nuts painted to match clothing.[68]

To those, particularly the young who had developed a taste for the pleasures of consumer culture in the first half of the twentieth century, the relentless need to make-do and improvise could be wearing. The *Manchester Evening News* remarked: 'Women are willing to help in every way and to give up any luxuries, but there is something about the lack of beauty aids that takes the starch out of their backbone.'[69] An article under the heading 'Raid the larder for beauty' encouraged readers to incorporate food products into their beauty routines. As manufacturing of makeup had been cut to a minimum, a range of unusual ingredients were put to use to try and replicate the real thing. Boot polish was used as mascara, powdered starch for face powder, beetroot juice was turned into lip colour. The supply of 'proper' lipstick, which was still made by hand and sold in wooden tubes to conserve metal for military requirements, was severely limited.[70] One Liverpool housewife advocated mutton fat warmed and rubbed into the skin as good for roughened hands and also made her own face cream by putting a few drops of cream from the top of the milk plus a few drops of olive oil into the shell of a broken egg, mixing it up and then putting it on her face. Improvisation and substitution seemed to know no bounds, with one young woman who worked in an aircraft factory using the transparent 'dope' from the paint shop as nail varnish and others utilising a homemade face pack made from Fullers Earth which was dark green in colour.[71] Desperation enticed some people to purchase black market products, many made in unhygienic environments, containing dubious if not dangerous substances such as lead and arsenic. The government was so alarmed it issued a short film, *Black Market Beauties*, showing the dangers of these products.[72]

Opportunism

Opportunism was a tactic which was particularly the preserve of the middle and upper classes and those with limited work commitments. Many with the resources to do so had purchased and hoarded items in the summer of 1939 and in the early months of the conflict before the shortages and rationing took effect. Ready cash and surplus disposable income enabled some to continue to engage in such activities throughout the war when desirable products randomly appeared. Esther Rowley, living in Exmouth, spotted a supply of lipstick and face powder in a local store in March 1941 and decided to: 'buy in a whole lot … as they are not making any more after this lot is sold up'.[73] Similarly, in 1943 a few lucky women were delighted to get hold of anti-sunburn lipstick produced for troops. Time as well as money was a factor in seizing opportunities, for example consignments of rare goods such as silk stockings sold out within hours to women who started queuing before dawn.[74]

The over eight million full time housewives[75] even if they did some voluntary work, were best placed to devote time to the acquisition of scarce items and pounce on any unexpected opportunities that arose. Women who worked long hours and undertook compulsory overtime in factories had little access to such opportunities. Having the time to 'shop-crawl' in the hope of acquiring a rare commodity or just to buy whatever was available was considered anti-social but also necessary as shortages increased. General scarcity of simple household goods such as matches, batteries and hairpins necessitated spot purchases of anything useful when seen in the shops whether needed at the time or not.[76] Once again, class, wealth and disposable income were crucial in providing resilience to rationing. Thus Clara Milburn, writing in 1944, summed up an approach to purchasing clothes that only the wealthy could adopt: 'Even if the price is high, it is always best to buy the thing that is right when you see it.'[77]

Opportunity often needed to be combined with creativity and imagination. Bryher (the nom de plume of the novelist Annie Winifred

Ellerman) recounted how she read in the newspaper one morning that the local zoo was selling the clippings from their camel's coats without coupons. She went to the zoo in her lunch hour, a sack was produced and filled with these clippings. Bryher sent them to Scotland and they were turned into six skeins of wool which she shared with her friend Oliver Sitwell. From her share she had a jacket made which was 'too hot even for me' so she passed it to a farming friend.[78] Parachute silk was a more widely used item to make both home furnishings and clothing – although it was hard to get hold of and not used as widely as popular memory suggests. In her letters to an Austrian refugee, Molly Rich recounted how, when helping a friend pack up to move house, she had observed 'a chair covered from the parachute of a shot-down airman. It is lovely, springy blue-green silk with a gold lining and bound with the blue cord held by the airman.'[79] More prosaically parachute silk was very suitable to be turned into underwear, not least because the source was unidentifiable, although until 1945 when parachute material was put on sale, commandeering it was a crime.[80] Material came from the most unlikely of sources with one enterprising seamstress even transforming a captured German flag into a dressing gown.[81]

The ability to take advantage of any material that came your way, legally or otherwise, depended on your ability to sew or employ the services of a dressmaker. Upon the outbreak of war many had to learn these skills quickly. Classes and exhibitions were rapidly organised by the women's organisations. Whilst many home dressmakers still stitched by hand, a few owned a sewing machine, some even powered by electricity; with many working-class homes not having electricity and the prohibitive cost of machines, once again class and wealth shaped the experience of wartime rationing. Purchasing a sewing machine had gained in popularity in the inter-war years when they had become more widely available, even on hire purchase. Kays Catalogue offered its 'Kays Famous Paragon British Made Sewing Machine' for a deposit of 6/6 and then 3/6 weekly or £6 15s in one payment, but with the Singer sewing machine factories in New Jersey and Scotland turned over to war production, sewing machines became expensive and hard to obtain.[82] This did not stop adverts for Singer Sewing Machines appearing in newspapers with the slogan: 'Furniture that helps to make furnishings.'[83] For many purchasing a sewing machine was a consumer fantasy that might enable them to take advantage of some of the opportunities that emerged in wartime Britain.

Conclusion

Ideas of the 'People's War' were embodied in the introduction of rationing and utility clothing and furnishings and brought the struggles of the Home Front firmly into the domestic space of the home. Rationing was intended to ensure everyone had the basic necessities of life without compromising production for the war effort. Government strategies were only however a starting point for housewives who continued to seek ways to express their individuality in clothing and home furnishings, even if many of their desires were not met until well into the post-war era. In wartime a range of tactics were employed: buy to last, make-do-and-mend, self-sufficiency and opportunism continued to ensure that the pleasures of clothing and furniture were sustained in wartime. They all relied upon a degree of creativity, resourcefulness and innovation from the housewife; what is also clear is that they required more than this. Time and money, more frequently the prerogatives of the wealthier classes, made all the difference when coping with the privations of wartime. Despite guidance, advice and sometimes the best of intentions, rationing was an area in which the ideals of the 'People's War' and 'everyone in it together' were severely compromised. Nevertheless, dreams, desires and fantasies about consumer products and shopping for pleasure did not disappear in wartime, although queues and shortages took their toll and dulled or moderated them a little. Dreams of dresses and carpets were replaced by fantasies of a new sewing machine, rag rugs, accessories and a refashioned hat. When the war finished, however, housewives looked to something a little more exciting but they had to wait well into the 1950s for their hopes and dreams to be realised.

Notes

1. M. Brown and C. Harris (2001) *The Wartime House*, pp 85–87.
2. E. Rappaport (2001) *Shopping for Pleasure*.
3. M. Andrews and M. Talbot (2000) *All the World*.
4. P. Bourdieu (1984) *Distinction*.
5. D. Ryan (2000) 'All the World and Her Husband', pp 10–22.
6. J. Winship (2000) 'New Disciplines', pp 23–42.
7. G. de la Bédoyère (2009) *The Home Front*, p 18.
8. G. Braybon and P. Summerfield (1987) *Out of the Cage*, p 243.
9. Vogue, http://www.vogue.co.uk/magazine/archive (accessed 20 February 2014).
10. P. Kirkham (1995) 'Beauty as Duty', pp 13–28.
11. H. Millgate (ed.) (2011) *Mr Brown's War*, p 233.

12. V. Hodgson (1976) *Few Eggs*, p 214.
13. S. Garfield (2006) (ed.) *Private Battles*, p 334.
14. R. Sword (1974) *Utility Furniture*, p 33.
15. R. Sword (1974) *Utility Furniture*, p 141.
16. J. Walford (2008) *Forties Fashion*, p 49.
17. S. Koa-Wing (ed.) (2007) *Mass Observation*, p 129.
18. A. Lurie, (1981) *The Language of Clothes*, p 5.
19. Mass Observation quoted in H. Reynolds (1999) 'The Utility Garment: Its Design and Effect on the Mass Market 1942–45', in J. Attfield (ed.), *Utility Reassessed. The Role of Ethics in the Practice of Design* (Manchester: Manchester University Press).
20. J. Scott, 'Deborah Kerr Shows Off the New Utility Clothes for Women', *Picture Post*, 28 March 1942, pp 18–19.
21. P. Kirkham (1999) Fashion, Femininity', p 143–154, p 150.
22. J. Gardiner (2004) *Wartime Britain*, p 572.
23. P. Nicol (2010) *Sucking Eggs*, p 164.
24. M. Brown and C. Harris (2001) *The Wartime House*, p 91.
25. R. Sword (1974) *Utility Furniture*, p 5.
26. J. Attfield, (1996) 'Give 'em Something Dark and Heavy', pp 185–201, p 190.
27. D. Sugg-Ryan (2011) 'Living', pp 217–244.
28. S. Reimer and P. Pinch (2013) 'Geographies', p 99–112, p 103.
29. Kays Catalogue in University of Worcester Special Collections, Spring/Summer 1944, p 122; Spring/Summer 1943, p 54.
30. Kays Catalogue Autumn/Winter 1939.
31. Kays Catalogue Autumn/Winter 1943, edition p 83.
32. M. Andrews (2012) *Domesticating the Airways*, p 104.
33. M. Brown and C. Harris (2001) *The Wartime House*, p 91.
34. Kays Catalogue Spring/Summer 1942, p 24.
35. F. Partridge (1999) *A Pacifist's War Diaries*, p 110.
36. C. McDowell (1997) *Forties Fashion*, p 109.
37. M. Andrews (1997) *The Acceptable Face*, p 110.
38. H. D. Millgate (ed.) (2011) *Mr. Brown's War*, p 233.
39. F. Partridge (1999) *A Pacifist's War Diaries*, p 194.
40. Kays Catalogue Autumn/Winter 1939, p 290.
41. G. Braybon and P. Summerfield (1987) *Out of the Cage*, p 243.
42. F. Hackney (2006) 'Use Your Hands', pp 23–38, p 26.
43. F. Hackney (2006) 'Use Your Hands', p 29.
44. J. Gardiner (2004) *Wartime Britain*, p 569.
45. *In Which We Live: Being the Story of a Suit Told by Itself* (1943).
46. Pathé News (1943) *Evening and Day Frock Issue Title is hi-de-hi.* Accessed via: http://www.britishpathe.com/video/evening-and-day-frock-issue-title-is hi-de-hi (accessed 11 October 2013).
47. S. Griffith (2009) *Stitching for Victory*, pp 157–158.
48. See painting by Christa Hook – 1941. Reproduced in M. Brown (2011) *Wartime Britain*.
49. C. McDowell (1997) *Forties Fashion*, p 98.
50. M. Andrews (2012) *Domesticating the Airwaves*, p 84.
51. C. McDowell (1997) *Forties Fashion*, p 98.
52. C. McDowell (1997) *Forties Fashion*, p 109.

53. A. Craigmayle (2013) *A Vicarage in the Blitz*, p 109.
54. J. Walford (2008) *Forties Fashion*, pp 100 and 129.
55. C. McDowell (1997) *Forties Fashion*, p 98.
56. C. McDowell (1997) *Forties Fashion*, p 83.
57. Mass Observation Archives File report 791 1 June 1941, p 4.
58. S. Hodge (2012) *The Home Front*.
59. R. W. Malcolmson (ed.) (2005) *Love and War*, p 169.
60. S. Griffith (2009) *Stitching for Victory*, p 154.
61. Oral memory quoted in S Griffith (2009) *Stitching for Victory*, pp 28–30.
62. S. Griffith (2009) *Stitching for Victory*, pp 28–30.
63. A. Kendall (1972) *Their Finest Hour*, p 47.
64. J. Walford (2008) *Forties Fashion*, p 106.
65. Kays Catalogue Spring/Summer 1945, p 174–175.
66. M. Brown and C. Harris (2001) *The Wartime House*, p 146.
67. E. R. Chamberlin (1972) *Life in Wartime Britain*, p 84.
68. C. McDowell (1997) *Forties Fashion*, p 103.
69. *Manchester Evening News*, 30 October 1940, p 4, quoted in C. Langhammer (2000) *Women's Leisure*.
70. M. Brown (2011) *Wartime Britain*, p 46.
71. N. Longmate (2002) *How We Lived Then*, p 279.
72. M. Brown (2011) *Wartime Britain*, p 46.
73. J. Folkes (2010) (ed.) *Dogs, Goats*, p 42.
74. V. Nicholson (2011) *Millions Like Us*, p 135.
75. H. L. Smith (1986) 'The Effect of the War', pp 208–229, 210.
76. K. Knight (2011) *Rationing in the Second World War*, p 173.
77. P. Donnelly (ed.) (1979) *Mrs. Milburn's Diaries*, p 246.
78. J. Hartley (ed.) (1994) *Hearts Undefeated: Women's Writing of the Second World War* (London: Virago) p 194.
79. A. Craigmayle (2013) *A Vicarage in the Blitz*, p 139.
80. C. McDowell (1997) *Forties Fashion*, p 97.
81. C. McDowell (1997) *Forties Fashion*, p 102.
82. S. Griffith (2009) *Stitching for Victory*, p 151.
83. M. Brown and C. Harris (2001) *The Wartime House*, p 71.

References

Andrews. M (1997) *The Acceptable Face of Feminism: The Women's Institute as a Social Movement* (London: Lawrence and Wishart).

Andrews. M (2012) *Domesticating the Airways: Broadcasting, Domesticity and Femininity* (London: Continuum).

Andrews. M and Talbot. M (2000) *All the World and Her Husband* (London: Cassell).

Attfield. J (2001) (ed.) *Utility Reassessed: The Role of Ethics in the Practice of Design* (Manchester: Manchester University Press).

Attfield. J (1996) '"Give 'em Something Dark and Heavy": The Role of Design in the Material Culture of Popular British Furniture 1939–1945', *Journal of Design History*, 9, 3, pp. 185–201.

Bédoyère. G de la (2009) *The Home Front* (Oxford: Shire Publications).

Braybon. G and Summerfield. P (1987) *Out of the Cage: Women's Experiences in Two World Wars*. (London: Pandora).

Bourdieu. P (1984) *Distinction* (Oxford: Routledge).

Brown. M (2011) *Wartime Britain* (Oxford: Shire Publications).

Brown. M and Harris. C (2001) *The Wartime House* (Stroud: Sutton Publishing).

Chamberlin. E R (1972) *Life in Wartime Britain* (London: B.T. Batsford Ltd).

Craigmayle. A (2013) *A Vicarage in the Blitz, The Wartime Letters of Molly Rich 1940–1944* (Appledore, Kent: Balloon View Publishing Ltd).

Dennys. J (2010) *Henrietta Sees it Through: More News from the Home Front*, reprint, originally published for *Sketch* in 1943 (London Bloomsbury).

Donnelly. P (ed.) (1979) *Mrs. Milburn's Diaries, An Englishwoman's Day-to-Day Reflections 1939–1945* (London: Futura).

Folkes. J (2010) (ed.) *Dogs, Goats, Bulbs and Bombs: Esther Rowley's Wartime Diaries of Exmouth and Exeter* (Stroud: The History Press).

Gardiner. J (2004) *Wartime Britain 1939–1945* (London: Headline).

Garfield. S (2006) (ed.) *Private Battles: How the War Almost Defeated Us* (London: Elbury Press).

Griffith. S (2009) *Stitching for Victory* (Stroud: The History Press).

Hackney. F (2006) '"Use your Hands for Happiness": Home Craft and Make-do-and-Mend in British Women's Magazines in the 1920s and 1930s', *Journal of Design History*,19,1, pp 23–38.

Hartley. J (ed.) (1994) *Hearts Undefeated: Women's Writing of the Second World War* (London: Virago).

Hodge. S (2012) *The Home Front in World War Two: Keep Calm and Carry On* (Barnsley: Remember When).

Hodgson. V (1976) *Few Eggs and No Oranges* (London: Denis Dobson).

Kendall. A (1972) *Their Finest Hour: An Evocative Memoir of the British People in Wartime. 1939–1945* (London: Wayland Publishers).

Kirkham. P (1995) 'Beauty as Duty: Keeping Up the (Home) Front', in P Kirkham. and D Thoms. (eds), *War Culture* (London: Lawrence & Wishart) pp 13–28.

Kirkham. P (1999) 'Fashion, Femininity and 'Frivolous' Consumption in World War Two Britain', in J Attfield. (ed.) *Utility Reassessed* (Manchester: Manchester University Press) pp 143–154.

Knight. K (2011) *Rationing in the Second World War: Spuds, Spam and Eating for Victory* (Stroud: The History Press).

Koa-Wing. S (ed.) (2007) *Mass Observation, Britain in the Second World War* (London: The Folio Society).

Langhammer. C (2000) *Women's Leisure in England 1920–60* (Manchester: Manchester University Press).

Longmate. N (2002) *How We Lived Then: A History of Everyday Life During the Second World War*. (London: Pimlico).

Lurie. A (1981) *The Language of Clothes* (London: Heinemann).

McDowell. C (1997) *Forties Fashion and the New Look* (London: Bloomsbury).

Malcolmson. R W (ed.) (2005) *Love and War in London. A Woman's Diary 1939–1942* (Ontario: Wilfred Laurier University Press).

Millgate. H (ed.) (2011) *Mr Brown's War: A Diary from the Home Front* (Stroud: The History Press).

Nicholson. V (2011) *Millions Like Us: Women's Lives During the Second World War* (London: Penguin).

Nicol. P (2010) *Sucking Eggs, What Your Wartime Granny Could Teach You About Diet, Thrift and Going Green* (London: Vintage Books).

Partridge. F (1999) *A Pacifist's War Diaries 1939–1945* (London: Phoenix).

Rappaport. E (2001) *Shopping for Pleasure* (Princetown: Princetown University Press).

Reimer. S and Pinch. P (2013) 'Geographies of the British Government's Wartime Utility Furniture Scheme 1940–1945', *Journal of Historical Geography*, 39, pp 99–112.

Ryan. D (2000) 'All the World and Her Husband: The Daily Mail Ideal Home Exhibition', in M Andrews. and M Talbot, (London: Cassell) pp 10–22.

Smith. H L (1986) 'The Effect of the War on the Status of Women', in H L Smith. (ed.), *War and Social Change* (Manchester: Manchester University Press) pp 208–229.

Sugg-Ryan. D (2011) 'Living in a "Half-Baked" Pageant', *Journal of Home Cultures*, 8, 3, pp 217–244.

Sword. R (1974) *Utility Furniture and Fashion, 1941–1951. The Geffrye Museum* (London: Inner London Education Authority).

Walford. J (2008) *Forties Fashion: From Siren Suits to the New Look* (New York: Thames and Hudson).

Winship. J (2000) 'New Disciplines for Women and the Rise of the Chain Stores in the 1930s', in M Andrews. and M Talbot (eds), *All the World and Her Husband* (London: Cassell) pp 23–45.

12
Idle Women: Challenging Gender Stereotypes on Britain's Inland Waterways During the Second World War

Barbara Hately-Broad and Bob Moore

Introduction

Debates about the mobilisation of women into employment during both the First World War and the Second World War have become an integral element of modern British social history. The subject was extensively examined in works by Arthur Marwick, Penny Summerfield and Harold Smith in the 1980s and 1990s,[1] all of whom focussed on the acknowledged extension of female labour into the workforce during the two wars and whether this improved their economic and social status at the same time as developing their confidence and self-consciousness. Whilst their work did not produce a consensus on the precise importance of war as an agent for this type of social change it served to prompt further studies that analysed, for example, women's employment in the inter-war period[2] and considered how their deployment as labour in Second World War affected their post-war lives.[3] In the wider literature on women drafted into the labour force during the 1939–1945 conflict, some areas of employment such as the Women's Land Army,[4] have received rather more attention than others. The fourfold increase in women deployed on Britain's railway network by 1945 and those working in the dockyards, has, for example, been largely ignored.[5]

Likewise, surveys of the ways in which women broke through gendered employment barriers during the Second World War have rarely spent time considering the inland waterways as a location of radical change or a beacon of future emancipation. Indeed, in the official war history of inland transport, canal carrying is given very little consideration and the contribution made by women to the industry only commands seven lines in a volume that runs to more than 600 pages.[6] Nonetheless, the shortage of labour in the industry led to a small number of women being newly trained and employed by canal carrying companies during the war to operate as all-female crews on the Grand Union Canal and latterly on other inland waterways. Despite their lack of attention in the official history, these women, often referred to unfairly as 'Idle Women' because of the blue and white IW (Inland Waterways) badge with which they were issued in lieu of uniform, were seen by the government at the time as 'carrying out essential work of great importance'.[7] This chapter seeks to explain how these women came to be employed and analyses the extent to which their new roles can be regarded as having altered gendered roles within the boaters' community.

By the end of the 1930s, the canal industry seemed to be in terminal decline – beset by continued competition from the railways and increasingly faced with a new threat from road haulage. If that were not enough, there were also tensions between the many canal companies owned by competing railway companies to whom they paid tolls to carry goods for a decreasing number of customers. Although attempts had been made by the state to reform and reorganise the industry, most notably the so-called Chamberlain Commission of 1921 and a further Royal Commission in 1930, little of substance was achieved. Despite some minor improvements, canals such as the Grantham Canal and the Thames and Severn had fallen into disuse, victims of both railway competition and poor maintenance.[8] Although an agreement had been reached between competing factions to eliminate price cutting, the overall level of traffic originating on the canals dropped from almost 16.5m tons in 1924 to just over 11m tons in 1938.[9] In addition, after the outbreak of war in September 1939, government planners regarded the British canal and inland waterway network as the least important of the various internal transport networks needed to serve the war economy.[10] The waterways were also susceptible to adverse weather conditions that could lay up boats for weeks or even months in the winter with an inevitable resultant loss of trade and income to those involved and this added an unwelcome element of unreliability for government planners to consider.

Perhaps because of these factors, canals had not featured heavily in the planning by the Committee for Imperial Defence for any future war. Thus it was only decided in March 1937 that the Ministry of Transport would take responsibility for them in a time of war.[11] There was no expectation that the total system would be taken into state control, because of the costs incurred by the Treasury in the Great War and the relatively poor value this was seen to have represented. However, the fact that railway companies, together with the waterways they owned, would automatically be mobilised as they had been in First World War meant that independent waterway companies needed some agreement that would protect their interests and their abilities to retain staff and compete for traffic against businesses whose rates were fixed by the state.[12] A compromise solution, that avoided full state control, was effected though the creation of the Canal (Defence) Advisory Committee (CDAC) to coordinate the industry through regional committees and to suggest policy on resource allocations, labour and the distribution of fuel to 'secure the best use of canals in the national interest in time of war'.[13]

Why the 'Idle Women' were needed

The first months of war saw an inevitable dislocation of traffic, with some regions reporting an initial shortage of traffic and boats being laid up, but this was replaced by complaints of labour shortages towards the end of 1939. The Severn and Canal Carrying Company (SCCC) and the East Midlands region both reported shortages largely because of better-paid employment in war industries such as aircraft building, and rates of pay that were uncompetitive with wages on the railways.[14] Conversely, the South West region continued to complain about a shortage of work and commented that the 'men resent being idle and are leaving for other work'.[15] This uneven pattern was combined with the problems associated with only partial government control of the industry. Whilst unwilling to subsidise the sector purely because it was ailing, the Ministry of Transport was prepared to make some concessions on the basis of its possible contribution to the war effort. Although this helped to temporarily stabilise the situation, many of their workers continued to be enticed away by 'more remunerative employment'.[16] Although the situation was partially addressed by designating all canal boatmen, bargemen, mates and steerers as reserved occupations exempt from military service, the government refused to restrict their movement to other industries.[17] These were, after all, private companies, and the state could not be seen to be favouring one enterprise over another.

Government perceptions of the canal system altered in the winter of 1940–1941 when railway and road haulage were hard-pressed to meet the demands of the war economy and the continued operation of the inland waterways was highlighted as an important alternative. Frank Pick, the

Vice-Chairman of the London Passenger Board, was commissioned to write a comprehensive report on the issue, which was published in May 1941, and led to the creation of a Central Canal Commission, replacing the CDAC.[18] Although this allowed for representation by the users of the network as well as the trade, and the renewal of the subsidy system to keep carriers and canal companies solvent, it failed to meet the real purpose of the government – namely to ensure continued investment in the waterway infrastructure to keep it operational in order to take the pressure off road and rail.[19]

Canal boat labour, already identified as an area of concern, had appeared as a regular item on the agenda of CDAC meetings.[20] Although its minutes for 15 March 1940 recorded that, as workers on the canals were exempt from military service, this would 'provide ample protection for all canal boatmen', this action had no effect in preventing men from the canals leaving for other, better paid employment.[21] As Mr Milford, the Transport & General Workers Union representative on the committee stated, 'the canal boat industry was not attractive so far as remuneration was concerned'.[22] This shortfall in labour was apparent across all areas, with Birmingham reporting a need for an additional 20 experienced men whilst T & W Wells of Stretford near Manchester needed up to 60 and the Grand Union Carrying Company a staggering 300.[23] However, the problem of a shortfall in the required labour force was not solely a result of the war; in 1937 the Ministry of Labour had begun a special drive to fill vacancies for canal boatmen but with 'practically negligible' results.[24]

At the outbreak of war, two possible solutions had been put forward. Firstly, the National Association of Canal Carriers' representatives to the CDAC suggested that, as in First World War, it might be possible to use labour battalions or pioneer battalions, even though this suggestion had already been rejected by the government in connection with dock labour. Secondly, it was suggested that labour requirements for the canals should be circulated to Labour exchanges who could then direct any suitable men on their registers to this area of employment, coupled with an organised training scheme. However, even in late 1939 the Ministry of Labour reported that it was 'not prepared to put in hand a training scheme for canal boatmen at the present time'.[25] Thus by December 1940, although the Labour Exchanges had been harnessed, the situation continued to worsen, with around 100 boats lying idle for lack of labour in the North Western, Grand Union and South Western areas.[26]

In early 1941 there was an apparent improvement when an article in the *Daily Mail* resulted in some 350 applications from potential boatmen. A government training scheme, with the incentive of a £10 subsidy for those who signed a contract of one year, added a further 125 registrations.[27] Frank Pick went on record as saying that it was 'unthinkable that a substantial number of suitable boatmen could not be obtained'.[28] However, even with a raised level of applicants, all did not go smoothly; in the South West region the main carrier in the area took on a number of new men but, '...unfortunately, they have not proved satisfactory and have voluntarily vacated the job.'[29] Of the 998 enquiries ultimately forwarded to carrier companies as a result of publicity in the press, 138 were offered work following interview but only a scant 13 remained in employment. A Ministry of War Transport memorandum in June 1941 stated that the applicants 'appeared to have little idea as to the hard manual labour involved' as the press had 'given rise to false impressions'.[30]

The same document also noted a Grand Union Canal Carrying Company (GUCCC) report that it had received 47 applications for employment from women. All of them had been informed that 'their offer of assistance [was] very much appreciated but at the present juncture [the company was] unable to avail [itself] of their services other than as members of family crews'. The report continues that, although in official circles there seems to be a view that the problem of lack of canal boat personnel could be solved by female labour, they could not agree with this and, as long as male labour was available, they would 'endeavour to exhaust this source before considering alternatives'. One of their main concerns was the loading and unloading of cargoes, currently being undertaken by male labourers but which might, in the near future, have to be undertaken by the boat crews themselves.[31]

A year later, the labour situation on the canals had deteriorated even further. The protection afforded boatmen as a reserved occupation was soon overridden when the needs of the Admiralty dictated it, and in the summer of 1942 'some hundreds' were called up.[32] In a last desperate attempt to find a (male) solution, a representative of the North West Regional Canal Committee suggested that Irish labour might be brought in but canal representatives generally felt that neither merchandise carriers nor coal traders would be 'disposed to employ inexperienced Irish labour'.[33] This reluctance was as least partly based on 'unfortunate' past experience including issues of discipline, damage to property and carelessness. Moreover, prior to the war, canal companies had been concerned about the infiltration of IRA agents following a bomb in a culvert crossing a canal at Wednesbury.[34] With hundreds of boats already lying idle and an employment rate of less than one per cent of all male applicants all other possible avenues had finally been exhausted and the carrying companies were forced to consider training and employing women to make good the shortfall.

Recruiting and training women for the boats

In fact, the canal boat industry's reticence to employ women had already been undermined. Towards the end of 1940, Daphne Marsh, with Molly Traill working as crew, had begun to use her own boat, the Heather Bell, to carry cargo, having converted it from its previous use as a family pleasure boat. In this enterprise they were assisted by various temporary third crew members who worked with them until, in April 1941, they were joined by Kit Gayford. Although the actual date at which they began carrying cargo is rather vague, a handwritten note from Daphne Marsh claims that she had been carrying both grain and flour for Townshends Flour Mills on the Worcester and Birmingham Canal since February of that year.[35]

Later in the same year, the Ministry of War Transport began to take a more active interest, writing directly to Daphne Marsh to report that the GUCCC was already interested in training women and asking if she would either act as trainer herself or if she could recommend someone as the Grand Union Canal Carrying Company would 'like to give the thing a trial'.[36] Daphne Marsh replied that the only people she felt could undertake this role were either herself or Molly Traill and, if there was sufficient need for training on the Grand Union Canal, and 'provided cargoes could be guaranteed and freights satisfactory', she was prepared to bring her own boat and train people as she worked, which she felt was the only practical way.[37] In fact, both the GUCCC and 'Severners' had been approached by the Ministry to try to interest them in such a training scheme as, however reluctant these companies were, they would 'have to make up their minds to employ women'.[38] A month later, R. H. Moll of the GUCCC replied that, as he had information that 'quite a number' of efficient female crews were already operating on the Grand Union system, he was 'not adverse to the suggestion at all'. He did, however, raise the question of where recruits would come from as they would need to be 'hardy people'.[39]

The SCCC response was that 'to work canal boats by female labour entirely [was] not a practical proposition', that they 'object[ed] to sending women on boats alone' and that they were not interested in the training proposal.[40] Although this reply seems to ignore the fact that the women were already operating boats alone in their area, there is a possibility that the objection was actually in relation to women working alone on rivers and tidal waters as the letter refers to the Severn as not being suitable for two women alone. If this was the case, it was a concern also expressed by other carrying companies dealing with estuarine or tidal waters. The North Eastern Regional Canal Committee, for example, felt that 'except in isolated cases where the master of a vessel has a wife who has grown up in contact with the water industry and is therefore capable of navigating a barge in easier places' the 'size of craft, river proportions of navigation and tidal waters' made the waters in their region unsuitable for the employment of women.[41] Similarly, boats utilised by the Leeds and Liverpool Canal Company had to cross the River Mersey to Birkenhead and operate within the Liverpool Docks and it had 'not been considered desirable to utilize women for this reason'.[42]

Despite these apparent setbacks, the suggestion of training women for canal work persisted, together with the question of how to attract suitable recruits. In March 1941, the Ministry of Information suggested that a photographer should be sent to take pictures of the 'two girls' at Worcester – actually Daphne Marsh and her mother – on their narrow boat for publicity purposes.[43] Although Daphne Marsh voiced some reluctance to this publicity and initially only agreed provided the photographs would 'not appear in the Daily Press (sic)', the Photographic Division felt that the photos had turned out so well it seemed 'a pity that they will not be available for publication in at least one of the illustrated weeklies.'[44] The Ministry of Information agreed to seek a general release from Mrs and Miss Marsh as: 'They would be doing a public service by permitting the further publication of the photographs because they are setting a fine example to women about the part they they (sic) can play in the war effort, and their example will encourage others.'[45]

After expressing some concern about technical errors, such as the use of the term 'barge' instead of 'boat' which would be 'evident to other boatmen and people who knew about the cut'.[46] Daphne Marsh finally agreed to this after her fears of misuse were set to rest by the Photographic Division who felt that there was not 'the slightest chance that they could be used for general advertising purposes.[47] In the event the Ministry of Information appears to have been correct in its evaluation that the Marsh's example would encourage others, as Margaret Cornish and Susan Woolfit both record that they applied for the scheme as a result of newspaper/magazine publicity.[48]

By May 1942 the training scheme on the Grand Union Canal Carrying Company was in operation with a number of women being trained to take charge of boats. Early reports indicated that 'this venture is likely to be successful' as crews for six boats were expected to be fully trained by the end of the summer.[49] However, at this stage, 'training' appears to have been somewhat rudimentary. Kit Gayford records that it was 'well into the second year [of the scheme]' before an 'organised system' for training had been developed.[50] Initially new recruits were given one full working trip to decide whether or not they wanted to stay and then one further trip which was seen as giving them 'enough grounding' before they were sent off to 'continue their learning the hard way'.[51] Margaret Cornish, who joined the scheme in early 1943, recorded the initial training journeys as being from Brentford or Limehouse to Tyseley, Birmingham then back by the 'Lower Road' on the Birmingham and Fazeley canal to the Coventry coalfields and through Hawkesbury and the Oxford Canal, carrying coal for factories.[52]

Eventually, new recruits were provided with a standard outline of the Training Scheme which was described as taking ' ... from 2 to 3 months, according to individual ability ... '.[53] Trainees were taught management of both the motor boat and the unpowered, towed butty, correct methods of loading and unloading, care of cargo, sheeting up and a 'certain amount of instruction in the care of the engine', although it was emphasised that trainees were not expected to act as mechanics as trained mechanics provided by the company would carry out all repairs. Margaret Cornish records that they were expected to know how to prime and swing the flywheel, how to grease bearings and check couplings for loose nuts and balls, watch levels in the bilges, keep pumps free from grit, maintain oil pressure, top-up and change batteries, and clean the filter for the water cooling system.[54]

During training, the women were paid £2 per week out of which they had to pay for all personal expenses, food and state insurance; after training, payments were made at agreed freight rates – approximately £10 per week to be shared between the three crew members with a guaranteed minimum wage of £3 per week for each trained crew member. The outline emphasised that earnings 'are dependent largely on your own efforts', that is, crews who worked hardest and completed more runs earned more.[55] Ration books were provided with an arrangement made that the trainees would be able to make purchases in any part of the country. Whilst stating that the work itself was 'not particularly strenuous', the long hours worked over a seven-day week, often in exposed conditions, made it 'imperative that only women of robust constitution and good health' should consider this type of employment.[56] During training, recruits were allowed one week's leave without pay at the end of each trip but once in employment no leave was granted after the firs trip, three days after the second trip and a further six days after two further trips. This pattern was then repeated, without pay, after every second and fourth trip if crews could be spared. All crews were allowed one week's paid leave per annum. The letter concluded by saying that 'transport [would be] an essential key to Victory (sic).[57]

Small numbers of women were also given the chance to work on other canals. Three female volunteers tried out a horse-drawn boat on the Gloucester and Sharpness Canal 'where they would not cause any disturbance', but apparently only completed a few trips.[58] In the North West, Canal Transport Limited, the major canal carrying company on the Leeds and Liverpool Canal finally agreed to consider training women after having exhausted the possibilities of using Irish labour. A number of boatmen's wives were already formally employed as mates, but a scheme was begun in February 1945 which had trained eight women by April and taken on another four, but their usefulness was limited by the almost immediate end of the war in Europe.[59]

The waterways as social change?

At first glance the waterways appears to be a classic example of women breaking into a new area of employment as a result of wartime labour shortages driven in part by a few highly motivated individuals and with some prompting and encouragement from the state, despite the prejudices and reservations of many in the industry. However, this reading obscures the fact that women had been an integral part of the canal carrying workforce for generations before 1939, habitually undertaking many of the tasks that the trainees were being taught. Although apparently dominated by men, the ability of canal carriers to earn a living had often relied on the involvement of whole families, including women and children. Whilst hard evidence for the extent of women's labour in the closed community of the boaters is difficult to trace, there are glimpses of their role included in the reformist literature of the later nineteenth century. These campaigning works were almost entirely concerned with the living conditions on the canal boats, the absence of literacy and education for the children, and the lack of religion and attendance at Sunday Schools, but contain occasional references to women as steerers on family-run boats.[60] The resultant pressure brought about the Canal Boat Acts of 1877 that sought to reform the worst excesses of poor living conditions for families on the boats and to regulate their operation through inspections.[61] *The Liverpool Journal*, in commenting on the possible consequences of the implementation of the act, recorded that four out of six coal barges coming down from Wigan to the Mersey were run exclusively by women and their children because their husbands had died, and the same article noted that the Bridgewater Navigation Company employed six women on its boats.[62] Later photographic evidence also shows women and children engaged in just about every activity necessary to operate a boat on the cut.[63]

As the canal carrying industry struggled to survive in the face of competition from railways and later also road transport, boatmen were increasingly driven to make their homes on the boats they operated, and also to rely on their wives and older children for labour rather than employing other crew members. However, despite new social legislation to protect other workers, these wives and children were not covered by the 1897 Workmen's Compensation Act, as they were deemed employees of the boatman and not of the carrying company. As a result, they do not appear in employment records and can only be enumerated from the inspectors' reports. At the outbreak of the First World War, in addition to the independently owned canal companies, other parts of the canal system which were owned by railway companies, were mobilised alongside the railways. However, there had been no recourse to the female labour employed in other forms of transport to make good the shortfall caused by war. This was in part because of the heavy nature of the work but also because the skilled status of the work involved was carefully guarded by its male practitioners. Any changes effected by the First World War were essentially temporary and made little difference to those earning their living on the waterways.

In the aftermath of war, pressure for reform of the canal industry reappeared – this time fronted by the Trade Union movement. The Annual General Council of the National Transport Workers Federation (NTWF) demanded both a 48-hour working week and an end to the 'living-in' system. The NTWF case was made by President Harry Gosling and Ernest Bevin, who described the canals as 'the most medieval industry [...] left in the country'. However, by employing only one man per boat, the owner also received the services of the wife (and the children) 'for nothing'. Although concentrating on the children as the Victorian social reformers had done, there is no doubt that the NTWF also recognised the role played by women in the canal carrying industry as unpaid elements within family-run boats. Research by the government departments of Health, Education and Transport indicated that on the Shropshire Union Canal some 90 per cent of boats were in the charge of a man and wife team.[64] Consequently, the civil servants at the nascent Ministry of Transport concluded that with the information then available, it would be 'impossible to consider the abolition of the living-in system.'[65]

Pressure from the NTWF led to a departmental enquiry in 1921 (commonly referred to as the Chamberlain Committee), that reinforced the conclusion that there remained large numbers of family boats on the inland waterways and they continued to press for reforms that would replace the unpaid labour of wives and children (who would then remain 'at home') with additional men brought in to crew the boats. As this reform would result in increased payments to the boatmen or an increased wage bill for the carriers to pay the additional manpower employed, it was inevitably unpopular with canal carriers already hard-pressed by competition from railways and increasingly from road haulage as well. Moreover, whilst happy to support some of the union demands, the proposal to remove women from the boats was decried by the boatmen themselves who, it was argued, 'would separate from the Union rather than separate from their wives.'[66]

Ostensibly, neither the Victorian social reformers nor the Trade Union movement had much power to affect conditions for women on the boats; their lives remained undeniably hard when compared with their sisters in other occupations and other family circumstances. The canal women on the boats may not have been recognised as being employed, but their contribution was certainly evident and indeed essential for their families to make a living on the inland waterways – either operating independently or under contract to the canal carrying companies. Aside from all the domestic duties associated with running a home and bringing up a family in extremely cramped and difficult circumstances, many of the women on the cut could have claimed that the Second World War trainees were doing no more than they and their sisters had done for generations. The replacement of horses by engines that needed maintenance created the potential for another male preserve, but even this was by no means universal. Likewise, steering the lead (powered) boat was also usually a male preserve, with the wife steering the unpowered butty – where there was greater space for cooking and for children. Yet whilst this may have remained the norm in the inter-war years, even the all-female crew supposedly pioneered by the trainees seems to have been in existence long before Daphne Marsh and Molly Traill began working the Heather Bell on the Worcester Canal in 1940. Leaving aside the references to boats run by women in the nineteenth century, the tradition of wives taking over the sole ownership and operation of boats on the death of their husbands continued into the twentieth century.[67] Thus a Mrs Sammy Saxton could be found on the Grand Union Canal steering boats registered in her name and with an all-female crew of daughters and nieces.[68]

Conclusion

Essentially, the women trained to work on canal boats during the Second World War did not break down any employment barriers that had not already been breached by force of economic or family circumstances in the previous century and a half. What marks them out from their predecessors is that they were part of a paid labour force with guaranteed minimum earnings and, like their sisters who went into other forms of industry, were largely middle-class outsiders with little or no knowledge of the closely-knit and isolated community they were trying to enter.

Notes

1. A. Marwick (1974) *War and Social Change*; A. Marwick (1988) *Total War*; H. L. Smith (1986) *War and Social Change*; Penny Summerfield (1989) *Women Workers in World War II*; Clive Emsley Arthur Marwick and Wendy Simpson eds. (1990) *War, Peace and Social Change*.
2. M. Glucksmann (1990) *Women Assemble*; S. Horrocks (2000) 'A promising pioneer profession?', pp 351–368; M. Savage (1988) 'Trade Unionism', pp 209–230.
3. A. Thomson (2013) 'Tied to the kitchen sink?', pp 126–147; P. Summerfield (1998) 'They didn't want women back in that job!', pp 83–104. P. Goodman (1998) 'Patriotic Femininity', pp 278–294; Susan L. Carruthers (1990) 'Manning the Factories', pp 232–256.
4. See for example, N. Tyrer (1997) *They Fought in the Fields*; S. V. Cook (2000) 'Emancipation of Exploitation?', pp 7–16; Emma Vickers (2011) 'The Forgotten Army', pp 101–112.
5. In real figures this represented an increase from 23,300 in 1939 to a peak of 93,300 in 1944. C. I. Savage (1957) *Inland Transport*, pp 620–621, p 651. On their history see, H. Wojtczak (2005) *Railwaywomen*; and A. Day (1998) 'The Forgotten "Mateys"', pp 361–380; A. Marwick (1977) *Women at War*, p 166.
6. C. I. Savage (1957) *Inland Transport*, pp 620–621.
7. C. I. Savage (1957) *Inland Transport*, pp 620–621.
8. C. Hadfield (1974) *British Canals: An Illustrated History*, 5th Edition (Newton Abbot: David and Charles) p 299.
9. C. I. Savage (1957) *Inland Transport*, p 21. These were the Departmental (Chamberlain) Committee on Inland Waterways (1921) and the Royal Commission on Transport (1930). C. Hadfield (1974) *British Canals*, p 302, gives figures of 17 million tons for 1924 and 13 million tons for 1938.
10. C. I. Savage (1957) *Inland Transport*, p 33. Indeed, it was thought that its chief value might be in the canal craft that might play a 'useful minor role in war'.
11. C. I. Savage (1957) *Inland Transport*, p 37.

12. 'English Canals', *The Economist*, 20 April 1940, p 735.
13. C. I. Savage (1957) *Inland Transport*, pp 82–85. Essentially this compromise was chosen because the Ministry of Transport did not feel it could sway the Treasury to accept the costs involved given the experiences of 1914–1918. Memorandum CDAC 1, p 1. The National Archives (TNA) MT52/240; 'English Canals', *The Economist*, 20 April 1940, p 735.
14. Memorandum CDAC 4 Regional Canal Situation Reports (East Midlands), p 1. TNA MT52/240.
15. Memorandum CDAC 4 Regional Canal Situation Reports (South West), p 2. TNA MT52/240.
16. Memorandum CDAC 6, p 1. TNA MT52/240. See also, 'The Canals Must Be Used', *Modern Transport*, 6 January 1940; and 'English Canals', *The Economist*, pp 735–736.
17. All canal boatmen were 'reserved' at 18, motor boatmen at 25 and boatmen and watermen at 25. It was therefore important for employers to describe their employees with great care. Canal Transport Ltd. to Mr J. Halliwell, 20 June 1940 and F. C. Bunn (Ministry of War Transport) to E. W. Bayliss (National Association of Canal Carriers), 2 November 1939. National Waterways Museum (NWM) BW168/236.
18. C. I. Savage (1957) *Inland Transport*, p 174.
19. C. I. Savage (1957) *Inland Transport*, p 445.
20. See, for example Canal (Defence) Advisory Committee meeting agendas January, March and May 1940. TNA MT52/45, 46 and 47 respectively.
21. Memo CDAC6, Canal (Defence) Advisory Committee Meeting, 15 March 1940. TNA MT52/46.
22. Minutes of meeting of Canal (Defence) Advisory Committee, 31 January 1940. TNA, MT52/45.
23. Memo CDAC 6, Canal (Defence) Advisory Committee Meeting, 15 March 1940. TNA, MT52/46.
24. In Hull, 25 men had been interviewed as a result of this drive but all had refused to accept the wages and conditions offered. Canal (Defence) Advisory Committee Meeting, 15 March 1940. TNA, MT52/46.
25. Note, F. C. Bunn, (Ministry of Transport) to Secretary, CDAC, 28 November 1939. TNA MT52/43.
26. Letter, 8 November 1940 Lionel Wood, The Severn Commission to Walter Sedgwick, Canal Association and Minutes of Canal (Defence) Advisory Committee Meeting 19 December 1940 respectively. NA, MT52/50.
27. Canal (Defence) Advisory Committee Meeting, 14 May 1941. TNA, MT52/52.
28. Canal (Defence) Advisory Committee Meeting, 27 February 1941. TNA, MT52/51.
29. Letter South-Western Regional Canal (Defence) Advisory Committee to S. W. Nelson, Ministry of War Transport. 25 June 1941. TNA, MT52/52.
30. Memorandum CDAC 20, Canal (Defence) Advisory Committee Meeting, 15 June 1941. TNA, MT52/53.
31. Memorandum CDAC 20, Canal (Defence) Advisory Committee Meeting, 5 June 1941. TNA MT52/53.
32. C. I. Savage (1957) *Inland Transport*, p 395; Central Transport Committee, Transport Position – Winter 1942–1943 (September 1942).

33. Letter, N. N. Bird, Liaison Officer and Secretary, North-Western Regional Canal Committee to Batten, Ministry of War Transport, 5 June 1942. TNA MT52/102.
34. Letter, P. Nadin, West Midland Regional Canal Committee to Sir Osborne Mance, Director of Canals, Ministry of War Transport, 17 June 1942. TNA MT52/102.
35. Daphne March, handwritten note, 20 October 1941.TNA MT52/102. Although the terms are often used interchangeably, a standard 'barge' has a beam of 14 feet, the Heather Bell, a narrow boat, was 70 feet long and only 7 feet in the beam as she had originally been built with the intention of being able to access Welsh canals where the locks were smaller. E. Gayford (1973) *The Amateur Boatwomen*, p 20.
36. Letter S. W. Nelson (Ministry of War Transport) to Daphne March, 21 October 1941. TNA MT52/102.
37. Letter Daphne March to S. W. Nelson, 21 October 1941. TNA MT52/102.
38. Letter S. W. Nelson to Daphne March, 27 October 1941. TNA MT52/102.
39. Letter, R. H. Moll, Grand Union Canal Carrying Company to S. W. Nelson, 4 November 1941. TNA MT52/102.
40. Letter, Severn and Canal Carrying Company Ltd, 25 November 1941. TNA MT52/102.
41. Letter, H. V. Riley, North-Eastern Regional Canal Committee to E. R. Batten. 21 July 1942. TNA MT52/102.
42. Letter, R. Davidson, Leeds & Liverpool Canal Company to General Sir Osborne Mance, Director of Canals, Ministry of War Transport, 9 November 1942. TNA MT52/102.
43. Note, Batten, Ministry of Information, 9 March 1941. TNA MT52/102.
44. Letter, R. Butt, Photograph Division to Fleetwood Pritchard, Ministry of Information, 28 April 1942. TNA MT52/102.
45. Letter, Fleetwood Pritchard, Ministry of Information to R. Butt, Photographic Division, 29 April 1942. TNA MT52/102.
46. Letter, Daphne Marsh to E. R. Batten, 8 May 1942. TNA MT52/102. Although these changes were apparently made to the captions on the photos, Butt continued to refer to 'barges' in his letters. The term 'barge' is only applied to boats with a beam of over 14 feet, the Heather Bell, which had been built to be able to access the narrower locks on the Welsh system had a beam of 7 feet. The term 'cut' is generally used by boatmen to refer to a canal. Despite the best efforts of the women to adopt the terminology of the boatpeople and adhere to its codes of behaviour and manners, and no matter how expert they became at handling the boats, the British Waterways Archive records that they remained 'trainees' throughout their time on the cut. British Waterways Archive. Outreach Pack – *World War II; The Home Front*, p 20.
47. Letter, R. Butt, Photographic Division to Fleetwood Pritchard, Ministry of Information, 13 May 1942. TNA MT52/102. These photographs are now held by the Imperial War Museum (IWM) Photographic Archive.
48. Cornish, M. (1986) 'The Wartime Trainees', *Waterways World*, May, pp 32–37. IWM 05/72A., Woolfitt, *Idle Women*, p 9.
49. Note Batten, Ministry of Information to Regional Canal Committees, 9 May 1942 and Letter, Batten to N. N. Bird, Manchester Ship Canal Company, 2 July 1942. TNA MT52/102.

50. E. Gayford (1973) *The Amateur Boatwomen*, p 15.
51. E. Gayford, (1973) *The Amateur Boatwomen*, pp 114, 115.
52. These factories included paper mills at Croxley and Kings Langley, Glaxo at Yiewsley and Heinz at Greenford. IWM 05/72A.
53. Ministry of War Transport standard letter to applicants for Training Scheme in E. Gayford (1973) *The Amateur Boatwomen*, p 140–141.
54. E. Gayford, (1973) *The Amateur Boatwomen*, p 20; M. Cornish, (1986) 'The Wartime Trainees', pp 32–37. IWM 05/72A.
55. Ministry of War Transport standard letter to applicants for Training Scheme in E. Gayford (1973) *The Amateur Boatwomen*, p 140–141.
56. E. Gayford (1973) *The Amateur Boatwomen*, p 140–141.
57. E. Gayford (1973) *The Amateur Boatwomen*, p 140–141.
58. H. Conway-Jones (1990) *Working Life*, p 163.
59. G. Wheat (1999) *Canal Transport Ltd*, (Mill Lane Publishing Reading) p 22; W. Freer (1995) *Women and Children of the Cut*, p 24, http://www.rchs.org.uk/trial/gwpf.php?wpage=about-us.
60. G. Smith (1875) *Our Canal Population. The Sad Condition of the Women and Children – with Remedy* (London: Haughton and Co.) p 46.
61. Canal Boats Act 1877 (40 & 41 Vict c.60) and Canal Boats Act (1877) Amendment Act 1884 (47 & 48 Vict c.75).
62. *Liverpool Journal*, 15 September 1877. http://www.old-merseytimes.co.uk/canalboatsact.html
63. See for example, IWM Photo Archive D21765, D21775 & D21781.
64. TNA MT6/2583/7 Memorandum attached to docket, 28 July 1919.
65. TNA MT6/2583/7 Memorandum attached to docket, 19 September 1919.
66. K.B. Sherwood 'The canal boatmen's strike of 1923' http://www.steamershistorical.co.uk/Web_FMC_Steamers/The%20canal%20boatmen's%20strike.pdf (accessed 12 November 2013) cites Ministry of Health, *Report of the Departmental Committee appointed to Inquire into the Practice of Living-in on Canal Boats in England and Wales and to report whether any alteration in the practice is required*, evidence of Rev. W. Ward, p. 840.
67. See M. Stammers (1993) *Mersey Flats*, p 157 who notes the role played by women on that waterway at the end of the nineteenth century.
68. E. Gayford (1973) *The Amateur Boatwomen*, p 13.

References

Carruthers. S L (1990) '"Manning the Factories": Propaganda and Policy on the Employment of Women, 1939–1947', *History*, 75, 244, pp 232–256.

Conway-Jones. H (1990) *Working Life on Severn and Canal. Reminiscences of Working Boatmen* (Stroud: Sutton).

Cook. S (2000) 'Emancipation of Exploitation? The Women's Land Army in the Second World War', *Minerva: Women and War*, 18, 2, pp 7–16.

Day. A (1998) 'The Forgotten "Mateys": Women Workers in Portsmouth Dockyard, England, 1939–1945', *Women's History Review*, 7, 3, pp 361–380.

Emsley. C Arthur Marwick and Wendy Simpson (eds) (1990) *War, Peace and Social Change: Europe 1900–1955. Book IV: World War II and its Consequences* (Buckingham: Open University Press).

Gayford. E. (1973) *The Amateur Boatwomen: Canal Boating 1941–1945* (Newton Abbot: David and Charles).

Glucksmann. M (1990) *Women Assemble: Women Workers and the New Industries in Inter-War Britain* (New York: Routledge).

Goodman. P (1998) '"Patriotic Femininity": Women's Morals and Men's Morale During the Second World War', *Gender and History*, 10, 2, 278–294.

Horrocks. S (2000) 'A Promising Pioneer Profession? Women in Industrial Chemistry in Inter-war Britain', *British Journal for the History of Science*, 33, 3, pp 351–368.

Marwick. A (1974) *War and Social Change in the Twentieth Century* (London: Macmillan).

Marwick. A (1977) *Women at War, 1914–1918* (London: Croom Helm).

Marwick. A (1988) *Total War and Social Change* (London: Macmillan).

Savage. C I (1957) *Inland Transport, History of the Second World War: United Kingdom Civil Series* (London: HMSO/Longmans Green).

Savage. M (1988) 'Trade Unionism, Sex Segregation and the State: Women's Employment in the "New Industries" in Inter-war Britain', *Social History*, 13, 2, pp 209–230.

Smith. H (1990) *War and Social Change: British Society in the Second World War* (Manchester: Manchester University Press).

Stammers. M (1993) *Mersey Flats and Flatmen* (Sudbury: Terence Dalton).

Summerfield. P (1989) *Women Workers in World War II: Production and Patriarchy in Conflict* (London: Routledge).

Summerfield. P (1998) '"They didn't want women back in that job!": The Second World War and the Construction of Gendered Work Histories', *Labour History Review*, 63, 1, pp 83–104.

Thomson. A (2013) '"Tied to the kitchen sink"? Women's Lives and Women's History in Mid-Twentieth Century Britain and Australia', *Women's History Review*, 22, 1, pp 126–147.

Tyrer. N (1997) *They Fought in the Fields: Women's Land Army – The Story of a Forgotten Victory* (London: Mandarin).

Vickers. E (2011) '"The Forgotten Army of the Woods": The Women's Timber Corps in the Second World War', *Agricultural History Review*, 59, 1, pp 101–112.

Wojtczak. H (2005) *Railwaywomen: Exploitation, Betrayal and Triumph in the Workplace* (Hastings: Hastings Press).

Woolfitt, Susan (1985) *Idle Women (Working Waterways)* (London: M.& M. Baldwin)

13

'Doing Your Bit': Women and the National Savings Movement in the Second World War

Rosalind Watkiss Singleton

Introduction

Almost 75 years after the outbreak of the Second World War there are aspects of life on the Home Front which have, as yet, received little scholarly attention. The economic contribution of the National Savings Movement and its function as a morale booster are both under-researched, although they were considered by the government as a method of encouraging national cohesion and 'securing from citizens, even of very moderate income, loans from their savings towards the severe expenses of war.'[1] The success of the movement in galvanising the population into saving is undeniable. Ostensibly, it seems that patriotism was a major factor in the scheme's success as '[t]here were a lot of patriotic feelings about, we would do anything to help the armed forces',[2] and '[e]veryone...wanted to rally round',[3] yet motives for supporting the movement are ambiguous. Although the government propaganda machine effectively publicised and garnered support for the project, complicated interplays of 'cultural and social factors play[ed] an appreciable part in savings patterns' at this time.[4] In the overall experiences of war the National Scheme has been virtually forgotten by many of the participants.

This chapter compares the stereotypical images and words on the propaganda posters with the oral testimony[5] of women from Birmingham and the Black Country, supplemented by the memoirs and autobiographies,[6] of those involved in the movement, to reveal the complex motivations for participation in the scheme. The 32 respondents from the Black Country who recounted their experiences of wartime saving were born between 1920 and 1940.[7] They were contacted through over 50s groups and clubs, local libraries, or they responded to an appeal published in the *Black Country Bugle*, a local history publication.[8] The vast majority of interviews were conducted in person, following an initial telephone conversation, letter or email. Mostly the reminiscences were of their personal involvement in the movement but the three younger respondents shared memories of their mothers' participation accompanied by evidence in the form of badges, photographs and Certificates of Honour and letters of appreciation from the National Savings Committee. Although virtually all respondents claimed that they 'wanted to do their bit for the country', to support both the troops and the war-effort, and this undoubtedly was true, they were pressured, sometimes unwittingly, by the National Savings Committees, society at large, and their communities to conform to accepted norms of patriotism and respectability.

'Let's save as hard as they fight'

The origins of the National Savings Movement lie in the economics of the 1914–1918 War. Finance was a perplexing dilemma and, from the conflict's initial stages, funding was of paramount importance. Conventional means, from increased taxation and a Vote of Credit to a War Loan, 'aimed at the conventional investor who, being already wealthy, merely became wealthier',[9] were deemed insufficient. The Parliamentary War Committee proposed to reduce borrowing and regulate spending and saving within the wider population; and harnessed the auspices of the Post Office to launch a War Loan designed to attract the smaller investor[10] – 'the humble man'.[11] In 1916, the War Savings Movement initiated the sale of sixpenny coupons which could ultimately be exchanged for a War Savings Certificate. As the working class were already familiar with the concept of making small-scale, regular investments to sickness, insurance and savings clubs their participation was feasible.[12] The scheme expanded beyond individuals into schools, churches and places of employment, administered by volunteers, supported locally and nationally by civil servants.

Despite depression and unemployment the National Savings Movement continued during the interwar years, its significance increasing with the imminence of war. In times of crisis 'the movement was acting as a stabiliser and giving people a proper sense of proportion'.[13] Following the declaration of war in September 1939, savings operations intensified. The War Office initiated a new Savings Campaign, reorganising and enlarging existing committees in order to mitigate, at least partially, against the effects of inflation.[14]

Slogans on hoardings and in advertisements – 'Save Your Way to Victory' and 'Lend to Defend the Right to be Free'[15] – exhorted the population to purchase savings stamps, exchanging completed books for savings certificates worth 15 shillings. Upon maturity, in ten years, the saver would receive 20s 6d; the tax-free interest rate being attractive to small investors.[16] Certificates could be cashed in earlier if necessary but deferral was encouraged on patriotic grounds.[17] The expenses of the war could not be defrayed wholly from taxes, requiring the modification of spending and voluntary saving. The Chancellor indicated that:

> It is more than ever important ... that the considerable flow of investment in National Savings Certificates and Defence Bonds, together with money deposited with the Post Office and Trustee Savings Banks, should steadily increase ... savings, of course, imply abstention from unnecessary expenditure. It is vital that ... man-power and material resources ... should be devoted to the supreme effort, and by abstaining from unnecessary expenditure people and institutions will make a considerable contribution to this vital objective.[18]

The Savings Movement was underpinned by a substantial and costly advertising campaign designed to stir the patriotic nature of the British public.[19] They were bombarded with images and text in newspapers and magazines, on hoardings and posters,[20] at the cinema, and on the radio, designed to encourage saving.[21] The intimations of the advertisements altered with the tenor of the war, becoming increasingly aggressive at the conflict's height.[22] Posters announced that 'The Fight is on!', exhorting 'we who stay at home' to 'turn out ... pockets and purses ... [and] put all you can into National Savings.'[23] The messages were unambiguous; saving was a duty for all non-combatants.[24] Sociological surveys and government-commissioned Mass Observation Surveys (MASSOBS)[25] demonstrated their success.[26] A 1940 survey announced that 'National Savings has shot up since the war'.[27] In 1941 another[28] concluded that National Savings propaganda 'has produced a general atmosphere in which it is the "done thing" to save',[29] a phrase reiterated within the oral testimony – 'it was the done thing, our boys relied on us'.[30] *The Times* proclaimed: 'Before the war it was the exception for the lower-paid worker to go in for national savings; now it has become a majority habit.'[31] The public conscience was gripped, 'Saving was by 1943 an even more obvious obsession than salvage.'[32] Saving numbers peaked in March 1944 at twelve million members – a third of the population.

The Post Office was most frequently recalled as the repository for the respondents' savings. Although it was 'popular with all classes'[33] its function as a depository for working-class savings,[34] and dispenser of Old

Age Pensions and stamps, ensured that the less well-off, who eschewed intimidating banks and building societies, were comfortable transacting their business within its environs.[35] It was 'the one government institution that most people regularly interacted with.'[36] Respondents confirmed that: 'Post Offices played a big part in the war', 'it was ideal', 'well, the Post Office was so convenient', and 'I already used the Post Office so it made sense to save there'.[37]

Although men and women were involved as savers and administrators within the movement, women played an increasingly prominent role, as committee members, savings group secretaries and collectors. With the escalation of the war the strategies used to promote saving and maximise contributions grew. Communal saving was deemed the most effective method of ensuring participation and bolstering morale, resulting in the formation of savings groups within schools, factories, shops, offices, and individual streets or neighbourhoods.[38] Miss YB 'thought that it functioned to boost morale as much as funds'.[39] Indeed, the Chancellor proclaimed that savings momentum 'must be continued and must also be matched with a like spirit in all sections of our community.'[40] The government encouraged employers 'to strengthen savings groups in industry',[41] issuing administration guidelines and illustrating ways to encourage savings through rewards and incentives.[42]

'All in it together'

Individual saving was undoubtedly important, and should not be underestimated; nevertheless, it was saving groups that respondents mentioned repeatedly. Group participation was an important factor in the savings process;[43] as a report into *The Economic Effects of the War* explained: people 'in factories are peculiarly good subjects for savings group propaganda. At work people are used to paying levies... for Trade Union payments or for schemes organized by their employers. In such cases the psychology of doing what everyone else does is highly operative.'[44] Group saving was effective because communities were already in situ and savings could be conveniently extracted at source, relieving employees of effort.[45] June Robinson recalled, 'well it was convenient, companies did all the work.'[46] MASSOBS confirmed that 'Savings Groups in the works have certainly been extremely successful.'[47] Success relied, partially, on the persuasive powers of the savings groups representatives – 'if they called a meeting in the canteen with the shop stewards on the platform, and a speech was made recommending Savings Certificates... it would do a lot of good.'[48] Colleagues provided mutual support and encouragement to savers;[49] 'when they started it [saving] at work it was a case of one and all'.[50] Respondents joined groups because 'the firm had asked them to, or everybody else did',[51] or, as Vera Harding claimed, because 'it was almost obligatory'.[52]

Savings groups flourished, their achievements explained because '[t]he forces of propaganda and social imitation favour National as against other savings methods, and they favour also the National Savings Group as opposed to private purchase of certificates.'[53] The impetus was sustained by targets, inter-firm and inter-community competitions and prizes.[54] Vere Hodgson delightedly exclaimed that her office savings target was 'doubled by Friday'.[55] Manufacturers, who awarded National Savings Certificates as prizes, revealed that Savings Leagues encouraged 'intensive internal competition'.[56] Successful groups won cups, shields, badges and approbation within the newspapers. Employers provided additional saving incentives by supplementing workers' contributions,[57] opening employee accounts or purchasing bonus certificates for regular savers.[58] Women agreed that '[t]he savings were very good. We used to buy government savings and they [employers] used to put shillings ... the bonds were fifteen shillings each and every fourteen shillings we saved they would give us a shilling – the company ... and you could put in as much as you could afford.'[59]

Outside the workplace, administration of a savings group permitted women who were otherwise excluded to support the war effort. Pauline Jones explained, '[p]eople wanted to be seen to be doing their bit to help.'[60] Volunteers were mostly 'housewives, often those ... who were the backbone of every form of service.'[61] In Knightsbridge, the Harrods in-store National Savings recruiting bureau 'met the needs of thousands of women who are seeking some way of offering their ... services to the country.'[62] Agents enlisted from within the community were ideally placed to encourage participation. 'Most people bought them'[63] because refusal was awkward, particularly if rebuttal could potentially be disseminated within the workplace or the neighbourhood. Housewives confirmed that non-participation was difficult as 'they call to the house for it'.[64] Martial language ('I called myself up – for the savings front')[65] and images made clear connotations between female savers and the conflict.[66] Readers were informed that a female savings collector standing at a neighbour's front door was ' ... on a mopping-up operation. A few houses are holding out – little isolated pockets of resistance to her Savings Group. She won't be satisfied until every member of every house is digging deep ... to do battle for Britain.'[67] Coercive in tone the adverts implied that failure to conform was tantamount to betrayal.

Propaganda 'produced a general atmosphere in which saving was the "done thing"';[68] correspondents confirmed that 'it was natural'.[69]

Consensual opinion is that working and lower middle-class women played a vital role in managing the family finances, bearing responsibility for economic decisions within the home until the post-war years.[70] Their role was to balance income with expenditure, avoid 'going into debt', and to save for emergencies.[71] John Beck's mother was 'chancellor of the family exchequer',[72] a statement endorsed by oral testimony and memoirs.[73] Since the spectre of the workhouse loomed over working-class communities, financial independence and self-sufficiency were inextricably linked to estimations of respectability,[74] which, although subjective, were partially correlated to a family's capacity to budget. Purchasing individual savings stamps was feasible for wives and mothers[75] who were accustomed to saving small weekly sums from the housekeeping in clubs and savings schemes. These contributions, and the acquisition of goods,[76] provided visible evidence of their financial and social status within the community.[77] 'Communal knowledge of a household's credit position affected both its community and self-esteem' and the women of the family were often responsible for the circulation of this information;[78] Marion Allen, and other respondents, revealed that 'everyone in the street knew your business [as] there were a lot of nosy parkers.'[79] Consequently, National Savings contributions also functioned as an important indicator of status, and women's potential role in the movement was recognised in direct appeals to them[80] as 'guardians of the wartime purse'.[81]

'Pulling together?'

If involvement in the scheme indicated the patriotism, financial stability and respectability of contributors, what Johnson described as the 'openness of almost all saving behaviour'[82] made refusal to participate virtually impossible as it signalled treachery and categorised families as less respectable. Respondents stated emphatically that failure to participate in the scheme indicated a lack of propriety. Mavis Morgan typically insisted that 'we all wanted to be part of the war effort, even as children' and only the most deprived families failed to contribute.[83] Olive Houlton recalled that refusal to join Ratcliffe's Savings Group applied solely to disreputable workers.[84] Colleagues and neighbours censured those who remained outside the scheme – 'we had no time for them'.[85] Indeed, Kindersley explicitly stated the campaign's intention to promote saving until abstinence would 'create a public opinion so strong that the blatant spender becomes an outcast'.[86] Nevertheless, other factors influenced popular support for the National Savings Movement. Rationing and shortages made conspicuous consumption virtually impossible, thus encouraging the saving of surplus income.[87] That scarcity of merchandise and empty shop windows 'made it difficult for them to spend their money'[88] was endorsed by Vera Harding – 'well, there was nothing in the shops'.[89] Similarly in recounting her regular weekly investments, June Robinson admitted 'mind you, there wasn't much to buy'.[90] Shortages of goods were corroborated by women who, unable to acquire trousseaus or furniture, purchased Savings Certificates. As Pauline Jones recalled, 'Saving was the only option when the shops were empty.'[91]

Conversely, some women were accused of purchasing unnecessary luxuries from their unprecedentedly high wartime wages.[92] One correspondent observed that 'there are young women … in their early twenties, with practically no experience or skill in industry, drawing £11 17s a week and spending every penny of it at night in drink, dancing and amusements. Does the Government … expect us to go on pinching and scraping and saving, as we have done, while it utters no clear word in public about this riot of waste which is going on under our very eyes?'[93] Concerned at the 'thoughtless spending' of highly paid women workers buying 'ornamental vases', paying 'three visits to hairdressers at 30s per visit', and generally wasting money, it was thought necessary to appeal to the 'social conscience'.[94] The introduction of the 'Squander Bug'[95] was a timely reminder that wasting money aided the enemy.

Furthermore, respondents also appreciated the personal financial benefits of the Scheme, such as the convenience of savings directly deducted from pay – 'I don't miss the 5/- a week' – 'I think it's a good investment'.[96] The 'ease and accessibility'[97] was also a factor, 'the returns were good and guaranteed', 'they were tax-free', and 'they were "safe" in the Post Office'.[98] Parliament was reassured that '[s]o far as small savings are concerned, in case there should be any doubt left … there is nothing in the new powers of the Government … which endangers money in any bank.'[99] Saving for the post-war years was also a consideration: 'it was a way of saving for the future';[100] indeed contributors to a Mass Observation (MASSOBS) report saw themselves as 'providing for a possible lean future',[101] or what Betty Johnson called 'a rainy day'.[102]

Conclusion

Whilst women's financial acumen in times of hardship and their contributions to the National Savings Movement, both in monetary and in organisational terms, are evident, their motives are perhaps less so. Undoubtedly the necessity to sustain morale, support the war effort, and defeat the common enemy motivated saving. Respondents on the Home Front identified with loved ones on the war front – 'We are warriors all';[103] as National Savings advertisements reminded readers, 'the photographs are watching'.[104] Patriotism undisputedly played a role within the Savings Movement, with most women rationalising their involvement in nationalistic terms.[105] However, there was immense pressure from within the workplace and the community to conform to accepted norms, which was endorsed in advertisements and the press.[106] Nevertheless, respondents refuted suggestions of coercion; the oral testimony reflected June Robinson's comments that people were 'encouraged not pressured' to save.[107] From the factories to Girl Guides or the Women's Voluntary Services, the camaraderie of savings groups echoed the zeitgeist of the era, and collective co-operation against the enemy. But, through their contributions women were also able to demonstrate the financial stability of their families to the wider community, thus providing evidence of both their patriotism and their respectability. The consensual opinion was that 'if you had a bit [of money] to save, then you were "somebody" and in any case we loved our country and needed to win the war,'[108] and 'we had a personal stake in ending the war',[109] 'we all wanted to be part of the war effort'.[110]

Notes

1. Sir J. Simon, Chancellor of the Exchequer, *Hansard*, vol. 353, cc. 1030, 21 November 1939.
2. *Oral Testimony*: MM (Willenhall).
3. *Oral Testimony*: JR (Bilston).
4. File Report 1053 'A Savings Survey (Working Class) by Mass Observation', December 1941, p 33.
5. For an examination of the oral testimony of women in the Second World War and the relationship between discourse and subjectivity, see P. Summerfield (1998) *Reconstructing Women's Wartime Lives*.
6. Memoirs and diaries from around the country are used to provide a more balanced assessment.
7. Twenty-seven women and four men took part in the project.
8. R. Watkiss (2011) 'Old Habits Persist, Change and Continuity in Black Country Communities: Pensnett, Sedgley and Tipton, 1945 – c. 1970', Unpublished PhD thesis, University of Wolverhampton.
9. K. G. Burton (1999) *A Penknife to a Mountain*, p 2.
10. K. G. Burton (1999) *A Penknife to a Mountain*, outlines the formation of the National Savings Movement between 1915 and 1920.
11. A. J. P. Taylor (1965) *English History*, p 88.

12. K. G. Burton (1999) *A Penknife to a Mountain*, p 3. For working-class spending and saving see P. Johnson (1985) *Saving and Spending*; P. Johnson (1985) 'Credit and Thrift'; J. Benson (2005) *Affluence and Authority*; J. Benson (1996) 'Working-Class Consumption', pp 87–99.

13. *The Times* 14 June 1939, p 8.

14. P. Summerfield (1986) 'The "Levelling of Class"', in H. Smith (ed.) *War and Social Change: British Society in the Second World War*, (Manchester: Manchester University Press), p 183. Debate within the Commons suggests that public financial contributions were more beneficial as a counter to inflation and to prevent unnecessary consumption than for their monetary value. http://hansard.millbanksystems.com/

15. *The Times*, 23 November 1939, p 5; J. Waller and M. Vaughan-Rees (1987) *Women in Wartime: The Role of Women's Magazines, 1939–1945* (London: MacDonald Optima) p 56.

16. *Hansard*, vol. 353, cc. 1030–1033, 21 November 1939.

17. Defence Bonds, bought in multiples of £5 to a limit of £1000, with an interest rate of 3 per cent, and National War Bonds 1946–1948 at 2½ per cent were also available.

18. Sir Kingsley Wood, Chancellor of the Exchequer, *Hansard*, vol. 568, 29 May 1940. 'It is also imperative that civilian consumption should continue to be curtailed and that every penny possible should be saved and lent to the State', *Hansard*, vol. 572, 21 June 1940.

19. S. Briggs (1975) *Keep Smiling Through*, p 172; Summerfield (1986) 'The "Levelling of Class"', p 183.

20. Z. Zeman (1978) *Selling the War*, 'The "total war" character of the Second World War meant that mass propaganda had to aim at the largest possible part of the population and convince it to be utterly loyal to the state', p 31.

21. K. G. Burton (1999) *A Penknife to a Mountain*, p 224.

22. N. Longmate (1988) *How We Lived Then*, p 378.

23. *Picture Post*, 8 June 1940, p 38.

24. *Picture Post*, 14 September 1940, p 8.

25. Mass-Observation founded (1937) to 'record the voice of the people', and study everyday behaviour in Britain. R. Fisher, R. Gap and A. Dobson (2011) 'Letters from the War Factory', pp 47–57; P. Summerfield (1985) 'Mass Observation: Social Research or Social Movement', *Journal of Contemporary History*, 20, 3, 213–229. Fisher et al. (2011) concluded that the findings of the MASSOBS do not necessarily reflect the actual experiences of women involved in war work. Summerfield examines the subjectivity and inherent bias in the work of MASSOBS.

26. C. Madge (1943) *War-time Patterns of Saving and Spending*, National Institute of Economic and Social Research Occasional Papers, IV, Cambridge University Press, p 1.

27. MASSOBS File Report 353, 'Wartime Spending and Saving by Mass Observation', 10 August 1940 p 3. The authors aspired to provide a 'representative' picture but were confined to Coventry and Islington because of time restraints.

28. MASSOBS File Report 1053. The extended survey included Oldbury, 'a Black Country Town' and was undertaken at the request of 'six advertising agents handling the propaganda of the National Savings Committee'.

29. MASSOBS File Report 1053, p 115.
30. *Oral Testimony*: OH (Tipton); PJ (Coseley); DB (Pensnett); DR (Sedgley).
31. 'Thrift in War-Time: How and Why Workers are Saving', *The Times* 21 April 1941, p 5.
32. V. Lynn (1994) *We'll Meet Again*, p 124; A. Calder (1996) *The People's War*, p 355.
33. MASSOBS File Report 1053 p 5.
34. Johnson (1985) *Saving and Spending*, pp 87–125; P. Bailey (1979) 'Will the Real Bill Banks', pp 338–353; B. Harrison (1982) *Peaceable Kingdom*, p 177.
35. H. Forrester (2010) *By the Waters*, p 290.
36. M. Heller (2013) 'The Development of Public Relations', p 339, CD-ROM.
37. *Oral Testimonies*,, JR (Bilston); VH (Wolverhampton); JC (Park Village); PJ.
38. MASSOBS File Report 1053, p 15. Reported that group savers were 'more qualitatively enthusiastic and more regular'.
39. *Oral Testimony*: YB (Pensnett).
40. Kingsley Wood, *Hansard*, vol. 568, 29 May 1940.
41. Rt. Hon. Oliver Lyttleton (1942) *War Saving in Industry* (National Savings Committee), p 6.
42. O. Lyttleton (1942) *War Saving*.
43. Z. Zeman (1978) *Selling the War*. Zeman indicated that the posters of all protagonists played on the psychological needs of the individual to belong to a group, p 32.
44. File Report 267, 'The Economic Effects of War' by Mass Observation 1940.
45. O. Lyttleton (1942) *War Saving*.
46. *Oral Testimony*: JR.
47. File Report 267, 1940.
48. File Report 267, 1940.
49. H. Forrester (2010) *By the Waters*, p 347; G. Parkes, (2012) 'The Contribution of Black Country Women to the Resolution of the Conflict of World War II', (University of Wolverhampton MA thesis). Winnie Parkes, employed by J. B. Brookes and Co. of Walsall, encouraged colleagues to contribute; receipts and letters of thanks testify to her commitment.
50. File Report 1053, p 15.
51. File Report 267, 1940.
52. *Oral Testimony*: VH.
53. File Report 267, 1940.
54. S. Bruley (ed.) (2001) *Working For Victory*, p 3. For example, the Government Training Centre at Waddon held a War Savings Prize sweep on Wednesdays (pay-day), as did numerous other places of employment; M. Hutchinson (2005) *A Penny Dip*, p 83. Schools awarded prizes of savings stamps and bonds for pupils' contributions to the scheme.
55. V. Hodgson, (1999) *Few Eggs*, p 463.
56. O. Lyttleton (1942) *War Saving*, p 12.
57. N. Longmate (1988) *How We Lived Then*, p 379: Bruley (2001) *Working For Victory*, pp. 99–100. Directors at Morrison's Engineering Works in Croydon opened Post Office Savings accounts for employees with 'an amount to be announced at Christmas'.
58. File Report 1053, p 123.
59. *Oral Testimony*: OH, clerical assistant.

60. *Oral Testimonies*: PJ; SH (Oldbury), 'Grandma and mother both went from house to house selling stamps.' Email 27 March 2013.
61. N. Longmate (1988) *How We Lived Then*, p 379.
62. 'Recruit Bureau' *Daily Mail*, 28 June 1940 p 5.
63. *Oral Testimonies*: PL (Great Bridge); BJ (Great Bridge); BH (Bloomfield); RK (Tipton).
64. File Report 1053, p 25.
65. *Picture Post*, 8 June 1940, p 38; 26 July 1941, p 3; 23 August 1941, p 3; 13 June 1942, p 23.
66. *Picture Post*, 26 July 1941, p 3; 9 August 1941, p 2; 23 August 1941, p 3; 6 September 1941, p 4. These continued throughout 1941 and 1942.
67. *Picture Post*, 26 December 1942, p 4.
68. File Report 1053, p 115.
69. File Report 267, 1940.
70. C. Chinn (1988) *They Worked All Their Lives*; P. Johnson (1985) *Saving and Spending*, p 87; R. Hoggart (1957) *The Uses of Literacy*, p 39; M. Tebbutt (1983) *Making Ends Meet*; D. Vincent (1991) *Poor Citizens*, p 146; S. O'Connell (2009) *Credit and Community*, p 13.
71. E. Roberts (1995) *Women and Families*; R. Watkiss (2011) 'Old Habits'.
72. J. Beck (2003) *Perhaps I'm Really Mervyn Davenport*, pp 93–94; M. Tebbutt (1983) *Making Ends Meet*, p 1.
73. J. M. Stafford (1990) *Light in the Dust*, p 22.
74. Inextricable links between respectability and saving meant that respondents saved regularly before the war, citing family influence. 'Well, mother was a saver and I started at school … when I went to work I carried on with the Post Office, so it made sense to have the wartime stamps.' *Oral Testimonies*: VH; MA (Tipton); PL; BJ; P. Johnson (1983) 'Credit and Thrift', p 169; P. Johnson, *Saving and Spending*; P. Bailey (1979) 'Will the Real Bill Banks', 336–353; R. Watkiss (2011) 'Old Habits'.
75. File Report 1053, p 15. 'Saving by stamps is much more frequently done by women.'
76. J. Lawrence (2013) 'Class', p 285.
77. P. Johnson (1983) 'Credit and Thrift'. Savings schemes, organised by a variety of institutions included 'diddlums', Christmas clubs, Friendly Societies, life insurance, sickness and death insurance. See P. Johnson (1985) *Saving and Spending*.
78. P. Johnson (1985) *Saving and Spending*, p 161.
79. *Oral Testimonies*: MA; PJ; BJ; BH.
80. 'I want to appeal to all women', *Daily Mail*, 3 July 1940, p 3,
81. R. Kindersley, 'Women Will Keep War Purse Full', *Daily Mail*, 22 May 1941, p 1; 'Direct Appeal to Women' *Daily Mail*, 3 July 1940, p 3. Kindersley was Chairman of the National Savings Committee from 1916–1920 and President between 1920–1946.
82. *Oral Testimonies*: P. Johnson (1983) 'Credit and Thrift', p 169.
83. *Oral Testimonies*: MM; EJ (Wednesbury – letter 13 April 2013); BJ, Betty fetched beer for her neighbour's husband and was rewarded with money to 'buy a stamp of my own' every week; VH.
84. *Oral Testimony*: OH.
85. *Oral Testimonies*: VH; PL.

86. 'Save or be Outcast' *Daily Mail*, 10 February 1941, p 2.
87. E. R. Chamberlin (1972) *Life in Wartime Britain*, p 100; H. Forrester (2010) *By the Waters*, p 290; N. Webley (2002) *Betty's Wartime Diary*, p 102.
88. A. J. P. Taylor (1975) *English History*, p 511; 'You've got to save a penny of two!' *The Black Country Bugle* 20 January 2005; M. Smith (2012) *These Wonderful Rumours*, p 218.
89. *Oral Testimony*: VH.
90. *Oral Testimony*: JR. Others used similar phrases.
91. *Oral Testimonies*: OH; PJ; BJ.
92. R. Broad and S. Fleming (2006) *Nella Last's War Diaries*, p 156; H. Forrester (2010) *By the Waters*, p 342.
93. Sir Godfrey Elton, *Hansard*, 30 September 1942, cc 427.
94. *Daily Mail*, 16 July 1942, p 3.
95. A malevolent cartoon character designed to deter unnecessary or frivolous spending.
96. MASSOBS File Report 1053, p 16.
97. MASSOBS File Report 1053, p 23.
98. *Oral Testimonies*: BJ; OH; PJ.
99. Kingsley Wood, *Hansard*, Finance Bill, 29 May 1940, c 568.
100. *Oral Testimonies*: MM; OH; JR.
101. MASSOBS File Report 267, 1940.
102. *Oral Testimony*: BJ.
103. N. Webley (2002) *Betty's Wartime Diary*, p 111.
104. P. Kitchen (ed.) (1990) *For Home and Country*, p 71.
105. MASSOBS File Report 1053, p 23.
106. *Picture Post* 13 July 1940, p 47; 17 May 1944, p 3; 17 June 1944, p 3.
107. *Oral Testimony*: JR.
108. *Oral Testimonies*: MA; BJ; VH.
109. *Oral Testimony*: FM (Willenhall)
110. *Oral Testimony*: MM.

References

Bailey. P (1979) "'Will the Real Bill Banks Please Stand up?" Towards a Role Analysis of Mid-Victorian Working-Class Respectability', *Journal of Social History*, 12, 3, pp 336–353.

Beck. J (2003) *Perhaps I'm Really Mervyn Davenport* (Middlesex: New Millennium).

Beck. P (1989) *A WAAF in Bomber Command* (London: Goodall Publications Ltd).

Benson. J (1996) 'Working-Class Consumption, Saving and Investment in England and Wales 1851–1911', *Journal of History and Design*, 1, 2, pp 87–99.

Benson. J (2005) *Affluence and Authority: A Social History of the Twentieth Century* (London: Hodder Arnold).

Braithwaite. B, Walsh. N and Davis. G (1986) *From Ragtime to Wartime: The Best of Good Housekeeping 1922–1939* (London: Edbury).

Briggs. S (1975) *Keep Smiling Through: The Home Front 1939–45* (London: Wiedenfeld and Nicolson).

Broad. R and S. Fleming (eds) (2006) *Nella Last's War: The Second World War Diaries of Housewife, 49* (London: Profile Books).

Bruley. S (ed.) (2010) *Working For Victory: A Diary of Life in a Second World War Factory* (Stroud: The History Press).

Burton. K G (1999) *A Penknife to a Mountain: The Early Years of the National Savings Committee* (London: National Savings Committee).

Calder. A (1996) *The People's War: Britain, 1939–1945* (London: Pimlico).

Cantwell. J (1989) *Images of War: British Posters 1939–1945* (London: HMSO).

Chamberlin. E R (1972) *Life in Wartime Britain* (London: B. T. Batsford).

Chinn. C (1988) *They Worked All Their Lives: Women of the Urban Poor in England, 1880–1939* (Manchester: Manchester University Press).

Donnelly. P (ed.) (2001) *Mrs. Milburn's Diaries: An Englishwoman's Day-to-Day Reflections, 1939–1945* (London: Futura Publications).

Fisher. R, Gap. R and Dobson. A (2011) 'Letters from the War Factory: Women Workers in World War Two', *Women in Society*, 1, Spring, pp 47–57.

Forrester. H (1994) *Lime Street at Two* (London: Harper Collins).

Forrester. H (2010) *By the Waters of Liverpool* (London: Harper Collins).

Fussell. P F (1990) *Wartime: Understanding and Behaviour in the Second World War* (Oxford: Oxford University Press).

Gardiner. J (2005) *Wartime Britain, 1939–1945* (London: Headline).

Garfield. S (2005) *We are at War: The Diaries of Five Ordinary People in Extraordinary Times* (London: Edbury Press).

Goldsmith-Carter. G (1974) *The Battle of Britain: The Home Front* (New York: Mason and Lipscomb).

Hampton. J (2010) *How the Girl Guides Won the War* (London: Harper Press).

Harrison. B (1982) *Peaceable Kingdom: Stability and Change in Modern Britain* (Oxford: Clarendon Press).

Heller. M (2013) 'The Development of Public Relations and Integrated Marketing Communications at the General Post Office, 1933–1939', *Proceedings of the 16th Biennial Conference CHARM Association – Varieties, Alternatives and Deviations in Marketing History* 30 May–2 June 2013, pp 339–341 CD-Rom.

Hodgson. V (1999) *Few Eggs and No Oranges: The Diaries of Vere Hodgson, 1940–45* (London: Persephone Books Ltd).

Hoggart. R (1957) *The Uses of Literacy: Aspects of Working-Class Life with Special Reference to Publications and Entertainment* (London: Chatto and Windus).

Hutchinson. M (2005) *A Penny Dip: My Black Country Girlhood* (London: Hodder and Stoughton).

Johnson. P (1983) 'Credit and Thrift and the British Working Class, 1870–1939', in Winter. J (ed.), *The Working Class in Modern British History: Essays in Honour of Henry Pelling* (Cambridge: Cambridge University Press).

Johnson. P (1985) *Saving and Spending: The Working-class Economy in Britain, 1870–1939* (Oxford: Clarendon Press).

Kitchen. P (ed.) (1990) *For Home and Country: War, Peace and Rural Life as Seen Through the Pages of the W.I. Magazine, 1919–1959* (London: Edbury Press).

Lawrence. J (2013) 'Class, "Affluence" and the Study of Everyday Life in Britain, c. 1930–1964', *Cultural and Social History*, 10, 2, pp 273–299.

Longmate. N (ed.) (1981) *The Home Front: An Anthology of Personal Experience 1938–1945* (London: Chatto and Windus).

Longmate. N (1988) *How We Lived Then: A History of Everyday Life During the Second World War* (London: Arrow Books).

Lynn. V (1994) *We'll Meet Again: A Personal and Social History of World War Two* (London: Sidgwick and Jackson).

Madge. C (1943) *Wartime Pattern of Spending and Saving* (Cambridge: Cambridge University Press).

Malcolmson. P and Malcolmson. R (eds) (2010) *Nella Last in the 1950s: Further Diaries of Housewife 49* (London: Profile Books Ltd).

Malcolmson. P and Malcolmson. R (2013) *Women at the Ready: The Remarkable Story of the Women's Voluntary Services on the Home Front* (London: Little Brown).

Maltby. J '"The Wife's Administration of the Earnings?" Working-Class Women and Savings in the Mid-Nineteenth Century', Working Paper 43 (The University of York February 2009) *The White Rose Research Online* http://eprints.whiterose.co.uk/8795/

Marwick. A (1976) *The Home Front: The British and the Second World War* (London: Thames and Hudson).

Milward. A S (1977) *War, Economy and Society 1939–1945* (Harmondsworth: Penguin Books Ltd).

Minns. R (2012) *Bombers and Mash: The Domestic Front 1939–45*, (reprint of 1980 edition) (London: Virago Press).

Nicholson. V (2012) *Millions Like Us: Women's Lives During the Second World War* (London: Penguin Books).

O'Connell. S (2009) *Credit and Community: Working-Class Debt in the United Kingdom Since 1800* (Oxford: Oxford University Press).

Opie. R (1985) *Rule Britannia: Trading on the British Image* (Harmondsworth: Penguin).

Pearsall. P (1990) *Women at War* (Aldershot: Ashgate).

Roberts. E (1995) *Women and Families: An Oral History, 1940–1970* (Oxford: Blackwell).

Samuel. R (ed.) (1989) *Patriotism: The Making and Unmaking of British National Identity Vol. III* (London: Routledge).

Sheridan. D (ed.) (2000) *Wartime Women: A Mass Observation Anthology* (London: Phoenix Press).

Smith. H L (ed.) (1986) *War and Social Change: British Society in the Second World War* (Manchester: Manchester University Press).

Smith. M (2012) *These Wonderful Rumours! A Young Schoolteacher's Wartime Diaries 1939–1945* (London: Virago).

Stafford. J M (1990) *Light in the Dust: An Autobiography, 1939–1960* (Stourbridge: Trustline Publishers).

Summerfield. P (1998) *Reconstructing Women's Wartime Lives* (Manchester: Manchester University Press).

Taylor. A J P (1975) *English History 1914–1945* (Oxford: Oxford University Press).

Taylor. M (1990) 'Patriotism, History and the Left in Twentieth-Century Britain', *The Historical Journal*, 33, 4, pp. 971–987.

Tebbutt. M (1983) *Making Ends Meet: Pawnbroking and Working Class Credit* (Leicester: Leicester University Press).

Vincent. D (1991) *Poor Citizens: The State and the Poor in Twentieth-Century Britain* (Harlow: Longman).

Waller. J and Vaughan-Reeves. M (1987) *Women in Wartime: The Role of Women's Magazines 1939–1945* (London: MacDonald Optima).

Webley. N (ed.) (2002) *Betty's Wartime Diary* (London: Thorogood).

Witkowski. T (2003) 'World War Two Poster Campaigns: Preaching Frugality to American Consumers', *Journal of Advertising*, 32, 1, pp. 69–82.

Zeman. Z (1978) *Selling the War: Art and Propaganda in World War II* (London: Oris Publishing).

14

Contemporary Images and Ideas of the Home Front

Maggie Andrews

Introduction

In the twenty-first century, conflict and war are geographically distanced from domestic life and civilians are neither endangered nor conscripted in Britain. Yet the Home Front and the domestic and local consequences of war have never had a higher profile. This can be seen in the storylines of television dramas, the popularity of the Military Wives Choirs and the introduction of the Elizabeth Cross which, since 2009, has been awarded to the next of kin of members of the armed forces who are killed on active service. The growing concern for families and wives of those serving in the forces and an interest in the domestic consequences of war is to a significant degree a direct consequence of the role that television plays in mediating war and conflict for public consumption. Broadcasting is a domestic medium; audiences consume television and radio in their homes. In the 1930s when radio shifted from being an 'unruly guest' to becoming 'a friend in the corner',[1] it adopted an intimate mode of address which placed the broadcaster unobtrusively at the listener's fireside. Since then broadcasting's linguistic style and the focus of many programmes has privileged personal and family concerns; domesticating and arguably feminising the airwaves. Thus the lexicon of images broadcasting provides for its viewers to witness and imagine war is frequently concerned with the consequences of armed conflict on home and families.

In recent years the Home Front has been subject to, what John Ellis suggests is, broadcasting culture's tendency 'to work through' issues until it 'exhausts an area of concern, smothering it in explanations from almost every angle'.[2] This chapter interrogates some of the 'working through' that has occurred in recent televisual representations of the

Home Front, paying particular attention to a domestic drama entitled *Homefront* (ITV 2012) and three heritage dramas. Series two of ITV's *Downton Abbey* (ITV 2012), the BBC series *The Village* (2013) and the second series of *Mr Selfridge* (ITV 2014) were all set on the First World War Home Front. The multiple story lines and characters of television drama series enable them to 'work through' and explore issues. Their narrative structure is inherently discursive, with different characters able to represent a range of sometimes competing perspectives. All these dramas draw upon familiar narrative tropes whereby stoic but tortured individuals' lives are marred by death, injury and abandonment as a result of war, but these tropes are also reworked by wider contemporary cultural preoccupations with relationships and marriage. They are framed by current conservative rhetoric that marriage and relationships are now in crisis compared to an illusive golden ageism of the past, where duty and responsibility to others apparently prevented marital breakdown.

In the complex cultural interweaving which occurs between the past and the present; there has been slippage in the popular imagination between the First World War and contemporary wars in Iraq and Afghanistan. This has occurred particularly since the 90th anniversary of the First World War armistice in 2008 which took place at a point when Britain had had troops in Iraq for five years and in Afghanistan for seven years. Arguably the length of these conflicts, with little sign of a positive outcome encouraged comparison with the First World War, which is often characterised as a stalemate of trench warfare as portrayed in the TV comedy *Blackadder* (BBC 1989). In the popular imagination both the Iraq and Afghanistan conflicts have, like the First World War, tended to be understood as a waste of young innocent lives. In all three conflicts a substantial level of blame for this is laid at the door of the elite: uncaring or incompetent generals in the First World War, politicians in the Iraq and Afghan conflicts. Recent television portrayals of all three conflicts link the Home and Fighting Fronts and draw attention to the emotional costs of war particularly but not exclusively for wives, mothers and children. Such representational paradigms are politically significant, both responding to and framing wider debates about British engagement in armed conflict in the twenty-first century.

The war industries: televising the Home Front

The visibility of the Home Front in contemporary culture is part of a wider twenty-first century obsession with war, conflict, and remembrance resulting in what Dorothy Sheridan has referred to as the war industries.[3] These cover a wide range of media texts, popular histories, heritage sites and trails, alongside a plethora of activities such as the Wartime in the Cotswolds event at the Gloucestershire and Herefordshire Steam Railway. The War Industries ensure that the First World War and Second World War have become what Landsberg describes as prosthetic memories; through which individuals in a society have 'intimate relationships with memories of events' even though they did not live through them.[4] Some have suggested that this interpretation in using the term prosthetic overemphasises the significance of memories, but arguably, without 'memories' of the two wars, people struggle to gain a sense of belonging in contemporary British culture.

It could be suggested that, in media and heritage industries, emphasis on the Home Front is more frequently used to provide a softer, more palatable version of the war industries and one intended to broaden their appeal to women. This is important for programme producers and for war-focussed tourist attractions such as the Imperial War Museum in London, Manchester and Duxford or the National Memorial Arboretum in Staffordshire, all of which want to increase their footfall. The Home Front appears sometimes to be reduced to a design stylisation used in advertising or on consumer items, adding a dash of retro or even kitsch to the many products sold in gift shops. Keep Calm and Carry On mugs, not to mention Carry on Caravanning adverts, dog door-mats saying 'Wipe your Paws and Carry On' and 'Dig for Victory' posters are examples of this phenomenon as are wartime cookery books and releases of Vera Lynn music. Jay Winter[5] and Dan Todman[6] have suggested such a 'memory boom' reflects a need to reach back in order to reassert identity in the face of the ever-quickening pace of modernity, but it is a more complex syndrome. The Home Front often evokes an appealing sense of community, the two wars are seen as a period when Britain was perceived to have greater international power and influence and a stronger sense of national unity than it does now. This may be a selective myth, as some of the chapters of this book have demonstrated, but at a time of economic crisis, alienation and austerity, it may be an appealing myth. Furthermore the Home Front is associated with a time in which everyday mundane, domestic tasks and skills were valued, considered to be of national importance. Many people find themselves having to undertake numerous domestic tasks with little thanks; of necessity they have to scrimp and save, avoid waste and make-do-and-mend. Little wonder that they demonstrate a nostalgia for a time when such efforts were not just noticed but praised, for as Wendy Wheeler has argued 'nostalgia isn't nasty' rather it is rejection of the status quo.[7]

A pre-occupation with the Home Front can be identified in a number of spaces and places of British popular television, although commercial imperatives mean that such programmes, created to entertain, frequently fall back on oft-repeated myths and iconography; for example, women working in munitions or becoming more liberated by war. Alternatively there is little space in popular television for the visceral and debilitating facial injuries many soldiers suffered in the First World War and how families tried to cope with them in the years that followed. The commercial imperatives of broadcasting companies create a need for a palatable and familiar version of the past for television; the viewing public are resistant, and indeed often reject, attempts to debunk the myths of war. A heritage text's authenticity is established, as Noakes points out, first and foremost in relation to other representations of the past on television or in films.[8] Thus there is a tendency to utilise familiar, even clichéd, iconography of both the Western and the Home Fronts to evoke the First World War. A sanitised, but familiar version of the trenches is, for example, evoked by barbed wire, sandbags, mud and no man's land with an absence of vegetation. Alternatively women working in factories, giving out white feathers to men who didn't enlist and nursing can be used to visualise the Home Front. Television can and does at times add complexity to such myths and images, stretching and reworking them as new nuances are introduced. Furthermore, television's established preoccupation with the dreams, desires, disasters and tensions of intimate relationships and everyday domestic life leads the medium to focus its portrayal of the horror of war through the emotional reactions of those at home coping with death, destruction and anxiety. Television is, however, entertainment and too much horror or stretching of popular myths and memories can produce a negative response from the audience.

A cultural association of the Home Front with Second World War has perhaps been affirmed through *Dad's Army* (BBC 1968–1977) repeats of which continue to be broadcast on a Saturday evening alongside, in recent years, drama series such as *Foyle's War* (2002–2012), *Landgirls* (2009–2012) and *Murder on the Home Front* (2011–2012). These televisual texts stretch and rework the representational paradigms of the British experience of 1939–1945 to include for example: a substantial amount of crime, anti-Italian riots, corruption, the death of evacuees, class divisions and antagonism, and the avoidance of conscription. Such representations offer welcome alternatives to the popular perception of the People's War' as a moment of national cohesion and apparent equality of sacrifice – a perception that has been challenged by a number of historians,[9] nevertheless the national narrative maintains that Second World War was Britain's 'good war', whilst First World War offers a less comfortable version of the past.

This may explain why, despite the popularity of the 1970s drama series *Upstairs Downstairs* (ITV 1971–1975), until recently the First World War Home Front has been more culturally marginalised. However as the generation of veterans from this conflict have died, television dramas, documentaries and culture more widely has turned its attention to the families of those who took part in the conflict. This can be seen in the spin-off to the BBC's popular family history programme *Who do you think you are* (2004–), entitled *My Family at War*. This series was initially broadcast by BBC1 to mark the 90th anniversary of the end of First World War and has been repeated in digital channels in the television remembrance season ever since. Each of four episodes followed two celebrities undertaking a journey to 'reveal' a family member's participation in the war. The family history boom this series taps into is also being harnessed by many archives services and by the Imperial War Museum's 'Lives of the First World War' project which is providing an online depository for individual life stories for the First World War Centenary Commemoration. ITV's more populist response to the First World War 90th anniversary was to broadcast a one-off heritage drama entitled *My Boy Jack* on Remembrance Sunday. This portrayed the devastation that followed the death on the Western Front of the novelist Rudyard Kipling's son. Its all-star cast and high production values guaranteed it a wide audience and since then images of the First World War Home Front have increasingly appeared in the popular 9pm Sunday evening slot.

Heritage drama and the First World War Home Front

Downton Abbey is one of British television's successes in recent years, audience figures in the second series reached 11.7 million and it has had critical acclaim, winning both Golden Globes and Primetime Emmy Awards. This success, in Britain, can in part be attributed to its ability to tap into and reinforce the cultural fascination with war. In *Downton Abbey*, First World War is experienced on a fictional Yorkshire country house estate through the lives of the Earl of Grantham, his wife Cora Crawley, Countess of Grantham, three daughters, relations and servants. The first series ended as First World War was declared; series two focussed on wartime and series three moved into the inter-war era endorsing the popular perceptions of the First World War as a pivotal moment for personal and social change and a 'liberator of women'.[10] Indeed the dialogue is littered with the Earl of Grantham making reference to how the old world order have been disrupted by war. His two youngest daughters take on new roles: in voluntary work, nursing and working on the land, heralded as challenging traditional femininity. One learns to drive, the other to cook. The house in *Downton Abbey* is a frequent visual reference point, in some respects one of the stars of the show, as the series name suggests. It is the family home, providing some credibility to Jeremy de Groot's argument that the past in heritage texts is 'homogenous, class ridden, visually rich and viewed through the twin lenses of quality and authenticity'.[11] Expensive production values, images of the house and idealised rural landscapes provide visual pleasures for the viewer and alongside humour ensure the programme is effortless viewing. However heritage texts are often more complex than they first appear.[12] Downton Abbey stretches and disrupts predominant cultural memories of the First World War by portraying war widows' poverty, the use of dodgy medical certificates to avoid conscription and self-inflicted Blighty wounds.

The opening images of the second series show Matthew Crawley, heir apparent to Downton, fighting on the Somme in 1916, a battle that operates as authenticating shorthand for the horrors of war. His thoughts, however, and the setting of the narrative quickly turn to home and Downton Abbey, an embodiment of his physical and symbolic home and the nation that is being fought for. The movement of the text between the home and war fronts continues until Matthew returns to Downton injured. The fluctuation of the narrative between the home and fighting fronts emphasises the consequences of war on men and their families. The idea that Downton is a symbolic home worth fighting for is shared across the classes in this inherently conservative text. Mason, one of the servants, goes off to fight willingly once kitchen maid Daisy has agreed to become his fiancé; saying he can face war with her to return to. The Home Front where he idealises her waiting for him is however the servants hall, below stairs. Mason returns injured and marries Daisy only on his deathbed, the wedding attended by the Dowager Countess symbolising cohesion across the classes. The interconnection between home and war fronts is also confirmed when Downton becomes a convalescence hospital; bringing the victims of war into the domestic home that is being fought for. The consequent disruption caused to the Earl of Grantham's family draws attention to the stretching, reworking and redefining of domestic lives in wartime.

Longing and unfulfilled desires are the overwhelming emotional focus of the narrative, both between the Earl of Grantham's eldest daughter

Mary and his heir Matthew and in a parallel relationship between the two servants, Anna and Bates. The narratives of both these couples suggest potentially emotionally intense and fulfilling relationships constantly thwarted by moral imperatives and by responsibility to others. Yearning, separation and duty, dominate and express a perceived 'structure of feeling'[13] of wartime within which many couples experience hardship, denial, separation or death. Government control of people's working and domestic lives is presented as having interfered with personal relationships, split couples up and placed uncertainty and geographical distance between partners when men volunteered or were conscripted.

The Home Front in *Downton Abbey*'s representations of soldiers as victims of war and in need of care is stretched when the servants set up a soup kitchen to feed demobbed, injured soldiers. There is a sense that the whole household, men and women are emotionally or physically damaged by war. Bates, the Earl of Grantham's valet, struggles with a war wound from the South African war; Mr Lang, a footman displays symptoms of shell-shock but the housekeeper reminds him: 'Mr Lang – you're not the only member of the walking wounded in this house'. The cook, Mrs Patterson, struggles to come to terms with her nephew's death at the hands of the British army for cowardice. The small number of soldiers who were 'shot at dawn' have become a familiar motif in drama, signalling the elite's responsibility for those who die in war. Other women whose lives had been scarred by war include Jane a widow and mother who is employed as housemaid, and Ethel who becomes a poverty stricken single mother after a brief affair with one of the convalescing officers staying at Downton. After the officer is killed, she struggles to support her child and turns to prostitution.

The Village made a more conscious attempt to stretch and rework popular memories of First World War by constructing the narrative from the perspective of the rural working class on the Home Front. Set in a Derbyshire village it recounts the affect of war on the family of a young lad, Bert Middleton, whose beloved elder brother Joe does not find participation in the war either glorious or heroic and when he fails to return to his regiment after being on leave he is arrested and shot by the military police. Rural life on the Home Front is not presented as idyllic but precarious, made up of incessant toil. The landed gentry are self-serving rather than benevolent and servants are exploited rather than cared for; in the large house servants turn their faces to the wall as the master goes past and the mental illness of the daughter and suicide of her father suggest that the old order is decaying in spite of the national emergency of war. Any sense of a satisfying conclusion to the conflict is undermined in the drama by the fear of the flu epidemic as the war ends.

There are few of the reassuring and familiar versions of the First World War, there is little humour and less paternalism, the new opportunities for women's work are short lived. Within this grittier version of the Home Front there are only fleeting moments of communality, one of which is the village bathhouse, a particularly female cultural space. Gossip, the discourse of the powerless,[14] and self-reliance are shown as enabling the villagers to survive a frequently miserable life on the Home Front. It is the grief and anxiety in the lives of the wives and mothers which are used to convey the horror of war. The emotional turmoil of Joe's mother's suffering continues even to the construction of a war memorial. The acceptance of the grief she shares with other families at the dedication of the memorial offers hope and some optimism. However this was in the last episode and by this point this rather grimmer and more challenging version of the past had seen its viewing figures fall to only five and a half million.

Mr Selfridge aimed to ape the success of *Downton Abbey* but only mustered half its audience.[15] Loosely based upon the life of an American-born entrepreneur who opened the Oxford Street department store Selfridges in 1908, it was aired by ITV in Britain and broadcast and jointly funded by Masterpiece in the USA. The series charted the ups and downs of the working and personal lives of Harry Selfridge within both his immediate family and his symbolic family of Selfridges' employees. Having the central, powerful character as an American shopkeeper, not a member of the landed elite, disrupts the associations between the Home Front and Britain being internationally powerful. Indeed the only aristocrat in the narrative, Lord Loxley, is an arch villain. He is abusive towards his wife and a war-profiteer, using his position on the Government Acquisitions Committee to replenish his family fortunes by taking bribes from manufacturers supplying shoddy boots to soldiers. This perhaps made the series less comfortable viewing, something that possibly influenced its viewing figures.

There is fluidity between Harry Selfridge's home and his workplace as the store experiences the adverse consequences of war when men enlisted and luxury purchases were curtailed. Selfridges and its employees struggle to survive emotionally and financially on the Home Front, despite Harry Selfridge's paternalism which is affirmed when he guarantees to re-employ men who enlist at the end of the war. In *Mr Selfridge*, women not only temporarily take over these men's jobs but also have their clothing redesigned so as to be less restricting when working. Thus *Mr Selfridge* reproduces familiar myths and tropes of wartime; there are also multiple representations of women struggling on their own, suffering and worrying, although not necessarily as a direct consequence of war. Harry Selfridge's escapades visiting Germany to spy for the British government ensures that both his store and his home are bereft by his absence; Lady Mae leaves her husband and Delphine is already divorced. Finally window-dresser Agnes anxiously waits for news of her brother missing on the Western Front, only to find her relief at his return is short-lived when she then says goodbye to her lover Mr Leclair who joins the French army. Whilst in *Downton Abbey* and *The Village* there is an assumption that despite pressures placed upon relationships, marriages will survive, the more modern and populist *Mr Selfridge* suggests in the Lady Mae and Delphine characters that this may not be the case. A perspective that lies at the very centre of portrayals of the contemporary Home Front.

Representing the contemporary Home Front

In recent years the term Home Front has been applied not to the whole nation but rather to the military bases and garrison towns in which service families live, as in ITV's 2012 drama-series *Homefront*. In the First World War, as Janis Lomas has demonstrated, economic provision for wives and children was an area of concern; in the twenty-first century contemporary media takes the financial security of military wives for granted and instead focusses on their emotional hardship. Several factors contribute to this including the assumptions that women are now more economically independent and if not, the government and the welfare state will provide financially for military families. Concern for the emotional welfare of families is also symptomatic of a new privileging of intimacy and emotions.[16] Expectations and ideals of marriage in the twentieth century, as Claire Langhamer has documented, have shifted; it is no longer acceptable for marriage to be considered merely a materially sensible and hopefully companionable arrangement. There is now a firmly established expectation that marriage and coupledom should be an emotionally intimate relationship that is mutually supportive, enriching and fulfilling for all parties.[17] Meeting such high expectations is somewhat challenging, particularly for those in the armed forces, and media portrayals of life on the contemporary Home Front tend to focus on the gap between the ideal and the lived experience.

The long running series ITV series *Soldier Soldier* (1991–1997) drew attention to the challenges facing modern soldiers' wives and children as they followed their husbands from posting to posting and coped with periods of separation. It was however at a point in time when the British army was not engaged in major conflict. *Homefront* has quite a different background, the Afghanistan war was then continuing and the Iraq war still had a place in the public consciousness. In the opening shots of the series, Louise, an army wife out jogging, spots the tell-tale signs that there is news of a soldier's death – an official car with an officer and welfare support are driving towards the base housing. Her anxiety for her husband is conveyed as she speeds up, racing for home, relieved to see the car go on past, only to discover it has called at the house of her friend Tasha. The struggles of Tasha and her family to cope with bereavement become one of the main storylines of the series. This is particularly poignant to the audience because they have regularly, between 2007– 2012, witnessed on the news the coffins of British servicemen flown into RAF Lyneham and driven through the Wiltshire town of Wootton Bassett. The image of hundreds of the general public lining the streets of the town heads bowed in silent tribute became an iconic and very televisual tribute to the dead.

Homefront is set in a small market town in the English Home Counties with a high street of individual shops and large leafy detached houses where officers live. The narrative focusses on four women, past, present and prospective army wives, whose sons or partners are fighting in Afghanistan. Men are not the objects of pity or victims of war, they are volunteers who choose this as a way of life with the women bearing the consequences. All four women are feisty, at one level independent yet they all give up work as impractical. They are portrayed as having been pushed into the traditional role of a non-working supportive wife by the demands of their husbands' job. Perhaps because this drama is set in an era when such a position is at odds with cultural assumptions of femininity and seems incongruous, it is questioned, particularly by Louise after she discovers her husband has been having an affair whilst on tour in Afghanistan.

The drama represents families and military marriages as inherently precarious relationships. Young mother Tasha, who is widowed in the first episode has started a clandestine relationship with her brother-in-law by the last episode, Louise separates from her husband due to his infidelity and irrational behaviour, Paula's husband suggests they end their marriage and acknowledges his awareness of her previous affairs. Divorcee Claire, engaged to an officer, panics, calls off the wedding and finally marries him as onlookers mutter she will need luck to cope as an army wife. Marriages, it is suggested, are placed under stress by emotional separation and the problems of communication when any phone call or chat on Skype that a woman shares with her partner could be their last one before a soldier is killed. It is suggested that honesty and intimacy, tropes of twenty-first century relationships, are compromised by warfare.

This perspective is not reserved for drama; similar themes run through the depiction of the Home Front in *Helmand: A War on Two Fronts* (BBC2 2010). This documentary featured the soldiers and their families of Second Battalion A Company of the Yorkshire Regiment as they experienced a six-month tour of duty in Helmand Province, Afghanistan. Shown in the nine o'clock evening slot it was followed by a discussion with some of the participants on *Newsnight*. Attention was drawn to how military service disrupts domestic life with initial images of wives saying goodbye to their husbands on their doorsteps at two o'clock in the morning. The problems of emotional separation were also acknowledged by one wife who pointed out that 'in his head he leaves me before he goes and doesn't come back when he returns'. The title's reference to 'fighting on two fronts' gives equal status to military combat and wives and mothers struggling on the Home Front. In the *Newsnight* discussion the presenter, Kirsty Wark commented: 'One of the striking elements of the film is that it is harder for the people back home'. Such a statement matches the strapline used to promote the series *Homefront* 'sometimes the toughest battles are on the home front'. Both are indicators of the cultural privileging of domestic life and relationships and an indication of half-hearted support for British military activities overseas.

Notwithstanding ambivalence about contemporary military conflicts, the struggles of military wives and widows do elicit public empathy. In twenty-first century Britain, where relationships and family breakdowns are not uncommon, they are not the only women coping with temporary or permanent separation from their partners. Military wives and widows are however the acceptable face of single parenthood. The popularity of the Military Wives Choir who performed at The Royal British Legion's Festival of Remembrance in 2011 and 2012 can in part be understood because their predicament as women coping on their own resonates in the popular imagination. They are 'single mothers' who are seen as victims, their lives are framed by their husbands' commitment to do duty and fulfill their responsibility to others, these women are suffering because their husbands are serving the nation. The choir conducted by Gareth Malone was drawn from a number of choirs set up on various military bases around the UK, to help women cope with loneliness on the Home Front. Their initial song, which was created by Paul Maelor from extracts of correspondence between the women and their spouses, was so successful that it dislodged that year's winner of the television talent show The X Factor from their expected Christmas number one slot. The words of this song, 'Wherever You Are', express yearning and the pain of separation. That the Military Wives and their successors, the Poppy Girls, performed at The Royal British Legion's Festival of Remembrance is indicative of how, in contemporary culture, the idea of the Home Front has become blurred with Remembrance. The pain of temporary separation for families involved in war is now intimately entwined with the pain of permanent separation caused by bereavement, with both contemporary portrayals of the Home Front and remembrance drawing attention to the domestic consequences of war and conflict.[18]

Afterword

The image and idea of the Home Front may now however be at a turning point. The multiplicity of programming being produced to mark the centenary of First World War will provide a wider lexicon of images of the conflict. As the BBC seeks to legitimate its role as a public service broadcaster and justify the licence fee in stringent economic times, it has a vast array of programming to be aired to mark the centenary. For example in April 2014 the BBC launched its 'World War One at Home' series, a project that has involved the creation of one thousand local stories about how the First World War was experienced at regional and domestic levels. Dramas and documentaries are also being produced; Radio 4 began broadcasting its daytime drama entitled Home Front in August 2014. Such programming alongside the withdrawal of British Troops from Afghanistan may shift the representational paradigms through which the Home Front is understood. For the moment the televisual portrayals of the contemporary and First World War Home Fronts ensure that the domestic consequences of conflict remain on the political agenda and thus play an important role in drawing attention to the unacceptable cost of war.

Notes

1. S. Moores (1988) 'The Box on the Dresser', pp 116–125.
2. J. Ellis (2000) *Seeing Things*, pp 79–80.
3. Dorothy Sheridan 'The Second World War Industry: Wartime Mass Observation and how we understand it today', WHN Women, War and Remembrance Conference at the National Memorial Arboretum, 13 March 2010.
4. A. Landsberg (2003) 'Prosthetic Memory', pp 144–161, p 148.
5. J. Winter (2006) *Remembering the War*.

6. D. Todman (2011) *The Great War*.
7. W. Wheeler (1994) 'Nostalgia Isn't Nasty'.
8. L. Noakes (1998) *War and the British*.
9. See for example A. Calder (1969) *A People's War*; S. Rose (2003) *Which People's War?*
10. See for example, A. Marwick (1988) *Total War*.
11. J. de Groot (2009) *Consuming History*, p 212.
12. C. Monk and A. Sargeant (2002) *British Historical Cinema*.
13. R. Williams (2001) *The Long Revolution*.
14. M. Tebbutt (2009) *Women's Talk?*
15. http://www.imdb.com/title/tt2310212/news
16. A. Giddens (1992) *Transformation of Intimacy*.
17. C. Langhamer (2013) *The English in Love*.
18. See for example A. King (2010) 'The Afghan War', pp 1–25; and J. Winter (2006) *Remembering the War*.

References

Calder. A (1969) *A People's War* (Pimlico: London).

Ellis. J (2000) *Seeing Things* (London: I B Taurus).

Giddens. A (1992) *Transformation of Intimacy in Everyday Life* (Cambridge: Polity Press).

Groot. J de (2009) *Consuming History* (Oxford: Routledge).

King. A (2010) 'The Afghan War and "Postmodern" Memory: Commemoration and the Dead of Helmand', *The British Journal of Sociology*, 61,1, pp 1–25.

Landsberg. A (2003) 'Prosthetic Memory: The Ethics and Politics of Memory in an Age of Mass Culture', in P Grainge. (ed.) *Memory and Popular Film* (Manchester: Manchester University Press) pp 144–161.

Langhamer. C (2013) *The English in Love* (Oxford: Oxford University Press).

Marwick. A (1988) *Total War and Social Change in the Twentieth Century* (Basingstoke: Palgrave).

Marr. A (2009) *A History of Modern Britain* (London: Pan Macmillan Publishers).

Monk. C and Sargeant. A (2002) *British Historical Cinema* (Oxford: Routledge).

Moores. S (1988) '"The Box on the Dresser". Memoirs of Early Radio and Everyday Life', *Media Culture and Society*, 10, 1, pp 23–40, reprinted in Mitchell. C (ed.) (2000) *Women and Radio Airing Difference* (London: Routledge) pp 116–125.

Noakes. L (1998) *War and the British: Gender, Memory and National Identity* (London: IB Taurus).

Rose. S (2003) *Which People's War? National Identity and Citizenship in Wartime Britain 1939–45* (Oxford: Oxford University Press).

Tebbett. M (2009) *Women's Talk?: A Social History of Gossip* (Leicester: Leicester University Press).

Todman. D (2011) *The Great War: Myth and Memory* (Reprint of 2005 Edition) (London: Continuum).

Winter. J (2006) *Remembering the War: The Great War Between Memory and History in the Twentieth Century* (New Haven: Yale University Press).

Wheeler. W (1994) 'Nostalgia Isn't Nasty: The Postmodernising of Parliamentary Democracy', in M Perryman. (ed.) *Altered States: Postmodern Politics and Culture* (London: Lawrence Wishart).

Index

Printed and bound by CPI Group (UK) Ltd, Croydon, CR0 4YY